INDIANAPOLIS MOTOR SPEEDWAY CORPORATION

BOARD OF DIRECTORS

Mari Hulman George
Chairman of the Board

Anton Hulman George
President & CEO

Katherine George

Nancy L. George

Jack R. Snyder

M. Josephine George

EXECUTIVE STAFF

Jeffrey G. Belskus
*Executive Vice President
& Chief Operating Officer*

John Newcomb
*Vice President,
Sales & Marketing*

Leo Mehl
*Vice President & Executive
Director of the Pep Boys IRL*

W. Curtis Brighton
Vice President & General Counsel

Fred J. Nation
*Vice President,
Corporate Communications
& Public Relations*

Peggy Swalls
Vice President, Administration

Laura George
Staff Advisor

Kenneth T. Ungar
Chief of Staff

SPEEDWAY STAFF

Don Bailey
Vehicle Coordinator

Kevin Forbes
Director of Engineering & Construction

Mai Lindstrom
Director of Public Relations

Dawn Bair
Manager, Creative Services

Lee Gardner
Director of Strategic Events

Bruce Lynch
Director of Retail Sales & Operations

Ellen Bireley
Museum Manager

Mel Harder
Director of Facility Operations

Buddy McAtee
Director of Sales

Dr. Henry Bock
Director of Medical Services

Pat Hayes
Controller

Richard McComb
Director of Finance & Administration

Jeff Chapman
Director of Marketing & Branding

Marty Hunt
Manager, Track Operations

Robert McInteer
Director of Safety

Kevin Davey
Manager, Licensing

Jeff Kleiber
Events Coordinator

Ron McQueeney
Director of Photography

Donald Davidson
Historian

John Lewis
Manager, Facilities

David Moroknek
Director of Licensing & Consumer Products

Chuck Ferguson
Director of Information Services

Gloria Novotney
Director of Credentials

PEP BOYS INDY RACING LEAGUE STAFF

Brian Barnhart
Director of Racing Operations

Lynn Greggs
Controller

Johnny Rutherford
Special Projects

Dr. Henry Bock
Director of Medical Services

Andy Hall
*Director of Corporate & Sponsor
Relations*

Lisa Sommers
Public Relations Manager

Mark Bridges
Technical Manager

Tiffany Hemmer
Assistant Manager of Administration

Jody Thomas
Administrative Assistant

Phil Casey
Technical Director

Joy Hudson
Receptionist

Chris Tracy
Registered Nurse

Joie Chitwood
Manager of Administration

Les McTaggart
Technical Consultant

Chuck Whetsel
Manager of Timing & Scoring

Kris Callfas
Corporate & Sponsor Relations Liaison

Nikki Miller
Executive Assistant

Al Unser
Driver Coach and Consultant

John Pierce
Safety Consultant

CONTENTS

First published in 1998 by MBI Publishing Company, 729 Prospect Avenue, PO Box 1, Osceola, WI 54020-0001 USA

© IMS Corporation, 1999

All rights reserved. With the exception of quoting brief passages for the purposes of review,
no part of this publication may be reproduced without prior written permission from the Publisher.

The information in this book is true and complete to the best of our knowledge. All recommendations are made without any guarantee on the part of the author or Publisher,
who also disclaim any liability incurred in connection with the use of this data or specific details.

We recognize that some words, model names and designations, for example, mentioned herein are the property of the trademark holder.
We use them for identification purposes only. This is not an official publication.

MBI Publishing Company books are also available at discounts in bulk quantity for industrial or sales-promotional use. For details write to Special Sales Manager at
Motorbooks International Wholesalers & Distributors, 729 Prospect Avenue, PO Box 1, Osceola, WI 54020-0001 USA.

Edited by: Paul Johnson
Designed by: Tom Heffron

Editorial Contributors: Jonathan Ingram, Donald Davidson, Bruce Martin, and Jan Shaffer
Photo Contributions by Roger Bedwell, Dave Edelstein, Steve Ellis, Jim Haines, Tim Holle, Todd Hunter, Darryl Jones, Walt Kuhn, Jerry Lawrence,
Linda McQueeney, Ron McQueeney, Mark Reed, Jef Richards, Steve Snoddy, and Leigh Spargur.

Printed in Hong Kong   ISBN 0-7603-0593-5

Thank You

DRAMA AND EXCITEMENT always surround the Indianapolis 500-mile race, and 1998 was no exception. To win at Indy takes skill, grit, and a dose of luck. Eddie Cheever displayed all of these traits and more when winning the 82nd running of the Indianapolis 500. Eddie had the drive of his life, and he was not to be denied. He survived a first-turn bump and several other close calls while driving his way to victory in one of the most incident-free races in history.

Eddie Cheever is another in a long line of deserving champions, and he is an eloquent spokesman for all of motorsports. A former Rookie of the Year and a nine-time qualifier, Eddie's experience paid off. Congratulations to him and to the other 32 drivers who made the 1998 Indianapolis 500 such an entertaining event.

Eddie's victory is just one of many exciting May events covered in this edition of the Indy Review. In words and pictures, the story of the Indianapolis 500-mile race is preserved for the ages. Thank you for your continued interest. Because of you and the millions of fans worldwide, the Indianapolis 500 is truly the "Greatest Spectacle in Racing."

On behalf of all the members of my family, the employees of the Indianapolis Motor Speedway, and the Pep Boys Indy Racing League, let me extend a sincere and grateful thank you to all of our fans, drivers, team members, car owners, and sponsors who made this one of the best Indy 500s ever.

Sincerely,

Tony George

Tony George
President

Indianapolis Motor Speedway

1998 IRL Pep Boys Championship Series

League Suppliers

All Sports Telemetry

Cold Fire/Firefreeze

Worldwide

Fastlane Footwear

Firestone

Goodyear

Hewlett Packard

Holmatro

Nissan

Oldsmobile

Perkin Elmer

Award Sponsors

Bart Wheels

BOSCH Spark Plugs

Champion Spark Plugs

Coors Brewing Company

EMCO Gears

Earl's Performance
Products

KECO Coatings

Klotz Special Formula
Products

MBNA Motorsports

Pennzoil

PPG Industries

Sprint PCS

STP Racing

Indy 200 Winner Tony Stewart	Walt Disney World Speedway	**January 24**
Dura-Lube 200 Winner Scott Sharp	Phoenix International Raceway	**March 22**
Indianapolis 500 Winner Eddie Cheever	Indianapolis Motor Speedway	**May 24**
True Value 500k Winner Billy Boat	Texas Motor Speedway	**June 6**
New England 200 Winner Tony Stewart	New Hampshire International Speedway	**June 28**
Pep Boys 400k Winner Scott Sharp	Dover Downs International Speedway	**July 19**
VisionAire 500k Winner Kenny Brack	Charlotte Motor Speedway	**July 25**
Radisson 200 Winner Kenny Brack	Pikes Peak International Raceway	**August 16**
Atlanta 500k Classic Winner Kenny Brack	Atlanta Motor Speedway	**August 29**
LoneStar 500k Winner John Paul, Jr.	Texas Motor Speedway	**September 20**
Las Vegas 500k Winner Arie Luyendyk	Las Vegas Motor Speedway	**October 11**

LEAGUE SPONSORS

Official League Sponsor
Official Auto Parts Store

Official Website Provider

Official Clothier

Official Fire Extinguisher

Official Sponsor

Official Soft Drink

Official Sponsor

Official Battery

Official PCS Provider

Official Pace Car

Official Trailers

Official Hotel

Pennzoil
Official Motor Oil

MCI
Official Long Distance Carrier

Canon
Official Camera

True Value
Official Hardware Store

Be sure to visit the official IRL website at www.indyracingleague.com

Team Menard Wields Magic at Disney

REIGNING CHAMP TONY STEWART TAKES IRL OPENER

by Bruce Martin

In the first two years of its existence, the Indy Racing League (IRL) entered the first race of the calendar year—the Indy 200 at Walt Disney World—faced with challenges. In 1996, the IRL staged its first-ever race with one-year-old or older cars, but the cars and engines were about the only old components. The IRL had a field of young, talented stars, the series was new, many of the teams were new, and the Walt Disney World Speedway was new. The IRL had struck out on its own to establish itself in the auto racing world. In 1997, the drastic changeover to a new engine/chassis package was difficult for teams and manufacturers as they struggled to prepare enough equipment in time to stage a race.

On both occasions, the IRL was able to overcome obstacles and build the series. That is why this year's Indy 200 was vastly different than the first two runnings at the 1.1-mile Walt Disney World Speedway. For the first time, the IRL

Jimmy Kite (7) and pole-sitter Tony Stewart had the crowd at Walt Disney World Speedway on its feet with their wheel-to-wheel racing in the 1998 IRL season opener.

Inset: Defending IRL Champion Tony Stewart started the new year on a winning note for Team Menard, winning the Indy 200 with aggressive driving and a smart fuel strategy.

5

At the start of the season, veteran Mark Dismore took advantage of the well-funded Kelley team behind him. Dismore led late in the race and stretched fuel economy to the limit. Forced to take on fuel, he handed the lead and the eventual win over to Stewart and finished a lap down in fifth position.

IRL crews showed-off midseason form during pit stops like this one during a caution period. Tony Stewart's crew (front) helped him retain the lead while on his way to the season-opening win.

opened a season with a sense of accomplishment and renewed optimism.

Not only has the IRL survived, it has shown signs of growth. With 31 cars entered for the January 24, Indy 200, it was the largest field ever for the event, which is run near the entrance to the Magic Kingdom at Walt Disney World. In fact, the IRL had to send three cars home because its rule book only allows 28-car starting fields on 1.0-mile ovals. And, for the first time, the IRL entered the season with a series sponsor—Pep Boys, who signed on for five years.

A Florida rain shower washed out pole qualifications for the Indy 200 on Friday, January 23, so the starting line-up was determined by 1997 IRL points standings and practice speeds from Thursday's two sessions.

Tony Stewart, the 1997 IRL champion, started on the pole for the race with Kenny Brack starting on the outside of the front row. Brack replaced Davey Hamilton at A. J. Foyt Enterprises (the points from last season go to the entrant not the driver). Brack's teammate, Billy Boat, started third, followed by Mike Groff and Arie Luyendyk.

With the first 20 positions filled from the 1997 points standings, the last 8 positions were filled based on practice speeds from non-points entrants. Scott Sharp, who was the fastest car at the Walt Disney World Speedway in preseason testing, started 20th alongside Scott Goodyear, and defending Indy 200 winner Eddie Cheever started 23rd. With only 28 cars starting the race, 3 didn't make the show—Billy

Roe, Jim Guthrie, and Affonso Giaffone.

Foggy and rainy conditions were prevalent on race day, but the moisture wasn't enough to keep the race from starting on time. And just like some of the rides at Disney World, the race itself was a roller coaster, with Tony Stewart dominating an action-packed race. This year, however, ended differently because Stewart was finally able to drive to victory at the demanding three-turn race track after coming close to winning at Disney the first two years.

Stewart's fearless driving style has made him one of the brightest young drivers in American motor racing. This was never more evident than in the Indy 200. Stewart successfully opened his defense of the 1997 Indy Racing League championship with the victory, the second of his IRL career. The native of Rushville, Indiana, passed his boyhood pal Mark Dismore entering the first turn on the 195th lap. One lap later Dismore ran out of fuel, taking him out of contention for the victory.

Stewart beat Jeff Ward, last year's Indianapolis 500 Rookie of the Year, by 8.579 seconds. Stewart drove his Team Menard G Force/Oldsmobile Aurora/Firestone package to victory at an average speed of 95.14 miles per hour. He led the race five times for 132 of the 200 laps and won $121,250 in a race witnessed by over 50,000 fans. Hamilton was third in his first race for Nienhouse Motorsports, followed by Stephan Gregoire and Mark Dismore.

"This track gave me the best memory of my life to finish second here in the first race; then to lose it the way we did last year, I really wanted to win this race

Two-time Indy 500 champion Arie Luyendyk qualified strong and started on the third row, but he fell back during the race, finishing eighth, three laps off the lead lap.

bad," Stewart said. "It was tough to beat Mark Dismore because he taught me so much about racing, and I used to drive go-karts for him when I was a kid."

After finishing a lap off the pace, Dismore was left to ponder what might have been if his team's fuel gamble had worked. Dismore made his last pit stop on the 127th lap and tried to make it to the finish without another pit stop. "I never even looked at the dash until I felt the thing stumble coming off of Turn 2," Dismore said. "I just put it out of my mind. I had the car in sixth gear and ran it as lean as I could without burning a piston. It almost worked." Because of this, Dismore, a native of Greenfield, Indiana, was left to watch his racing protégé get the fame and glory with the victory in Saturday's race.

"Tony and I have known each other for 20 years, ever since he was a little, little kid," Dismore recalled. "We spent a lot of time together in a van pulling trailers to go-kart tracks. His father, Nelson [Stewart], all of us are real tight. It's like we are family. Tony is a competitor, and so am I. When you get on the track, you still love him, but you want to whip him. It's a unique relationship.

"The kid is a natural. He is God's gift behind a steering wheel. He knows what to do. Nothing is planned; it's all reaction. He just knows what to do with the steering wheel and what his butt tells him and relays that to his team, and they give him a good car." Stewart displays an air of cockiness involving his racing career, but Dismore doesn't take the credit for that. "No, that is something Tony has developed himself," Dismore said. "I didn't teach him that."

Jeff Ward ran red-hot in his new Tabasco G-Force entry, using its Aurora power to take second place. The former motocross champion hoped it was his first step toward the 1998 IRL title.

Robbie Buhl (3) threw up his hands as if to say "what happened?" after he and Raul Boesel (30) got together. Both restarted, but finished poorly: Boesel was 18th, Buhl was 20th.

The road to Stewart's eventual win was slowed a bit by cold, windy, and damp conditions that were responsible for many of the cautions as cold tires did not adhere to the race track, causing several spins. But unlike last year, there were no injuries as the new safety modifications appeared to have solved some of the problems. There were 10 caution periods for 77 laps, including several strange incidents, beginning with Robbie Groff's crash at the start of the race when the torque of the engine whipped his car around into the wall (he later admitted he hadn't warmed up the tires).

A few laps into the race another incident occurred involving Roberto Guerrero. He went from sixth to second position entering the first turn on the first lap of the race. When the race was restarted following the Groff incident, Guerrero took the lead when he passed Stewart on the seventh lap. He was in the lead until the 13th lap when Eliseo Salazar spun coming off the first turn. As Guerrero tried to drive by, he was hit by Marco Greco as he was trying to avoid Salazar's car. The incident took both cars out of the race.

Accidents and cautions continued throughout much of the remaining race as well. While leaving the pits, Raul Boesel tried to get around the slower car of Kenny Brack and crashed into Robbie Buhl. Billy Boat was another driver who crashed on a restart; he was involved in a collision on the front straight, making impact with the pit retaining wall on the 105th lap. While all this was going on behind him, Stewart appeared to be in complete charge of the race. But on the 132nd lap, Buddy Lazier charged into the lead, passing Stewart in the third turn. Lazier stayed in the lead until his loose race car spun coming off the first turn on the 160th lap and crashed into the infield retaining wall.

Stewart was back in front but pitted with Hamilton and Ward on the 167th lap while Dismore stayed out and assumed the lead. The gamble nearly worked, but Dismore was unable to stretch the fuel mileage to the end as 50,000 fans cheered Stewart to victory. "We were setting Mark Dismore up a little bit for the end," said Larry Curry, team manager for Team Menard. "We count everybody's laps on fuel, and we knew Mark Dismore hadn't been in the pits since Lap 127. You can't run 73 laps in these cars on a load of fuel."

The victory by the defending IRL champion was a great start for the 1998 season. "One of the things we focused on in the winter is we have won

The eventual third-place finisher, Davey Hamilton of Las Vegas ran full-throttle all the way, but had to settle for a podium finish rather than the win.

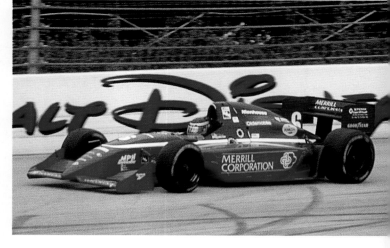

a championship, we sat on a lot of poles, but I told the guys in a team meeting we have to win more races," Curry said. "So here we are. This was the first year since I had been at Team Menard since 1993 that we didn't lose one employee. That is how you win races and championships, and that is what we will keep working on."

After finishing second to Buzz Calkins in the first-ever IRL race at Disney in 1996 and dominating last year's race before a broken oil line knocked him out while leading, Stewart and Team Menard could finally celebrate a victory at Disney World. "To be so close here for a couple of years, it means a lot to bring it home here," Stewart said. "As soon as I made it through the final turn, I said, 'Hey, we made it through Calamity Corner; all I've got to do is aim between the concrete walls, and we'll win it.' As I crossed the line I said, 'This is a big weight lifted off my shoulders.'"

With the burden removed, team owner John Menard thinks of even greater things to come for his team in 1998. "This is a track that has showcased our team, but we never really got the brass ring until today," said Menard. "We are real, real happy the way things turned out. We had a great race at the end with Buddy Lazier and then with Mark Dismore. That was a fantastic race. For us to dominate the race today and win, I hope, is a harbinger of how the season will go. We really needed this as a team."

It was also what the IRL really needed as it began its third season. Safety took a huge leap forward for the open-wheel, oval-track series. Although there was a number of crashes that accounted for 10 caution periods, there were no injuries. The IRL could take that as a sign that the new safety measures added to the race cars are paying off.

IRL Vice President/Executive Director Leo Mehl saw the circuit's third season get off to a fast start. Twenty-eight drivers started the race and fans saw the lead change hands eight times.

OFFICIAL BOX SCORE
PEP BOYS INDY RACING LEAGUE
Indy 200 at Walt Disney World Speedway
Saturday, January 24, 1998

FP	SP	Car	Driver	Car Name	C/E/T	Laps Comp.	Running/ Reason Out	IRL Pts.	Total IRL Pts.	IRL Standings	IRL Awards	Designated Awards	Total Awards
1	1	1	Tony Stewart	Glidden/Menard Special	G/A/F	200	Running	52	52	1	$91,900	$29,350	$121,250
2	24	35	Jeff Ward	ISM Racing	G/A/G	200	Running	40	40	2	54,900	5,650	60,550
3	19	6	Davey Hamilton	Nienhouse Motorsports	G/A/G	200	Running	35	35	3	65,500	11,250	76,750
4	15	77	Stephan Gregoire	Chastain Motorsports	G/A/G	200	Running	32	32	4	54,100	250	54,350
5	22	28	Mark Dismore	Kelley Automotive/LearJet/Valvoline	D/A/G	199	Running	30	30	5	27,900	8,000	35,900
6	20	8	Scott Sharp	Delphi/Futaba/AMD/Kelley	D/A/G	198	Running	28	28	6	22,800	750	23,550
7	4	10	Mike Groff	Jonathan Byrd's VisionAire Bryant Heating & Cooling	G/A/F	198	Running	26	26	7	43,700	0	43,700
8	5	5	Arie Luyendyk	Sprint PCS/Radio Shack	G/A/F	197	Running	24	24	8	42,700	0	42,700
9	17	99	Sam Schmidt	BG Product/Truck Air Racing Special	D/A/F	195	Running	22	22	9	42,700	0	42,700
10	7	18	John Paul Jr.	Klipsch/V-Line Overhead Door/ Earl's Perf Products	G/A/G	194	Running	20	20	10	41,700	850	42,550
11	27	20	Tyce Carlson	Keco	D/A/G	192	Running	19	19	11	18,600	0	18,600
12	26	15	Eliseo Salazar	Reebok R&S MK V	R/A/G	187	Running	18	18	12	17,600	0	17,600
13	2	14	Kenny Brack	AJ Foyt PowerTeam Racing	D/A/G	174	Running	17	17	13	38,600	0	38,600
14	10	12	Buzz Calkins	Bradley Food Marts/Sav-O-Mat	G/A/G	168	Running	16	16	14	37,500	0	37,500
15	8	91	Buddy Lazier	Hemelgarn/Delta Racing	D/A/G	165	Accident	15	15	15	36,500	0	36,500
16	28	7	Jimmy Kite	Royal Purple Synthetic/ Synerlec/Scandia	D/A/G	149	Half shaft	14	14	16	35,500	0	35,500
17	21	4	Scott Goodyear	Pennzoil Panther G-Force	G/A/G	132	Suspension	13	13	17	12,400	0	12,400
18	9	30	Raul Boesel	Beloit/Fast Rod/Team Losi/ McCormack Motorsports	G/A/G	128	Running	12	12	18	34,400	0	34,400
19	13	17 R	Brian Tyler	Chitwood Thrill Show Dallara	D/A/G	121	Accident	11	11	19	33,400	0	33,400
20	14	3	Robbie Buhl	John Manville/Menard Special	G/A/F	100	Electrical	10	10	20	32,400	0	32,400
21	3	11	Billy Boat	Conseco AJ Foyt Racing	D/A/G	72	Accident	9	9	21	32,400	0	32,400
22	18	19	Stan Wattles	Metro Racing Systems/NCLD	R/A/G	64	Accident	8	8	22	32,400	0	32,400
23	11	40	Dr. Jack Miller	Crest Racing	D/I/F	59	Handling	7	7	23	32,400	5,000	37,400
24	23	51	Eddie Cheever Jr.	Team Cheever	D/A/G	48	Engine fire	6	6	24	10,400	0	10,400
25	16	97	Greg Ray	TKM-Mercury Outboards	D/A/F	29	Accident	5	5	25	32,400	0	32,400
26	6	21	Roberto Guerrero	Pagan Racing DallaraOldsmobile	D/A/G	13	Accident	4	4	26	32,400	0	32,400
27	25	16	Marco Greco	Phoenix Racing	G/A/F	12	Accident	3	3	27	10,400	0	10,400
28	12	27	Robbie Groff	Blueprint Racing	D/A/F	0	Accident	2	2	28	32,400	0	32,400
			Menard Engines									600	600
			Brayton Engineering									800	800
											TOTAL - $1,000,000	$62,500	$1,062,500

Time of Race: 2:06:07
Margin of Victory: 8.579 seconds
MBNA America Lap Leader: #1 Tony Stewart

Average Speed: 95.14 mph
Fastest Lap: #14 Kenny Brack (Lap 57, 164.903)

Legend: R-Indy Racing League Rookie   Chassis Legend: D- Dallara; G- G Force   Engine Legend: A- Oldsmobile Aurora; I- Nissan Infiniti   Tire Legend: F- Firestone; G- Goodyear

Pep Boys Indy Racing League
Championship Series

PHOENIX INTERNATIONAL RACEWAY

Kelley Racing Takes the Desert Mile

SCOTT SHARP WINS WITH HELP FROM A FRIEND

by Jan Shaffer

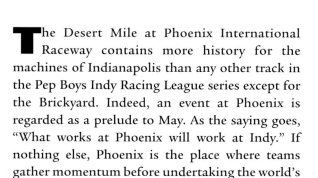

54th RUNNING INDY RACING LEAGUE
DURA-LUBE 200
PHOENIX INTERNATIONAL RACEWAY. MARCH 20-22, 1998

PEP BOYS
INDY RACING LEAGUE

Arizona fans saluted Scott Sharp as he took the checkered flag in the glorious desert sun. One year earlier he had finished a disappointing 16th in the Phoenix race.

Inset: After beating Tony Stewart in a late-race sprint to the finish, race winner Scott Sharp (in hat) was congratulated by teammate Mark Dismore (second from left). On the last restart, the field bunched up behind Dismore as Sharp screamed away toward victory.

The Desert Mile at Phoenix International Raceway contains more history for the machines of Indianapolis than any other track in the Pep Boys Indy Racing League series except for the Brickyard. Indeed, an event at Phoenix is regarded as a prelude to May. As the saying goes, "What works at Phoenix will work at Indy." If nothing else, Phoenix is the place where teams gather momentum before undertaking the world's oldest and most prestigious auto race.

So when the Dura-Lube 200 rolled around on March 22, 1998, the teams and drivers had Indy in the back of their minds, but were focused on conquering the Desert Mile. Phoenix fans witnessed the impressive form of Jeff Ward as he worked his way to his first career pole position. In the race itself, Scott Sharp beat Tony Stewart to the flag, claiming the victory. With a better understanding of the track by teams and drivers and further engine and chassis developments, the second race of the year was a story of speed.

With his Conseco Dallara-Aurora running beautifully, Billy Boat finished a strong third at Phoenix. The podium finish catapulted him to sixth place in the IRL points table as teams headed for Indy.

Increased speeds were foreshadowed the previous month at the third annual "Test of the West." At the "Test," seven drivers bettered Stewart's 1997 pole speed of 170.012 miles per hour, led by Sharp's lap of 174.893.

Practice rounds at Phoenix yielded substantial gains in performance, and lap records were shattered. After practice had been completed, six drivers bettered the 1997 pole speed. In a wild qualifying show, 32 drivers battled tooth and nail for the 28 starting positions. With new IRL rules governing provisional starters allowing for 28 starting positions, the number of qualifying cars would tie the largest-ever field at Phoenix, equaling the size of the group that took the green on April 10, 1994.

In all, eight drivers held the pole position at one time during qualifying. Ten bettered the previous year's pole speed. The field was the second closest in the 54-race history of Indy-style racing at Phoenix. Fortunately, a last-ditch effort by rookie David Steele to make the field was successful.

Tyce Carlson started the qualifying with a lap at 154.879 mph, followed by Greg Ray at 167.903 mph. Robbie Groff then checked in at 163.957 mph, with Mark Dismore pushing the bar to 169.221 mph. Eliseo Salazar was the first to better the 1997 pole speed with a lap at 171.241 mph. Four drivers would hold the pole, ever so briefly, in the first five qualifiers.

The smiles show that team owner A. J. Foyt and driver Billy Boat know they've got their car working well as the new IRL season heats up. Next stop: Indianapolis.

Jimmy Kite turned a lap at 172.282 mph to unseat Salazar, followed by Stewart who reached 172.505 mph just 2 minutes later. After four others posted qualifying runs, Billy Boat, in front of his hometown fans, nudged Stewart off the No. 1 starting spot with a lap at 172.521 mph. Following outings by Dr. Jack Miller and Marco Greco, Jeff Ward went to the line for his first qualification attempt and posted a first lap speed of 172.753 mph, which was good enough to stand.

Others took their shots. Buddy Lazier, Kenny Brack, and Davey Hamilton all reached the 170s but couldn't overturn Ward's run. Qualifying was suspended for 28 minutes to allow David Steele one last chance after his crew repaired his damaged mount from a crash. His first lap didn't get it done, but his second was 165.069 mph, good enough to bump Miller from the show and gain him his first Indy car start. Ironically, the defending Phoenix 200 Champion, Jim Guthrie, and Robbie Groff fielded by Blueprint Racing were both bumped.

The field was separated by just 8.106 miles per hour, an IRL record and the closest in 33 years at the legendary mile track. The closest Indy field in Phoenix International Raceway history came on March 28, 1965, with A. J. Foyt on the pole and the late Norm Hall in the 24th starting spot, separated by only 7.469 miles per hour.

Jeff Ward, whose best previous start was seventh for the 1997 Indianapolis 500, was quite satisfied with his results. "Qualifying isn't my forte, so I'm very pleased with this lap," Ward said. "We had a good practice this morning and knew there was something left in the car, although we didn't know how much. This is a nice change from Orlando, where we were at the back and never really got into the race."

"I didn't even know Boat bumped Stewart," he added. "Norm Johnson asked if I wanted to take some wing out to go for the pole, but I knew I had a good car and didn't want to change it. I've never been used to laying the wings back and going for outright speed."

Billy Boat, a newcomer to Phoenix in 1998, had a run good enough for the outside of the front row. Other newcomers to the Dura Lube 200 included David Steele and J. J. Yeley, both in their first Indy car race, and Jimmy Kite, Tyce Carlson, Brian Tyler, Dismore, Ward, and Greg Ray.

Newcomers and all were subjected to a hot spring day in the desert on race day. When the Dura Lube 200 started, the temperature was 85 degrees, and the track temperature was 122 degrees. As expected, Ward got the early lead, but Eddie Cheever, who started 20th, gained nine positions in the first three laps before Buddy Lazier brought out the first caution when he hit the Turn 4 wall.

Ward led the first 25 laps before turning the lead over to Tony Stewart, when he pitted on Lap 48. Boat took command at the front of the pack for six laps. On a Lap 55 restart, Cheever jumped ahead of Boat for the lead, having made the long pull from the rear. Boat got the edge back on Lap 61, but soon came Stewart to take it back on Lap 67.

By this point, several contenders had fallen by the wayside as the result of accidents. Lazier, Yeley, Hamilton, Steele, Arie Luyendyk, Salazar, and Sam Schmidt had all been involved in mishaps, and Dismore was on the sidelines for repairs.

Race winner Scott Sharp (8) passed J. J. Yeley (44) easily here, but Sharp faced a fierce duel with Yeley's Team Menard teammate Tony Stewart in the race's closing laps.

Along with changing tires and spinning wrenches, sophisticated IRL race teams utilize complex data acquisition equipment and laptop computers for performance analysis during testing and qualifying.

Scott Goodyear didn't qualify well (14th position), but he ran well at Phoenix, moving up to finish sixth. It was a heartening improvement from his 17th-place finish in the first race.

Racing veteran Sam Schmidt of Las Vegas showed his open-wheel savvy by improving steadily on his 13th-row starting position all the way to a career-best seventh-place finish.

Tire technicians from Firestone and Goodyear enable IRL drivers to put the rubber to the road. With the circuit's variety of track configurations and climates, the technicians' advice on tire set-up is always valuable.

Once in the lead, though, Stewart went on a tear. He lapped sixth-place Cheever at the halfway mark, but Kenny Brack was staying in his mirrors. On Lap 147, Stewart led Brack by only .80 of a second. On Lap 150, five cars were on the lead lap, with Sharp, Boat, and Stephan Gregoire trailing the leaders. Gregoire continued to impress. With minimal testing and a tiny budget, he consistently clawed his way towards the front of the field. Starting in 22nd position, he broke into the 5th position on Lap 60, briefly held 2nd, and eventually finished 4th.

Sharp went on the offensive and took over the lead from Stewart on Lap 171 when Stewart pitted for tires

under the caution. It would be a long, hard fight to move up to the front for Stewart, but when the race went green again, he sliced through the pack. Brack and Mike Groff tangled to bring out the final caution on Lap 186. The field closed up behind the pace car with Sharp at the front, Sharp's teammate Dismore in second, Stewart in third, closely followed by Boat.

When the track went green, Sharp dropped the hammer and sprinted away from the pack while Dismore slowed dramatically, forcing Stewart and Boat to

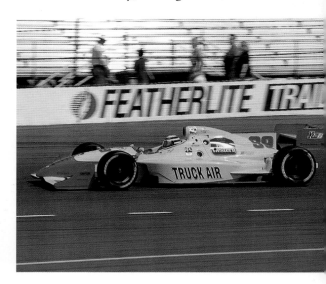

slow. Both drivers worked past Dismore and gave chase, but there was no overhauling Sharp, who won by 2.366 seconds with Stewart and Boat the only other drivers on the lead lap. Stewart claimed Dismore held him up, and later the IRL issued fines and took points away from Sharp to equalize him with Stewart at 43 points earned for the race.

"Mark Dismore slowed me down so much on the restart I had to put my clutch in or else I would've stalled the motor," Stewart said. "We'll never know if I could've caught him or not." Dismore disputed Stewart's charges. "Tony couldn't keep up with me in the last few laps," Dismore said. "If he could've passed me, he would've passed me." But it was Sharp's day and a first win for Kelley Racing. It was Sharp's second in IRL competition, the other coming in 1996 at New Hampshire.

"[On the radio] I asked Tom [Kelley, car owner] how quick Tony was and found he was not any quicker, and I was actually pulling away," Sharp said. "At the last restart, Mark was pulling away as well. Mark wasn't going to run Tony off the road, but he wasn't going to do him any favors

either. I lost here at Phoenix with a penalty [another year] when I had almost a lap lead, so what goes around comes around. I still think I would've beaten Tony even without Mark being there."

For Tom Kelley, the win was sweet. "We ran the dice today with one less pit stop," he said. "Today, our pit stops were great, and Scott picked up a couple of places. We're focusing on running this team like a business, and practicing pit stops is one of the things you need to do to be a top-notch team."

For others, it was also a good day. Boat's third-place finish was the best among those who had not previously started an Indy race at Phoenix. Stephan Gregoire and Scott Goodyear earned their best finishes ever at Phoenix, with fourth place and sixth place, respectively. And Sam Schmidt's seventh was his career IRL best.

And it was on to Indy.

For Stephan Gregoire, consistency at Phoenix was both good and bad. However, he posted his second-straight fourth-place finish.

OFFICIAL BOX SCORE
PEP BOYS INDY RACING LEAGUE
Dura-Lube 200 at Phoenix International Raceway
Sunday, March 22, 1998

FP	SP	Car	Driver	Car Name	C/E/T	Laps Comp.	Running/ Reason Out	IRL Pts.	Total IRL Pts.	IRL Standings	IRL Awards	Designated Awards	Total Awards
1	8	8	Scott Sharp	Delphi Automotive Systems	D/A/G	200	Running	43	71	3	$91,900	$14,850	$106,750
2	3	1	Tony Stewart	Glidden/Menards/Special	G/A/F	200	Running	43	95	1	76,900	19,400	96,300
3	2	11	Billy Boat	Conseco AJ Foyt Racing	D/A/G	200	Running	37	46	6	43,500	4,000	47,500
4	22	77	Stephan Gregoire	Chastain Motorsports	G/A/G	199	Running	32	64	4	54,100	11,250	65,350
5	1	35	Jeff Ward	ISM Racing	G/A/G	199	Running	33	73	2	49,900	45,600	95,500
6	14	4	Scott Goodyear	Pennzoil Panther G-Force	G/A/G	199	Running	28	41	8	44,800	10,000	54,800
7	25	99	Sam Schmidt	Best Western Gold Crown Racing Special	D/A/F	198	Running	26	48	5	43,700	0	43,700
8	13	30	Raul Boesel	Beloit/Fast Rod/Team Losi/McCormack Motorsports	G/A/G	197	Running	24	36	12	42,700	0	42,700
9	17	12	Buzz Calkins	Bradley Food Mart/Sav-O-Mat	G/A/G	197	Running	22	38	11	42,700	0	42,700
10	20	51	Eddie Cheever Jr.	Team Cheever	D/A/G	196	Running	20	26	18	19,700	0	19,700
11	18	97	Greg Ray	Aptex Mercury Marine	D/A/F	192	Running	19	24	21	18,600	0	18,600
12	12	3	Robbie Buhl	Johns Manville/Menards/Special	D/A/F	187	Running	18	28	17	39,600	0	39,600
13	27	20	Tyce Carlson	Immke Automotive Group/Immke Racing	D/A/G	186	Running	17	36	13	38,600	0	38,600
14	5	14	Kenny Brack	AJ Foyt PowerTeam Racing	D/A/G	185	Accident	16	33	14	37,500	0	37,500
15	24	10	Mike Groff	Jonathan Byrd's VisionAire Bryant Heating & Cooling	G/A/F	177	Accident	15	41	9	36,500	0	36,500
16	15	28	Mark Dismore	Kelley Automotive	D/A/G	175	Running	14	44	7	35,500	750	36,250
17	28	17 R	Brian Tyler	Syan Racing Dallara	D/A/G	168	Running	13	24	22	34,400	0	34,400
18	4	7	Jimmy Kite	Royal Purple Synthetic/ Synerlec/Scandia	D/A/G	129	Running	12	26	19	34,400	250	34,650
19	21	18	John Paul Jr.	PDM Racing, Inc.	G/A/G	126	Accident	11	31	15	33,400	0	33,400
20	16	16	Marco Greco	Phoenix Racing	G/A/F	122	Running	10	13	24	10,400	0	10,400
21	26	23	Paul Durant	CBR Cobb Racing	G/A/G	99	Engine	9	9	25	10,400	0	10,400
22	23	22 R	David Steele	rsm Marko	D/A/F	59	Engine	8	8	26	10,400	0	10,400
23	6	15	Eliseo Salazar	Reebok R&S MK V	R/A/G	58	Accident	7	25	20	32,400	0	32,400
24	19	5	Arie Luyendyk	Sprint PCS/Radio Shack/Qualcomm	G/A/G	58	Accident	6	30	16	32,400	0	32,400
25	10	44 R	J. J. Yeley	Quaker State Menards SRS	D/A/F	45	Accident	5	5	30	10,400	2,500	12,900
26	7	6	Davey Hamilton	Nienhouse Motorsports G-Force/Aurora	G/A/G	45	Accident	4	39	10	32,400	0	32,400
27	11	21	Roberto Guerrero	Pagan Racing Dallara/Oldsmobile	D/A/G	44	Transmission	3	7	29	10,400	0	10,400
28	9	91	Buddy Lazier	Hemelgarn Racing/Delta Faucet	D/A/G	9	Accident	2	17	23	32,400	0	32,400
			Menard Engines					800	800				
			Brayton Engineering					600	600				
										TOTAL -	$1,000,000	$110,000	$1,110,000

Time of Race: 2:02:18.735

Margin of Victory: 2.366 seconds

Fastest Lap: #1 Tony Stewart (Lap 43, 163.666)

Average Speed: 98.11 mph

Fastest Leading Lap: #1 Tony Stewart (Lap 43, 163.666)

PPG Pole Winner: Jeff Ward

True Value Pole Winning Chief Mechanic: Norm Johnson/ISM Racing

MBNA America Lap Leader: #1 Tony Stewart

Coors Pit Performance Winner: #4 Scott Goodyear/Panther Racing

Legend: R-Indy Racing League Rookie   Chassis Legend: D- Dallara; G- G Force; R- Riley & Scott   Engine Legend: A- Oldsmobile Aurora; I- Nissan Infiniti   Tire Legend: F- Firestone; G- Goodyear

A successful short-track veteran, Jack Hewitt was an Indy 500 rookie in 1998, meaning he had to pass his rookie test before attempting to qualify for the race.

Opening Day marked a major departure in Speedway tradition. Practice and qualifying for the "Greatest Spectacle" in racing was shortened to one week instead of two weeks; and no one knew quite what to expect. "It's been a little different for me like it has been for everyone," said Speedway President Tony George. "Last week, it seemed we should have been doing what we have in the past. But having the bad weather reinforces that the decision was the right one."

When the track went green at 11:07 A.M. under sunny skies, Mike Groff took the #10T Jonathan Byrd's VisionAire Bryant Heating & Cooling entry out first, completed two laps, and returned to the pits. In the past, Dick Simon entries have conducted a ceremony of their own. The drivers on the team vie for the honor of being the first car out on the track to practice. But it was not to be for Simon, who worked with Marco Greco and Phoenix Racing. "Well, it's impossible to beat someone that starts in one of the first pits," Simon said. "How do you make up for a half-mile? Jonathan [Byrd] has worked with me before, so he knows what it means to me. In reality, he was trying to beat Dick."

Rookie Jack Hewitt's opening day run didn't go according to plan. He hit the outside and inside walls of Turn 4 in the #18 Parker Machinery entry and logged in the month's first crash. "I entered the corner too high and got into the slow part of the track and couldn't get down," Hewitt said. "I just did it wrong. They were telling me to not get excited. They put a little push in the car so I would have to back off in the corners, and I didn't back off enough."

Hewitt's car caught fire in the incident, and a group of crewmen from Pagan Racing-Jack Pegues, Greg Elliff, Doug Barnes, Brett Andrew, and Barry Walkup-were the first to reach him with water and fire extinguishing equipment. "It looked like he needed a little help," said Elliff.

Later, rookie Jimmy Kite hit the wall in Turn 4, damaging the right front of the #7T Royal Purple Synthetic/Synerlec/Scandia entry. "We had a problem with the car pushing in Turn 1 all day," Kite said. "If I could make it through there, I knew it would be okay. On that lap, I made it through [Turns] 1, 2, and 3 and was halfway through [Turn] 4, and it just stopped turning."

Meanwhile, a group of established IRL front runners came out of the gate fast, led by Robbie Buhl with a lap at 219.325 miles per hour in the #3 Johns Manville-Menards Special, Arie Luyendyk at 219.207 in the #5T Sprint PCS-Radio Shack-Qualcomm entry, and Scott Sharp at 219.101 in the #8 Delphi Automotive Systems machine. The three-plus Jimmy Kite at 218.765 miles per hour-were faster

Nineteen sixty-three Indy 500 winner Parnelli Jones was one of six past winners honored during the Parade of Champions at IMS. Jones drove his Agajanian Willard Battery Special for a practice day crowd.

than the 1997 pole speed of 218.263 by Luyendyk. "I think you're looking at the whole front row at 220-plus," Buhl said. "The conditions are kind of tough today. It's windy and gusty in Turn 4 and coming off of [Turn] 1. You never know what it's going to be like on Pole Day, so you've got to run."

The Speedway was officially back to the real business of the 82nd running of the Indianapolis 500, with a long list of special events being held at the Speedway during the month of May (and even back into April). More than 19,000 students had visited the track at IMS School Days in April during the historic first open test at the Speedway.

On this, the opening day, Mari Hulman George, the Speedway chairman, presented a check for $50,000 to the Indiana Special Olympics as part of the 18th annual "Save Arnold" barbecue in the Speedway's Flag Lot. Parnelli Jones also took his historic car "Calhoun," in which he won the 1963 edition of the 500, around the 2 1/2-mile oval as part of the Speedway's new Parade of Champions. "To be honored is tremendous," Jones said. "You feel like you're a part of this place.

I've been here every year since 1960."

And 35 cars had taken to the track, running 933 laps in a fast and furious session.

DAY-AT-A-GLANCE

Date:	Sunday, May 10
Temperature:	High 74°
Drivers on Track:	32
Cars on Track:	35
Total Laps:	933

TOP TEN DRIVERS OF THE DAY

Car	Driver	Speed (mph)
3	Robbie Buhl	219.325
5T	Arie Luyendyk	219.207
8	Scott Sharp	219.101
7T	Jimmy Kite	218.765
51	Eddie Cheever Jr.	218.066
28	Mark Dismore	217.759
6	Davey Hamilton	216.648
1T	Tony Stewart	216.570
44	J. J. Yeley	216.403
77	Stephan Gregoire	216.351

Three-time winner Bobby Unser thrilled the crowd watching practice on Day 2 by taking his 1968 winner, the Rislone Special, for some hot laps around the famed oval.

The on-track action heated up as teams dialed in their cars and started turning in quicker lap times on the second day of practice. Tony Stewart, Robbie Buhl's teammate at Team Menard, blazed the trail with a lap at 223.703 miles per hour in the #1 Glidden-Menards Special as 43 cars went on the track for 1,221 practice laps in one of the busiest days ever at the Speedway.

"Mid-220s," Stewart said when asked to predict the pole speed. "No one will run 228 to 230. I can't tell you exactly, but it'll be around 223, 224. The increase in speed from '97 was multifold. Eighty percent of it is motor, 10 percent aerodynamics, and 10 percent tires."

Scott Sharp was next fastest at 222.107 miles per hour in the #8 Delphi Automotive Systems entry. "Today, we just went out to see what kind of speed we had in the car," Sharp said. "We had a few minor engine problems in both of our cars, so it limited the number of laps we could run."

Sweden's Kenny Brack followed at 222.080 in the #14 AJ Foyt Power Team Racing machine. He took a methodical and progressive approach to practice at the Speedway. "We just started today," he said. "For us, the car is quick straight out of the box. We're going to play along and see where we end up for the rest of the week."

Veteran Danny Ongais, who first raced at Indy in 1977, crashed following a spin during a practice run. He wasn't seriously injured, but the medical staff prohibited him from qualifying.

Unfortunately, Danny Ongais encountered a setback. Ongais spun while exiting Turn 3 in the #81 Team Pelfrey entry, and he hit the outside wall, warranting a trip to Methodist Hospital for a precautionary evaluation.

Meanwhile, Team Cheever was busy gearing up for their campaign at the Speedway. Rookie Robby Unser, son of three-time Indy 500 Champion Bobby, signed on to handle the driving chores of the Team Cheever entry. And Eddie Cheever, the team's owner, secured Rachel's Potato Chips as a sponsor for his own car.

"Every time his dad comes around, it scares me," Cheever joked. "I wonder what I did wrong." Robby responded, "Me too."

"Robby has a long way to go and a lot of things to do," Bobby said, "but so far, everything is going good. You've got to finish this race, that's really important. The first three years [of my Indy career], I saw a lot of pretty girls and a lot of press, but I didn't finish."

The elder Unser was the former champion who took a drive around the track on this day as part of the Parade of Champions. He drove two laps in the Rislone Special that carried him to victory in 1968. Sixty-one cars were now at the Speedway, and 46 drivers had passed physicals. Eight drivers exceeded 220 miles per hour on this day.

The week-long shootout continued.

DAY-AT-A-GLANCE

Date: Monday, May 11
Temperature: High 75°
Drivers on Track: 35
Cars on Track: 43
Total Laps: 1,221

TOP TEN DRIVERS OF THE DAY

Car	Driver	Speed (mph)
1	Tony Stewart	223.703
8	Scott Sharp	222.107
14	Kenny Brack	222.080
11T	Billy Boat	222.008
99	Sam Schmidt	221.588
51	Eddie Cheever Jr.	220.870
4	Scott Goodyear	220.604
3	Robbie Buhl	220.383
28T	Mark Dismore	219.111
53	Jim Guthrie	218.946

The teams and drivers put their machines into maximum overdrive and gave everyone a glimpse of their potential as the battle for the pole position started to take shape. As fate would have it, a contest between two powerhouse IRL teams, Team Menard and AJ Foyt Power Team Racing, unfolded.

Tony Stewart was again the quickest, turning a lap at 223.691 miles per hour in the Team Menard Dallara just 14 minutes before the track closed for the day. But Kenny Brack was second in the #14T AJ Foyt Power Team Racing entry at 221.593, and Billy Boat, in the #11 Conseco AJ Foyt Racing machine, was fourth at 220.060.

The talk again went to what it would take. "Whatever I can get," said Stewart. "There could be a 3-mile-per-hour difference between what I think and what it is, based on the weather. I don't care if we run 200 miles per hour; I just care if we get the pole. Then I'll be happy. For some strange reason, Foyt always seems to pull about 3/10ths [of a second] out of his hat for qualifying, so we'll see."

The Foyt camp was noncommittal. "We're making small changes here and there, and the car is getting better and better," Brack said. "We only ran once, and it was during the heat of the day."

Teammate Billy Boat stated, "Today was mainly a day of experimentation. We were trying different things and looking for a good handle on a race setup."

Elsewhere in Gasoline Alley, some made progress, and some had problems. Greg Ray and Thomas Knapp Motorsports announced they had lost their primary sponsor. Ray had actually lost the sponsor the previous day. After a story appeared in the Indianapolis Star, a member of the Speedway's Safety Patrol gave Ray $20 and a business card. The card was taped to the car. "It's our first cash sponsor," Ray said.

Pelfrey Racing was looking for a driver as Danny Ongais wasn't cleared to drive after his accident on Day 2. "We've talked to a few guys, Steve Kinser, John Paul [Jr.]," said Pelfrey crew chief Don Basala. "We're in communication with [Vincenzo] Sospiri as well."

The rookie field was getting acclimated to the track and the rigors of driving at the Speedway. Rookie Andy Michner got on the track for the first time with the Syan Racing team. "The car wasn't ready to go until last night," Michner said. "For the limited laps we ran, I'm kind of content with it."

Jack Hewitt, sidelined since Day 1 while the PDM Racing crew made repairs, was looking for-ward to a return to the track. "By doing the final phase [of the driver's test] tomorrow, we'll be working our way up to qualifying speed," Hewitt said.

First-timer Danny Drinan took a harrowing ride in the #24 D. B. Mann Development car, hitting the wall in Turn 1 late in the day. "We had just changed the rear wicker tab before that lap, and it just caught me by surprise," Drinan said. "I hope they can fix it. The damage looks pretty superficial. I just feel bad for Dave Mann and the team."

Two-time 500 winner Gordon Johncock was the daily honoree in the Speedway's Parade of Champions, taking two laps around the track in the STP Oil Treatment Wildcat that he took to Victory Lane in 1982 after a fierce battle with Rick Mears. "I wasn't going fast enough [on the exhibition lap], that's for sure," Johncock said. "I've got to thank the fans for all the support and memories, because without them, we wouldn't be here."

When Greg Ray's sponsorship program fell through, he took any and all financial support. He taped the cash and donors' names to his sidepod. By race day, though, the big bills were gone, used to buy food.

DAY-AT-A-GLANCE

Date:	Tuesday, May 12
Temperature:	High 77°
Drivers on Track:	35
Cars on Track:	43
Total Laps:	1,342

TOP TEN DRIVERS OF THE DAY

Car	Driver	Speed (mph)
1	Tony Stewart	223.691
14T	Kenny Brack	221.593
8	Scott Sharp	220.092
11	Billy Boat	220.060
97	Greg Ray	219.952
28T	Mark Dismore	218.989
35T	Jeff Ward	218.744
4	Scott Goodyear	218.314
5T	Arie Luyendyk	218.314
3	Robbie Buhl	218.113

A family atmosphere makes the track a great place to be during May. Kids of all ages have fun meeting the stars of open-wheel racing and watching their thrilling high-speed runs.

Tony Stewart took the day off, leaving the search for speed and the top of the ladder to Billy Boat and Scott Sharp. Boat registered a lap at 221.691 miles per hour in his spare #11T Conseco AJ Foyt Racing entry and a 220.751 in his primary car. The speeds were sandwiched around Sharp's, who recorded a lap in Kelley Racing's #8T Delphi Automotive Systems machine at 221.517.

"The thing that helped me the most today was talking to A. J. last night about the different lines that you can take around this track," Boat said. "With all of the cars that have run this month, there's a lot more rubber down and a lot more grooves. I was having a little trouble finding the right line. That's the benefit of having a four-time winner as your team owner. He's not shy about telling you what you do wrong."

Once again, Boat practiced in the heat of the day. "You always want to run faster, but we're kind of happy because we've been going out in the heat of the day," Foyt said. "Our goal is to try to qualify as well as possible and also to win the race. That's why we've been doing all of this running in the middle of the day at race time."

Meanwhile, Stewart and Team Menard were regrouping. "We had all of the engines out of Tony's car today," said Larry Curry, the team's director of racing. "We've had a little engine trouble. We wanted to take a breather. We wanted to pull back a little bit. He'll be back out tomorrow."

Jack Hewitt, bidding for his first 500 start at age 46, got back on the track for the first time since Opening Day. "We haven't got up to speed," Hewitt said. "The handling is 100 percent better, but we dropped a cylinder, so we pulled the motor. We're going to go out early tomorrow and finish it [the final phase of the driver's test]. It's great just being here, just being a part of the show, like the yellow shirts, the mechanics, the reporters. Just being part of the show."

The D. B. Mann team decided to go for it and repair the car that rookie Danny Drinan had crashed on Day 3. "Dave Mann is stepping up," said Jimmy Drinan, Danny's brother who served as the team's chief mechanic. "After the wreck, he's a little strapped for cash, but he's going ahead with the program."

Three-time 500 winner Johnny Rutherford was honored in the Speedway's Parade of Champions. "We're seeing a great metamorphosis," said Lone Star J. R. "If there's any one place in the world that's based on tradition, this is it. And we're seeing the transition from that great tradition to some new traditions. I'm proud to be involved with the IRL and with the Indianapolis Motor Speedway because that's what made the name Johnny Rutherford what it is, if it's anything today."

DAY-AT-A-GLANCE

Date:	Wednesday, May 13
Temperature:	High 83°
Drivers on Track:	33
Cars on Track:	34
Total Laps:	1,194

TOP TEN DRIVERS OF THE DAY

Car	Driver	Speed (mph)
11T	Billy Boat	221.691
8T	Scott Sharp	221.517
5T	Arie Luyendyk	220.464
14T	Kenny Brack	220.135
97	Greg Ray	219.539
28T	Mark Dismore	219.298
3	Robbie Buhl	218.739
15	Eliseo Salazar	218.097
16	Marco Greco	218.050
43	Scott Goodyear	217.812

With two days to go before pole qualifying, teams stepped up preparations for running the cars in qualifying trim. Joe Gosek and Scott Harrington passed refresher tests, and Jack Hewitt became the 10th rookie to complete the final phase of his driver's test with little time to spare.

In a turn of good sportsmanship, Gosek and Team Liberty got a helping hand from Jonathan Byrd-Cunningham Racing. When the Team Liberty car wasn't ready for track time, the Byrd-Cunningham team lent Mike Groff's backup car to Gosek for the refresher.

"The car was very comfortable," Gosek said of the Groff mount. "I've got to thank Jonathan Byrd . . . to allow me to use their car was an honor."

"Mike Deer, who owns Joe's car, is a good friend," Byrd said. "He's a good friend to all of racing, and they're in a little bit of a tight spot. He's helped our team in the past. It was a chance to return the favor."

"I can't thank the Jonathan Byrd-Cunningham team enough," Deer said. "It's in the true spirit of Indianapolis. That's what it's all about."

Also on this day, John Paul Jr. was named to drive the #81 Team Pelfrey entry vacated by the injured Danny Ongais. Paul was reunited with Team Pelfrey car owner John LaRue. The two attended Delta High School, just outside Muncie, Indiana, together.

When asked if he knew the last driver to replace Danny Ongais at Indy, Paul replied, "Yes, I do. That happened to be Al Unser [in

Rolled out of the garage without its front suspension cover and its engine cowling, Buddy Lazier's car shows some of the complex technology that makes up an IRL race car.

Eventual Rookie of the Year Steve Knapp waited out the rain from the seat of his well-covered car. He qualified on the eighth row but drove to an impressive third-place finish.

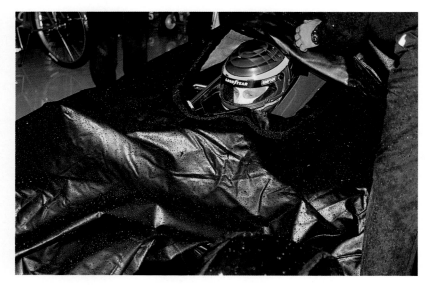

miles per hour in his Team Menard primary car just 2 minutes before the track closed. Kenny Brack was just a tick behind at 223.264 in the #14 AJ Foyt Power Team Racing entry. And Greg Ray came out of nowhere, sponsor problems and all, to turn the third quickest speed at 222.717 in the #97 TKM-Genoa Racing machine.

"Foyt's going to have to work harder if he wants the top spot," Stewart commented.

"Just when you think you've got this thing figured out," said Team Menard director of racing Larry Curry, ". . . you know Foyt will have his cars toward the top and then comes Greg Ray out of nowhere. This is going to be a very interesting qualifying day on Saturday."

1987]. He was walking around without a ride and ended up winning the race." It was also Al Sr.'s record-tying fourth win at the Indy 500.

Veteran Hideshi Matsuda, known for putting cars in 500 fields with little practice, was named to the #54 Beck Motorsports entry. It was his first venture in a normally-aspirated Indy Racing League car. "The engine has big torque," Matsuda said. "At 7,000 [rpm], the car jumps. I'm trying to bring it up slow to get used to the torque. When I let off, I call it nose-diving. The car slows down real fast when you let off."

With qualifications looming ahead, competition for the pole tightened.

For the third time in five days, Tony Stewart turned the fastest lap with a circuit at 223.430

And to end the practice session, in the last half hour Jimmy Kite backed into the Turn 4 wall in the #7 Royal Purple Synthetic/Synerlec/Scandia entry. Kite was uninjured, but the team had a lot of work ahead of itself to repair the car for qualifying.

Al Unser was honored this day in the Speedway's Parade of Champions, driving a pair of ceremonial laps in the Cummins Holset Turbo machine that carried him to his fourth win at Indy in 1987. "This is still the biggest and greatest race there is," Unser said.

Every car lined up for qualifying goes through an intense tech inspection to ensure it meets IRL safety and competition standards. Buzz Calkins' car was scrutinized here before a qualifying run.

DAY-AT-A-GLANCE

Date:	Thursday, May 14
Temperature:	High 87°
Drivers on Track:	38
Cars on Track:	46
Total Laps:	1,024

TOP TEN DRIVERS OF THE DAY

Car	Driver	Speed (mph)
1	Tony Stewart	223.430
14	Kenny Brack	223.264
97	Greg Ray	222.717
15	Eliseo Salazar	221.637
8T	Scott Sharp	220.577
3	Robbie Buhl	220.399
16	Marco Greco	220.189
91T	Buddy Lazier	219.587
51	Eddie Cheever Jr.	219.282
28T	Mark Dismore	219.234

Tony Stewart and Kenny Brack staged an intense duel for the top spot on the speed charts, and Billy Boat suffered a setback as teams jockeyed for position on the day before pole qualifying.

There was a lot on the line for pole qualifying day. A quick run on Pole Day is essential for starting up front and getting good track position early in the race. It also reduces the chances of being involved in a first turn altercation because there are more cars behind you rather than in front of you. There was a sizable reward up for grabs as well. The PPG Pole Award of $100,000 cash, a $27,000 Chevrolet Camaro convertible, and a $12,000 Harley-Davidson XL 1200 were on the line.

Stewart again posted the day's top lap at 223.797 miles per hour in the #1 Glidden/Menards Special, but Brack was right behind at 223.464 miles per hour in the #14 AJ Foyt Power Team Racing entry.

When asked about qualifying and the pole, Stewart had the following to say:

The pole speed? "Whatever the pole speed is going to be, it's going to be," Stewart replied.

More pressure with just two days of qualifying? Stewart: "Pole Day is still Pole Day."

How would you handle a bad qualifying draw? Stewart: "Larry Curry [Team Menard director of racing] knows what he's doing. When he says it's time to go, I'll get in the car and go."

The Foyt team also threw its two cents in the pot. "I think we have a shot [at the pole]," said Brack. "The car is definitely up to it, and I'm up to it. The one guy who has the best [air and track] condition at the time will get the pole."

Brack's next closest competitor on Day 6 was Billy Boat. In the morning, Boat hit the Turn 3 wall with his primary #11 Conseco AJ Foyt Racing entry, sustaining heavy right-side damage. He came out later in his backup. "It just didn't turn," Boat said. "I was going down into Turn 3 like every other lap, and the car just went straight." In his backup, Boat fashioned a lap at 221.691 miles per hour, third fastest of the day.

Greg Ray was again nearby with a lap at 220.626 miles per hour in the #97 TKM/Genoa Racing machine. And from news reports of the gift of $20 and a business card to help sponsor Ray, others materialized. "I'm very surprised at how much the media has opened their arms to us and helped us out," Ray said. "I'm surprised at all of the business cards I've received and the $20 bills."

Joe Gosek took his first laps in the #29 Liberty Special, which carried a tribute to the late Garry A.

Hoffman, a photographer at Indianapolis Raceway Park and a Frito-Lay delivery employee who was shot during a robbery at a convenience store and later died. Hoffman was an A. J. Foyt fan, and his tombstone carries a color etching of the car Foyt drove to his fourth victory in the 1977 Indianapolis 500. "It's really neat because Garry never got to drive a race car," said Sharon Henselmeier, Garry Hoffman's sister. "But now, he'll be on one, looking down smiling, hopefully."

Taking a wild ride on the sixth day at the Speedway was Jack Hewitt who did two half-spins without making contact in Turn 2.

Tom Sneva was the honoree of the Speedway's Parade of Champions, taking two laps around the 2 1/2-mile oval in the Texaco Star that carried him to victory in 1983. Asked why Indy was special, Sneva responded, "It's hard to explain why. There's some electricity in the air when they come around to start this race."

Pole Day awaited.

Joe Gosek of Oswego, New York, attempted to qualify for his second Indy 500, but a broken gear thwarted his second and final attempt.

DAY-AT-A-GLANCE

Date:	Friday, May 15
Temperature:	High 85°
Drivers on Track:	43
Cars on Track:	53
Total Laps:	1,633

TOP TEN DRIVERS OF THE DAY

Car	Driver	Speed (mph)
1	Tony Stewart	223.797
14	Kenny Brack	223.464
11T	Billy Boat	221.691
97	Greg Ray	220.626
8T	Scott Sharp	220.610
5T	Arie Luyendyk	219.925
28T	Mark Dismore	219.909
3	Robbie Buhl	219.673
99	Sam Schmidt	219.170
15	Eliseo Salazar	218.898

The morning practice did little to clear up the question of who would win the pole position for the 82nd running of the Indianapolis 500. Billy Boat turned a lap at 223.836 miles per hour in the #11T Conseco AJ Foyt Racing entry. It was the fastest of the event and the fastest lap turned at the Speedway with the Indy Racing League's new formula. But Tony Stewart came close with a circuit of 222.442 miles per hour in the #1 Glidden/Menards Special car. One driver, Paul Durant, was taken out of pole contention when he hit the wall at the exit of Turn 1 in the #23 CBR Racing entry.

When actual qualifications began, Speedway rookie Jack Hewitt was first up. Both Hewitt and Eddie Cheever, the first to attempt qualifications, waved off with laps in the 215-mile-an-hour range.

The first qualifier was John Paul Jr., who fashioned a four-lap run of 217.351 miles per hour in the #81 Team Pelfrey car. The team had come back from its earlier crash. "The fact that the car crashed on Tuesday and ran [2]18s today says a lot," Paul said. "It's a testimonial to the team."

Sam Schmidt was next and checked in at 219.982 miles per hour in the #99 Best Western/Gold Crown Racing Special. "We struggled with a lack of motor all week," Schmidt said. "Today, the car really stuck to the ground. I think we should have no problem running all day [in the race] at 215 or 216. I think track conditions and lack of a tow like you have in practice contributed to the slower speeds."

Robbie Buhl became the first qualifier to exceed 220 with a run at 220.236 miles per hour in the #3 Johns Manville/Menards Special, even though his first two laps were in the 219 bracket. "Every lap was on the rev limiter," Buhl said. "We lost our qualifying motor yesterday, so we're pretty happy."

Tony Stewart was next, and the crowd waited with anticipation. Although he got the pole for the moment with a run of 220.386 miles per hour in the #1 Glidden/Menards Special, speeds were clearly slowing from the morning practice. "There's nothing left for me to do right now but just wait," Stewart said. "I wish we could have run a [2]22 like we did this morning. But as warm as it got from the time we practiced this morning until now and knowing how much I had to get off the gas, it was a pretty good [run] I think, still."

A pair of rookies, Steve Knapp and Donnie Beechler, brought the number of qualifiers to six. Knapp averaged 216.445 miles per hour in the #55 ISM Racing Dallara, the third machine in the team's stable. Beechler managed 216.357 miles per hour in the #98 Cahill Auto Racing entry. It would not only be their first 500 but their first in an Indy car.

"It hasn't even sunk in yet," said Knapp. "I'm still thinking about what I was doing during the run. This has been a dream of mine since I was a kid. Now it's complete. We all talked before the run, and they said to keep your foot on the floor for four laps, and you'll make it in. That's what I did."

"To be honest, for years I wanted to go stock car racing," Beechler said. "I always liked Indy cars, but with the previous organization they were out of reach. I raced with Ken Schrader and saw him getting stock car rides, so I thought that was the only way for me to go. But when [car owner] Larry Cahill gave me the opportunity, I jumped at it."

Billy Boat (center) enjoyed his pole-winner awards with team owner A. J. Foyt (right). It was the first Indy 500 pole for a Foyt car since A. J. won the pole in 1975.

Billy Roe put the #33T Royal Purple/ProLink/Scandia car in at 215.781 miles per hour. "We were a little disappointed we didn't get to work on the car," Roe said.

After Scott Sharp waved off after a lap at 218.240 miles per hour, Mark Dismore, his teammate at Kelley Racing, put together a solid run of 218.096 miles per hour in the #28T Kelley Racing entry. "The car was a really good car, and I thought we could do 220s," Dismore said. "But on the first lap, I looked down and saw [2]19.4. I knew I was in trouble because the car was pushing."

Then came another contender in the form of Kenny Brack, A. J. Foyt's first driver to attempt to qualify. Brack became the field's ninth qualifier with a four-lap average of 220.982 miles per hour in the #14 Foyt Dallara, which was good enough to unseat Stewart from the No. 1 starting spot. When asked about driving Foyt's prestigious No. 14, Brack jokingly said, "Yeah, it's hard to drive that car. You really got to do well, you know? Last year, I learned how big this event is. You have to focus on what you're doing here. Being with A. J. here is easier because he knows all there is to know."

Next came Robby Unser. With his cousin two-time Indy 500 winner Al Unser Jr. giving him a thumbs-up, he took the #52 Team Cheever machine to a run of 216.534 miles per hour to qualify for the first time at Indy. "This is an emotional time for me," Robby Unser said. "The hardest thing for me right now is to hold back the tears. Getting in this show is all I want. It's the life I've chosen." In doing so, he became the sixth member of the legendary family to make a 500 field.

Disaster struck rookie Jimmy Kite on the next scheduled run. Kite slammed into the Turn 1 wall on the first lap of the run. He was uninjured, but his team had suffered another setback. "Our plan is to have another car out there late this afternoon for Jimmy," said Team Scandia manager Luke Wethington. "It looks like it will be [teammate] Billy's [Roe] backup. We have no idea right now what happened. It looks like the car just got up into the gray and pushed up into the wall."

Scott Goodyear followed, driving the #4 Pennzoil Panther G Force for a new team co-owned by NFL quarterback Jim Harbaugh. Goodyear's run of 218.357 miles per hour was solidly in the show. "We found a consistent race car today and also the limit for the G Force, which is 218 or 219," Goodyear said. "I had a little push on the first lap, but I used the weight jacker in the car to make adjustments. The wind made things really tricky."

After Dr. Jack Miller waved off, Davey Hamilton qualified the #6 Nienhouse Motorsports G Force Aurora at 219.748 miles per hour. "All week, we were working with our race setup to get the car competitive," Hamilton said. "I qualified with a race setup. I like going fast but going fast when it counts. We have a lot of downforce in the car, and I didn't want to risk it." Andy Michner followed and waved off after two laps.

Then came Billy Boat, who would be shooting at the pole speed that Brack, his teammate, currently held. Boat turned in a four-lap average of 223.503 miles per hour in the #11T Conseco AJ Foyt Racing machine to unseat Brack from the No. 1 starting spot. "You don't want to show your hand [in practice]," Boat said. "When we went out this morning, I knew we could run 224 today. The only problem I had was in Turn 1 with the wind. I was real loose, and I knew I'd have to run through it because I was okay in the others [turns]. On the fourth lap, I lost it in Turn 1, and I held my breath three times."

Marco Greco pulled into the pits before taking the green flag, then Eliseo Salazar went out in the #15 Reebok Riley & Scott MK V, but the racing gods weren't with him. On his first qualifying lap, Salazar did a three-quarter spin and hammered the Turn 1 wall. He suffered a bruised left shoulder and was transported to Methodist Hospital for X-rays.

After Roberto Guerrero waved off, 1996 IRL co-champion Buzz Calkins posted a four-lap average of 217.197 miles per hour in the #12 International Star Registry/Bradley Food Marts car. "It's always the longest 2 minutes and 45 seconds of your life

This is one of the powerplants that propels IRL cars to speeds in excess of 215 miles per hour. The Nissan Infiniti engine is undergoing considerable development to bring it up to the level of rival engine builder Oldsmobile.

here," Calkins said. "It's a relief to be in the field. This morning when we ran, I thought it would be possible to run consistent 218s. It's getting slick out there, so we have to be happy considering how we were running 48 hours ago."

Buddy Lazier, the 1996 Indy 500 champion, was next and qualified at 218.288 miles per hour in the #91 Delta Faucet/Coors Light/Hemelgarn Racing entry. "We went a little too aggressive," said Lazier. "I had some huge corrections and some anxious moments in [Turn] 1. I can't go any quicker. I'm wide open."

Rookie J. J. Yeley was next and put together the top rookie run to that point with a four-lap average of 218.044 miles per hour in the #44 One Call Communications/Quaker State/Menards/SRS entry. "We had a problem on the tech pad, so I didn't get to sit and think about it [qualifying hype]," Yeley said. Yeley was the 16th to qualify, and his run ended the original qualifying line, leaving others to search for speed later.

The first of those was Johnny Unser, 2 hours later. He ran three strong 217-plus laps in the #9 Hemelgarn Racing car, but the car quit in Turn 2 of the final lap. "It just sputtered and shut off," Unser said. But he came back 46 minutes later to record a run of 216.316 miles per hour. According to Unser, "We just had a miscalculation and ran out of gas. There's nothing worse than running out of gas on the way to work." In between Unser's runs, Tyce Carlson had a mishap with the #20

Immke machine, hitting the Turn 1 wall during practice. He was uninjured, but the car was extensively damaged.

Rookie Andy Michner was the first to push in line for the final end-of-the-day scramble at 4:43 P.M. He became the 18th qualifier with a run of 216.922 miles per hour in the #17 Konica/Syan Racing Dallara. He said waiting until later made a difference in his second bid to make a 500 field. "It did," Michner said. "We knew the car had speed in it. I just wanted to get in the show. It's a dream come true. The 500 has always been on my mind."

After Jim Guthrie waved off, Scott Sharp took to the track in his #8 Delphi Automotive Systems Dallara. Sharp's first two laps were faster than 220, but he settled into a four-lap run of 219.910 miles per hour. "It felt great on the first lap," Sharp said. "I thought I had 221s, but I got a big push. We had problems all day long. Lots of drama for the team, so it's good just to be in the show now."

Stan Wattles was next driver to take to the track, but he waved off. Cheever came back for a second attempt in the #51 Rachel's Potato Chips car and posted a run of 217.334 miles per hour. "I'm not happy," Cheever said. "I'm just going to take it and smile. My car was very loose. Last night it was good. Today it decided to misbehave. That's the worst our cars have run all week."

Mike Groff waved off, then Greg Ray came to the line. The pole was still within reach, but it would take a hot run late in the day to do it. Ray's first lap was 222.728 miles per hour, and he followed with three laps at 220-plus for a 221.125-mile-per-hour average to split the Foyt teammates and take the middle spot on the front row. "Earlier in the day, I thought it was too hot, and we had some handling problems," Ray said. "I'm so happy for this small team. This is our Cinderella story. Every boy dreams about running the Indy 500."

Salazar, back from Methodist Hospital where X-rays proved negative, went out and waved off after three laps in his backup mount. Then came Jack Hewitt for his second try, and the popular 46-year-old short-track veteran put the #18 Parker Machinery entry into the show with a run of 216.540 miles per hour, getting in the field for his first 500. "Everybody just stuck behind me," said Hewitt. "My team believed in me. Johnny Rutherford, Tony George, Gary Bettenhausen, and Big Al [Unser]—they all helped me out. There are 400,000 people here, and I've got enough emotion for every one of them now.

This is not how you want to end a qualifying run—on the hook. The IMS Safety Team prepares the car of Jimmy Kite for the long, slow ride back to the garage.

If I wasn't so old and stiff, I'd probably be doing flip-flops down the pit road. It's unbelievable."

Roberto Guerrero, also on a second try, put the #21 Pagan Racing Dallara Oldsmobile into the field with a run of 218.900 miles per hour. "The team worked so very hard," Guerrero said. "We're just happy that we're finally in the race. In the middle of the week, I was worrying about that. We did so many laps around this place . . . it has finally paid off."

Two-time winner Arie Luyendyk was next but mustered only 214.618 miles per hour on his first lap and waved off. Jim Guthrie made it into the show with a run of 216.604 miles per hour in the #53 ISM Racing G Force. "We took out some downforce and found a couple miles per hour," Guthrie said. "We'd like to be further up, but now we can start the race and have a chance to finish." After Guthrie's run, Stephan Gregoire and Lyn St. James tried to find the necessary speed but waved off as well.

Marco Greco, who had aborted before starting a qualifying attempt earlier in the day, went out and registered a four-lap average of 217.953 miles per hour. "I'm really pleased," Greco said. "We had a few problems in the morning. We put a new engine in and went straight out to qualifying. We had no practice. It [the engine] is shy 200 revs."

As the final qualifier, just 4 minutes from the end of the day, Dr. Jack Miller returned and qualified the #40 Crest Racing entry—the only Nissan Infiniti-powered car to do so—at 217.800 miles per hour. "Nissan has stuck with us, and we stuck with them, and it paid off today," said Miller. "It's been a struggle. I knew all along that Nissan was going to work."

When the dust cleared, 26 drivers had qualified for the 500. Boat, Ray, and Brack made up the front row, all second-year drivers. In doing so, the young lions of the IRL tied an interesting Indianapolis 500 record for the least experienced front row in history. That record had belonged solely to the 1935 Indy 500's starting front row, with pole sitter Rex Mays making his second start, Al Gordon in the middle making his third, and Floyd Roberts on the outside making his first.

For A. J. Foyt, it was the first time one of his cars had taken the pole since he drove one himself to the No. 1 starting spot in 1975. For Boat, he was the first second-year driver to win the pole since Rick Mears in 1979. "Winning is what matters," Foyt said. "You have good years and bad years. Things straightened out for us today. Qualifying is a starting point. You don't win the race on qualifying day."

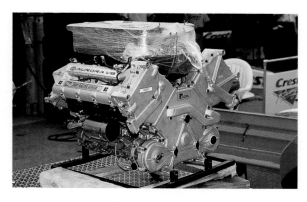

Forty-two qualification runs were attempted, a record for first-day attempts, breaking the mark of 38 set on May 12, 1984. Others were left with a single thought: What would it take to make the field?

And to make this first day of qualifying complete, four-time winner A. J. Foyt drove ceremonial laps in the Bowes Seal Fast car that took him to his first 500 win in 1961.

The Oldsmobile Aurora is the most dominant and prevalent engine used in the Indy Racing League. Although the Aurora engine has powered every IRL race winner to victory, the Nissan Infiniti continues to gain ground on the Olds.

DAY-AT-A-GLANCE

Date:	Saturday, May 16
Temperature:	High 82°
Qualification Attempts:	42
Qualifiers:	26

POLE DAY QUALIFIERS

Car	Driver	Speed (mph)
11T	Billy Boat	223.503
97	Greg Ray	221.125
14	Kenny Brack	220.982
1	Tony Stewart	220.386
3	Robbie Buhl	220.236
99	Sam Schmidt	219.982
8	Scott Sharp	219.910
6	Davey Hamilton	219.748
21	Roberto Guerrero	218.900
4	Scott Goodyear	218.357
91	Buddy Lazier	218.288
28T	Mark Dismore	218.096
44	J. J. Yeley	218.044
16	Marco Greco	217.953
40	Dr. Jack Miller	217.800
81	John Paul Jr.	217.351
51	Eddie Cheever Jr.	217.334
12	Buzz Calkins	217.197
17	Andy Michner	216.922
53	Jim Guthrie	216.604
18	Jack Hewitt	216.540
52	Robby Unser	216.534
55	Steve Knapp	216.445
98	Donnie Beechler	216.357
9	Johnny Unser	216.316
33T	Billy Roe	215.781

For rookie Stan Wattles, even the 10th row is a great place to start because it means you're in the show. Wattles qualified 29th, putting him next to two-time winner Arie Luyendyk.

Day 8 of the 1998 Indy 500 promised to be one of the most interesting "Bump Days" in memory—good for some and devastating to others.

When the day started, 26 cars were qualified for the 82nd running of the 500. The questions that remained were: who would fill the remaining 7 spots in the 33-car starting field? And how would they get them? In the morning practice, some competitors were quickly up to speed. Jeff Ward was fastest at 219.149 miles per hour, and two-time Indy 500 Winner Arie Luyendyk was just a tick behind at 219.127 miles per hour. Raul Boesel and Scott Harrington were both in the 218 bracket.

With the temperature at 78 degrees Fahrenheit, Boesel was first to go when the track opened for qualifications and put the #30 Beloit/Fast Rod/Team Losi/McCormack Motorsports entry in the field with a smooth run and a four-lap average of 217.303 miles per hour. "It's been a very long week," Boesel said. "We struggled quite a bit and had major problems almost day-to-day. We dropped a little bit of speed from the first laps. In Turn 4 the car started to react differently, and I lost a lot of grip."

Rookie Stan Wattles was next and ran his fastest laps of the month to record a run of 217.477 miles per hour in the #19 Metro Racing Systems machine. "It's quite a relief," said Wattles. "We've worked very hard at assembling this team, getting the Riley & Scott [chassis] up to speed, myself up to speed. The 217 was the fastest we've

run yet. That's the way to do it, have the 217 in qualifying, not in practice."

After Mike Groff and Eliseo Salazar waved off, Luyendyk then took the #5T Sprint PCS/Radio Shack/Qualcomm car into the field at 218.935 miles per hour. It was the same car in which he won the 1997 Indianapolis 500, and it is the first G Force produced by the manufacturer. "Yesterday, the moment I went out of the pits to practice, the motor wouldn't run," Luyendyk said. "The second motor wouldn't run in the afternoon qualifying either. The crew put in a motor today, the last one we had available, which had way too many miles on it to be crisp. But it performed."

Jeff Ward put together the fastest run of the day up to that point at 219.086 miles per hour in the #35 ISM Racing entry to become the month's 30th qualifier. "It was easy," said Ward. "The car stuck like glue. It wasn't a white-knuckle run. There was a lot left in the car."

The next potential qualifier, Scott Harrington, saw his month come to an end against the Turn 1 wall in the #66 LP Racing machine. The crash left the LP team in a scramble to find another car because it had sold the team's #99T backup to Tyce Carlson's team the previous day. As the day played out, nothing was available. After Danny Drinan waved off, Eliseo Salazar returned for the third and final time in the #15T Reebok Riley & Scott MK V and qualified at 216.259 miles per hour. Salazar's run ended the first wave with 31 qualifiers. The two remaining spots and any bumping would come later in "Happy Hour."

Those festivities started early, when Claude Bourbonnais went to the line at 4:31 P.M., and others trailed into the tech area after him. But Bourbonnais and Joe Gosek waved off attempts. Stephan Gregoire, the third in the final qualifying line of May, recorded a run of 217.036 miles per hour in the #77 Blue Star/Tokheim/Estridge/Miller-Eads entry. "We've been struggling," Gregoire said. "The push started on the second lap, but the car ran consistent. We lost time with the engine. It was our fault, not the engine builder's. The Calkins' helped us out last night."

After Hideshi Matsuda waved off, Jimmy Kite took the #7 Royal Purple Synthetic/"Synerlec"/Scandia Dallara on to the track and delivered a solid run of 219.290 miles per hour to end his month of adversity. Kite pumped his fist continuously on his cool-down lap as he made the field after three trips to the Speedway's walls. His speed would hold up as the fastest for a rookie in the field. "The team never gave up," Kite said. "Anytime something happened, I got back up. Boy, am I going to have a good seat for the race. I'm praising the guys every minute. It's been a roller coaster every day. You second guess. You ask yourself, 'Is it really meant to be? Am I supposed to be in the 500?' Just when it seems nothing goes right, everything goes right." Kite was also the 33rd qualifier, filling the starting grid, with just more than an hour left in qualifications.

For many drivers, the search for speed proved futile. Lyn St. James, Bourbonnais, Gosek, Matsuda, and Drinan all waved off attempts in succession. Billy Roe's speed of 215.781 miles per hour was on the bubble. With 37 minutes left in time trials, Mike Groff went out and bumped Roe with a run of 216.704 miles per hour in the #10 Jonathan Byrd's VisionAire Bryant Heating & Cooling entry. "We had a rough week," said Groff. "It came down to the wire. The guys rose to the occasion. The crew never doubted. They kept my confidence level up. I've never done this 'fourth day' [Bubble Day]. I don't like it. This is the toughest I've ever had it."

Durant and Gosek waved off (Gosek's for the third strike), before Roe went out with 24 minutes left in the #33 Royal Purple/ProLink/Scandia machine and registered a run of 217.835 miles per hour to bump Salazar. "We went out and qualified the backup car [Saturday]," Roe said. "Everybody thought a [2]15.8 would be good enough, so we just took it." After Kite's accidents, the Scandia team

Indy 500 veteran Mike Groff found the speed to make the show, qualifying for the last row. He fared much better on race day, moving up to finish 15th.

did some mixing and matching to have a car ready for Kite and another ready for Roe. Drinan waved off on his third strike, and St. James recorded a too-slow run of 215.642 miles per hour.

With 4 minutes to go, Salazar, in the Wattles backup, went to the line. After two laps in the 211 range, he was waved off by stewards after observers reported the car smoking. "What can I say?" asked Salazar. "We all tried so hard. We started this week with the fourth quickest time, then the crash. It seems no matter what we tried, it was not enough. I can't thank the guys enough—Riley & Scott, Reebok, Nienhouse, and Stan Wattles' group pitching in at the end. We just ran out of time."

Sixty-nine qualifying attempts had been made by 44 cars over two days. The field average was 218.305 miles per hour, slightly better than Luyendyk's pole speed from 1997. Forty-two drivers had been on the track during the busy week. The final practice and Race Day were all that remained.

DAY-AT-A-GLANCE

Date:	Sunday, May 17
Temperature:	High 85°
Qualification Attempts:	27
Qualifiers:	8

BUBBLE DAY QUALIFIERS

Car	Driver	Speed (mph)
7	Jimmy Kite	219.290
35	Jeff Ward	219.086
5T	Arie Luyendyk	218.935
33	Billy Roe	217.835
19	Stan Wattles	217.477
30	Raul Boesel	217.303
77	Stephan Gregoire	217.036
10	Mike Groff	216.704

For Eliseo Salazar, May was a roller coaster. He crashed on Pole Day, came back to qualify, then got bumped by Billy Roe. A last-minute qualifying attempt ended as his car started smoking; he ended up as a race alternate.

Front-row starter Kenny Brack demonstrated that he would be a factor in the race. He set the fastest lap time during Carburetion Day, the last practice session before the 500.

On Carburetion Day, a very close field went through its final paces to prepare for the 82nd running of the Indianapolis 500. It was the final 2 hours of practice followed by three days of anxious waiting for the "Greatest Spectacle" in racing. This gives the teams ample time to devise and analyze their race strategies. They make final preparations, test settings, and finely hone the race setups.

Stephan Gregoire was first out when the green light flashed on. Once again, A. J. Foyt's cars were setting the pace. When all was said and done, Kenny Brack was the fastest with a lap at 220.994 miles per hour with teammate Billy Boat at 219.181 miles per hour. Tony Stewart was next at 218.999 miles per hour, followed by Greg Ray, Arie Luyendyk, and Scott Goodyear in the 217 bracket.

"We had a small brake fluid leak," Brack said. "But that's what 'Carb Day' is for, to find the smallest glitches and get ready for Race Day."

Stewart was reveling in the event, the history, the tradition, and the special aura of the Indianapolis Motor Speedway. "It's just a great honor to be a part of the Indianapolis 500," he said. "Hopefully on Sunday, we'll just take the car to the front, but this race takes a little longer than a couple of laps to get to the front."

Arie Luyendyk, the defending Indy 500 champion, would have to start far back in the pack. "I think with the field being tighter than it was in '96, it's going to be difficult to get to the front," he

said. "As far as the race goes, I'm going to lay back in the beginning rather than attack. You're not going to see me out there running real hard in the first couple of laps. We'd like to go to the front, be there, and stay there. It really depends on how the race unfolds. The approach will be pretty sensible, all-in-all."

Ray expressed his concerns about starting in the middle of the front row. "It's an uncomfortable place to be, anytime you're in the middle of two cars," he said. "You're trapped between a rock and a hard place. I'd rather be inside second row. You never know what's going to happen when you're in the middle. Bottom line is you just have to deal with it. You can't plan a race."

Carburetion Day is also the day for the annual Coors Indy Pit Stop Challenge in which the pit crews chase a $40,000 top prize. In the final, Panther Racing, with driver Scott Goodyear, beat Team Menard and the crew of Robbie Buhl. The Panther team's stop was 12.307 seconds, but the team was assessed a 5-second penalty for a loose wheel connection. Buhl's team didn't leave the pit box and posted no time. "This is our day, right here," said Kevin Blanch, Goodyear's chief mechanic. "We've been practicing for four days, 2 hours a day. We thought we could do an 11 [-second stop]. We've been practicing in the mid-12s." The Panther victory ended a two-year reign of Galles Racing and was the first victory of any kind at Indianapolis for Goodyear who has finished second twice in the 500. The contest among the crews always sends a message for Race Day. "The guys are pumped up," Goodyear said. "They've been pumped up for a week now. Pit stops are huge. I think we showed today that when it comes down to the last pit stop of the race, getting in and out can definitely make the difference."

For newcomers, however, there is always some apprehension. "Everyone I talked to told horror stories, so I talked to [Gordon] Johncock, [Johnny]

Rutherford, [Al] Unser, and [Arie] Luyendyk about what it was like," said rookie Jimmy Kite. "I've started other races in these cars before, but this is my first time starting this far back."

For Jack Hewitt, pit stops would be new, and the PDM team had a "penalty system." "I've got to stop killing the motor when I leave the pit," Hewitt said. "Each time, it costs me five cases of beer."

Other announcements took place as well. John King, a mechanic for AJ Foyt Racing, was honored with the inaugural "True Grit" Award, a $5,000 prize check from Chris Paulsen to acknowledge a dedicated mechanic in the 500. Gary Knovak of Carrollton, Texas, won an Oldsmobile Aurora as part of the Pep Boys "Road to Indy Sweepstakes."

Danny "Chocolate" Myers, the gas man for seven-time NASCAR Winston Cup champion Dale Earnhardt, was scheduled to be the fueler for one of A. J. Foyt's machines on Race Day, doing double duty that day with the Coca-Cola 600 at Charlotte later that night.

"Just to walk in this place, it's a thrill," Myers said. "It always has been. If you're a racer of any kind, whether you're a drag racer or in NASCAR, you're going to watch the Indy 500."

Foyt put Race Day in perspective, saying, "One thing about Indianapolis, it doesn't matter who you are. Nothing is guaranteed here."

DAY-AT-A-GLANCE

Date:	Thursday, May 21
Temperature:	High 78°
Drivers on Track:	33
Cars on Track:	33

TOP FIVE DRIVERS OF THE DAY

Car	Driver	Speed (mph)
14	Kenny Brack	220.994
11T	Billy Boat	219.181
1	Tony Stewart	218.999
97	Greg Ray	217.754
5T	Arie Luyendyk	217.229

Scott Goodyear's Panther Racing team won the Coors Indy Pit Stop Challenge to earn bragging rights, $35,000 in cash, and $5,000 for the Youth Links charity. Goodyear called the win "a good omen."

Indianapolis 500 History

35 and 65 Years Ago

by Donald Davidson

ACTION SOUTH TURN

In 1933, the Indianapolis Motor Speedway's first turn had a very rural appearance. The Speedway instituted several key changes for the 21st running of the Indy 500. To qualify, racers had to complete 10 time-trial laps instead of 4, and the car engines had to have a starter.

For the second year in a row, Studebaker of South Bend, Indiana, took advantage of the rules favoring production engines by entering a five-car team. The 1932 Rigling & Henning chassis sported streamlined bodies, while their reliable Studebaker President engines carried them to finishes of 7th, 9th, 10th, 11th, and 12th.

INDIANAPOLIS MOTO
FLOOD MAY 1933

When heavy rains caused the Turn 1 creek to overflow during practice, drivers Ernie Triplett and Deacon Litz brought out a canoe.

JUST BEFORE THE START

To encourage more entries during the Depression years, the starting field was increased from the traditional 33 cars, and a record 42 took the green flag in 1933.

The Speedway no longer issued number 13 after the early 1920s—although Louis Schneider, the somewhat antagonistic 1931 winner, applied for it several times without success. He tried to force the issue in 1933 by showing up with it painted on his car, but officials made him change it to 22 shortly after this shot was taken. The apparent bad luck omen may have taken its toll as Schneider suffered an engine problem coming down the track for the start and never completed a lap. He is the only driver ever to have finished 42nd in a 500.

LOU SCHNEIDER

LOUIS MEYER MOTOR-WINNER EQUIPPED WITH WINFIELD CARBURETERS

LOUIS MEYER AT FINISH EQUIPPED WITH WINFIELD CARBURETERS

Although the specifications were designed to encourage the use of production engines, winner Louis Meyer used a 258-cubic-inch straight-eight Miller racing engine, equipped with Winfield carburetors.

Times were hard in 1933, and as a result the Speedway's purse took a dramatic cut. Louis Meyer's second win paid him only $18,000, which was barely one-third of that earned by Billy Arnold in 1930.

The Chrysler 300 pace car pulls off, and the 1963 Indy 500 is underway.

Turn 4 looked quite a bit different in 1963; the entrance to the pits was several hundred yards to the south.

Largely due to the enthusiastic efforts of American road racer Dan Gurney, Ford Motor Company joined forces with Britain's Colin Chapman and entered a team of lightweight, rear-engined Lotus chassis powered by production-based 4.2-liter Ford engines that utilized pushrods and carburetors. While Gurney wound up seventh after making two pit stops, Scotland's Jim Clark (above) stopped only once on his way to an amazing second-place finish.

Two of the five rear-engined cars entered by legendary hot rodder and drag racer Mickey Thompson featured tiny wheels utilizing revolutionary and controversial wide low-profile tires commissioned by Thompson. As strange as these looked when 50-year-old veteran Duane Carter qualified for the 1963 500, they were destined to become commonplace on high-performance street cars in a very short time.

Parnelli Jones started on the pole for the second year in a row and led 167 of the 200 laps on his way to the win.

After losing a wheel and hitting the north-end wall only 18 laps from the finish, the very popular Eddie Sachs returned to the pits on foot, bringing the wheel with him.

A major controversy broke out late in the race when a tiny horizontal split developed in the side of an externally-mounted oil tank on the car of leader Parnelli Jones. The tank emitted a fine vaporized spray for a few laps, but it ceased once the level had fallen below the split. A couple of drivers spun out from the oil on the track, and officials were taken to task for failing to display the black flag. While many people were in an uproar over the outcome, runner-up Jim Clark, who backed off in anticipation of the black flag which never came, was more than sporting the following morning in his admiration for Parnelli's victorious drive.

Inset:
These eyes have seen many seem-ingly sure wins snatched away by cruel fate. But at the 1998 Indianapolis 500, first-time winner Eddie Cheever saw the checkered flag wave for him.

A Dream Becomes Reality

EDDIE CHEEVER CAPTURES AN EPIC INDY 500

by Bruce Martin

The Indianapolis 500 is the ultimate test for Indy car drivers and machines, and the ultimate prize in all of motorsports. Winning the Indy 500 is a monumental achievement that has represented the pinnacle of many legendary driver's careers. In the Indy 500s of the recent past, it has been veteran drivers who have conquered the high-speed, 500-mile sprint race over the constantly changing 2.5-mile superspeedway oval. These drivers have attained the ultimate goal in racing because they possess a special blend of experience, cunning, aggression, race strategy, and flat-out speed. Arie Luyendyk, Buddy Lazier, Al Unser Jr., and Emerson Fittipaldi are among the elite group of drivers who have won the Indy 500 over the past several years. All of these tremendously talented drivers have a vast amount of racing experience and, specifically, Indy 500 racing experience to draw upon. (The only exception to this rule is 1995 Indy 500 champion Jacques Villeneuve, a phenomenally gifted race driver who finished second in his rookie outing in 1994 and won the race in 1995.)

Eddie Cheever drove the race of his life, a drive he was always capable of but had never realized. He stormed from his 17th-place starting position to the lead by Lap 68, but not without some heart-pounding excitement. Cheever was bumped from behind in Turn 1 early in the race.

The number board on the right reads:

12 | 22
13 | 44
14 | 16
15 | 40
16 | 8
17 | 5
18 | 2
19 | 7
20 | 53
21 | 52
22 | 18
23 | 55
24 | 98
25 | 9
26 |
27 | 35
28 | 3
29 | 19
30 | 30
31 | 77
32 | 10
33 | 33

Wet conditions and a threat of rain delayed the 82nd running of the "Greatest Spectacle in Racing." But when pole-sitter Billy Boat (11) led the field to the green flag, the race was on.

In 1998, Eddie Cheever, a Formula One, CART, and IRL veteran, joined this elite group of drivers. This was the race when everything came together for Cheever; his race car, experience, and ability were put to the ultimate test, and he came out on top. Cheever, a driver with considerable ability, never seemed to capitalize on opportunities or realize his true potential. For a driver who has endured so many heart-breaking losses in his career, the victory was particularly sweet. Winning the 82nd Indianapolis 500 was definitely a tremendous redemption. To secure victory in this fabled race, Cheever fended off challenges from John Paul Jr. and 1996 Indianapolis 500 winner Buddy Lazier. In the end, no one could match Cheever's pace, and he finished 3.1 seconds ahead of Lazier in front of 400,000 fans. Rookie Steve Knapp defied early predictions and was a factor throughout the race finishing third, followed by Davey

Hamilton in fourth, and rookie Robby Unser, driving for Team Cheever, in fifth.

Heavy rains fell in the Indianapolis area two days before the race and caused a 45-minute delay in the running of the 82nd edition of the "greatest spectacle" in racing. The delay created a higher level of anticipation for fans and competitors. Finally, at 11:40 A.M. CDT, Mari Hulman George uttered the famous words, "Gentlemen, start your engines." The 33 cars in the starting field roared to life and took the parade lap. Parnelli Jones, 1963 winner of the Indianapolis 500, drove the pace car to lead the field to the green flag.

AJ Foyt Conseco driver Billy Boat forged ahead of Greg Ray and Foyt teammate Kenny Brack in the drag race to Turn 1. As the field funneled into the first turn, drivers bumped and nudged each other as they searched for the best line. Rookie and SRS Racing Team driver J. J. Yeley was tapped from behind by another rookie, Jack Hewitt. In the process, Yeley made contact with Cheever, forcing Cheever sideways. Yeley spun and avoided banging into the wall, but the incident brought out the yellow flag. Both Cheever and Yeley were able to make it around the race track and back into the pits for service.

A race that held so much promise almost ended before it started. "I got punted from the back in the beginning and went through the first corner sideways," Cheever said. "I thought, 'This is so stupid. I have a good car.' It wiggled one way, then wiggled another way, and all of a sudden it was straight, and I continued."

On the restart, Boat retook the lead, but he was under heavy pressure. Ray followed closely, only 0.30 seconds back, and Stewart hounded Ray only 0.60 seconds out of the lead. Boat was able to hold his pursuers at bay for 12 laps. He made a valiant effort to stay out front but succumbed to Ray, relinquishing the lead on the 13th lap. Next it would be defending IRL champion Tony Stewart's turn to wrest away the lead. On the 21st go-around, Ray surrendered the lead when Stewart roared up the inside as the two racers headed into Turn 1.

But one lap later Stewart's engine let go, putting him out of the race. "We were running the race we wanted to," said Larry Curry, the team manager for Team Menard. "We wanted to just sit back. All of the sudden, bang, no warning, no telemetry, nothing. It just went." Stewart finished last in the 33-car field. Stewart's car was stranded in the first turn, which brought out the yellow flag and prompted almost the entire field to pit for service. After Stewart's demise, AJ Foyt PowerTeam driver Kenny Brack took over the top of the leader board for the next 36 laps.

Greg Ray and Billy Boat also suffered from mechanical gremlins. Greg Ray's transmission failed on the 32nd lap, and he became the second-straight leader to exit the race. Attrition continued as Boat lost the transmission in his Dallara/Oldsmobile Aurora engine at the rear of the field, ending his race on Lap 49.

Someone who wasn't deterred, even by the opening lap "bump" that sent him back to 31st position, was Eddie Cheever. He was on a mission. He regrouped and charged hard, slicing through the pack. One by one, Cheever picked off the cars in front of him. From Lap 20 to 30, Cheever rose from 21st place to 9th, setting some blistering lap times in the process. Cheever overtook Davey Hamilton during Lap 45 on the front straight for 2nd and then set his sights on the lead. On the same lap, the second Menard car, driven by Robbie Buhl, was eliminated from competition by an engine failure.

On Lap 47 the race was restarted, and Buzz Calkins led the field. As they entered the third turn, Sam Schmidt attempted to overtake Hamilton. The unsuccessful maneuver sent Schmidt's Dallara/Aurora spinning and forced other drivers to take evasive action. Jim Guthrie, Mark Dismore, Billy Roe, Roberto Guerrero, Stan Wattles, and Marco Greco were all caught up in the melee. Dismore, Roe, Wattles, and Guthrie were all sidelined due to extensive damage to their cars. But Guthrie's crash was the most horrific. He lost control at the apex of the turn, skimmed across the grass, and slammed head-on into the third-turn wall. Guerrero's Dallara Aurora incurred damage during the accident, but it was repaired, and he continued.

The race was restarted on Lap 64 with Brack leading, but he couldn't hold on. It was obvious Cheever's setup and tires were working well. He screamed past Brack on the 68th lap. By the end of the lap, he had opened over a 1-second advantage. John Paul Jr. was sitting in third, 1.8 seconds behind the leader, and Luyendyk was fourth, 2.6 seconds behind. Paul was on the move as well, coming from 16th position up to 4th. On Lap 69, he overtook Sharp for third.

For rookie Steve Knapp, simply making the Indy 500 starting grid was a dream come true. The undreamable dream—winning the race—almost came true as the Salem, Wisconsin, racer finished third.

Lazier, Cheever, and Knapp behind.

When the front runners pitted in the latter half of the race, the lead changed hands from one racer to another. On Lap 114, Paul scooted into the pits for service, and Hamilton took over the number one position. When Hamilton headed to the pits, Cheever acquired the lead from Lap 117 to 122. Cheever stayed out the longest and eventually pitted on Lap 123.

The Flying Dutchman, Arie Luyendyk, was demonstrating the speed and poise that earned him two Indy 500 victories. He was flying up the order and attempting to become the first driver to win back-to-back Indianapolis 500s since Al Unser in 1970 and 1971. Starting in 28th, Luyendyk blitzed the field, working his way into fourth by Lap 70, despite the fact that he was experiencing clutch problems. When Cheever ducked into the pits on Lap 84, Luyendyk inherited the lead for one lap.

On Lap 109, Paul led Hamilton by 5 seconds and Robby Unser by 11.3 seconds, with Luyendyk,

By Lap 130, Luyendyk was in second and stalking Paul for the lead.

A few laps later, Cheever and Paul staged a thrilling dogfight for the lead. Paul was the leader as late as the 146th lap but handed over the lead to Luyendyk when he pitted on the 147th lap.

Three laps later, Luyendyk made his pit stop, and the crew got him out in just 13.8 seconds. It was then, however, that he had a stroke of bad luck. He had not been able to use first and second gears for some time, but he could not find any gears after his pit stop. "I knew this was going to

Rush hour. No fewer than 28 cars entered the pits en masse during this early-race caution period, making pit row the busiest stretch of Indiana pavement on the Memorial Day weekend.

get us sooner or later," Luyendyk radioed to his crew after stalling between Turns 1 and 2. "The clutch isn't pulling. That's it."

"It was just feeling so good out there in front," Luyendyk said as his crew tried to repair the problem. It was not to be his day, however.

At about the same time Luyendyk was trying to return to the race, sixth-place runner Robby Unser was trying to pit for tires and fuel. Unser, like other drivers, had been struggling with mechanical maladies throughout the race. He had been racing without his Dallara's rear brakes for almost the entire race. To make matters worse, he missed his pit on Lap 148 and wasted valuable time. He was forced to make another lap before he pit on the 149th lap. When safety cars were removing Luyendyk's car from harm's way, Unser had gone two laps down.

By the caution on Lap 157, only three cars remained on the lead lap—Cheever, Lazier, and Knapp. They were able to pit under the caution and continued to run in that order following the Lap 157 restart. Cheever and his Goodyear-shod Dallara/Oldsmobile Aurora took firm command of the race and put fourth-place driver Paul a lap down on Lap 163. Railing off the corners and pulling away, Cheever and his machine established them-

selves as the combination to beat. But Cheever's run to the checkered flag was not to go unchallenged. Lazier had been reeling off some quick laps and was methodically closing in on Cheever. On Lap 174, he was trailing by 2.9 seconds. Knapp was back in third, 9.6 seconds behind, and didn't have the pace to be a contender. Lazier appeared to be the only driver who could challenge Cheever for the win.

On Lap 176 another crash interrupted green-flag racing. Stephan Gregoire brushed the Turn 4 wall bringing out the caution flag and bunching up the pack. The leaders pitted on the 177th lap, and Cheever was able to get out of the pits ahead of Lazier and kept his lead. John Paul Jr., who was running fourth on Lap 177 one lap down, stalled his engine during his pit stop. His crew pushed him back to his pit area and refired the car, but the clutch failed once again on Paul's car, ruining what may have been one of the best races of his career. The crew refired the engine five times, but Paul was unable to get out of the pits. Finally, on the sixth try, the crew was able to get the car refired, and Paul made it back onto the track.

"I stalled it on the first yellow and didn't lose any positions," Paul said. "After that, I tried to keep the throttle up and engage gear with the throttle on it. That last time, it cooked the clutch

In 1997, rookie Kenny Brack (14) crashed out of the race without completing a lap. In 1998, the Swede qualified third-fastest and even led the race before ending up with a sixth-place finish.

Talented rookie Robby Unser—whose car owner, Eddie Cheever, won the race—ran impressively and finished fifth. Incredibly, Unser was only the second-best rookie finisher, as first-timer Steve Knapp took third.

and took forever to find a way to start it. I finally got it in fourth gear. They must have started the thing five or six times. It was frustrating. We had a really good car. I was getting an opportunity to run up front here and to possibly be in contention to win the race on the last restart. It's hard to accept that you have thrown it away. But once you get going, you have to put it behind you and concentrate on the job. Even being two laps down, you don't want to ruin anyone's day out there. You want to be professional about it. I'm sure I'll have bad nights about it."

"There is nothing I could say or do that is going to change what happened," Paul added. "I believe I had tremendous opportunities. I wasn't holding on for dear life, and I had a car that was capable of winning the race."

The green flag flew on the 179th lap, but the field only made it through the second turn before rookie Jack Hewitt made contact with the wall to bring out another caution flag. Cheever's lead had been erased. The race was restarted on 182 with Cheever ahead of Lazier and Knapp. On the fol-

lowing lap, Lazier pulled up behind Cheever's gearbox and looked for a way through. Cheever dropped the hammer and slowly pulled away from Lazier. As the laps wound down, Cheever increased the gap between him and his competitors, and on Lap 189 he had a 3.1-second lead over Lazier. Unfortunately, Marco Greco's engine blew up on Lap 190, bringing out yet another yellow flag.

When the green flag waved with the final five decisive laps remaining, Cheever was leading. This is the time when champions are separated from the rest of the field. Cheever had to reach into his racing repertoire and use everything he had—skills, experience, and savvy. The wily veteran rose to the occasion and swiftly responded to the pressure.

On the final restart with five laps to go, Cheever drove low, then high, trying to break the draft Lazier was trying to hold on to. Using the high racing line, Cheever wrung all he could out of his Dallara, taking his car all the way out to the wall on the exits of the corners. Foot by foot and yard by yard, Cheever opened up a gap on Lazier.

Three-time Indy 500 winner Bobby Unser (right) offered pre-race advice to his son Robby, a rookie who showed talent and maturity en route to a fifth-place finish. By contrast, as a rookie in 1963, Bobby crashed on the third lap.

With an abundance of experience behind him, Scott Goodyear's prospects in the 1998 Indy 500 looked promising. He had a competitive team with a good chassis and engine package and the 10th position on the starting grid. But while running near the front on the 25th lap, his clutch failed.

In the last four laps, his lead steadily increased, but Cheever was giving his crew fits with the chances he was taking. On Lap 196, he led by 1.1 seconds, increasing it to 1.9 seconds on Lap 197. However, during that lap, he had quite a moment. He drove high out of a turn and almost brushed the wall, but he kept his composure and control of the car and forged on. "I wasn't going to finish second," Cheever said. "I was either going to win it or not finish it at all."

By Lap 198 he increased the lead to 2.1 seconds, and on Lap 199 it climbed to 2.7 seconds. In the run to the checkered flag, Lazier wasn't able to get on even terms with Cheever. He developed an oversteer condition which prevented him from picking up the pace. He thought he had an opening when Cheever drove high in the fourth turn and nearly brushed the wall three laps from the finish. "He was up against the wall for sure," Lazier recalled. "I was just trying to push him

For the second straight year, Davey Hamilton started from the eighth position. He put in another solid performance by finishing fourth in the 1998 race and advanced two positions over his 1997 finish. Hamilton has shown the speed and consistency to be a potential threat for the win in future Indy 500s.

because we didn't have anything more than what we were running. That was as hard as we could run. We were picking up a big push. I used up all my sway bars. I almost hit the wall trying to catch Eddie a couple of times."

But Lazier wouldn't have enough to overtake the victorious Cheever. Winning only his second IRL event, Cheever was both excited and relieved.

"I was sure it was going to break, and I had no reason to think that, other than past history," Cheever said. "When we lost the race in Nazareth for A. J. Foyt and ran out of fuel with two laps to go, it was heartbreaking. I was thinking, 'Don't break, don't break, please don't break.' I had to take that risk the last 20 laps of running with a shorter gear, which I knew was not very healthy for the engine. The Braytons [Brayton Engineering, which builds Cheever's engines] have done one hell of a job for the engine, and I ran it hard all day long. It ran well. There are so many gremlins that come into your head when you are running. "There was a crosswind that changed about 20 laps from the end. I got hit with this crosswind, and the sound of the engine changed. At that point, you are imagining a bunch of things that aren't really happening. You are always wondering what will happen.

"About 50 laps from the end, I went to the front and tried to go through as many miles as I could without using the car, so I was running a very high gear most of the day. The crew called me and told me he [Lazier] was gaining, so I had to take the risk of running in fifth gear, which is really not that good on the engine. I really thought he had the legs to run me down, so on those restarts, I was very worried if he got me, he would be able to pass me again.

"My car was tremendous in traffic all day long. It was very good on restarts. Arie Luyendyk was very quick when I was behind him, but he didn't look that good in traffic. There were a lot of people capable of running quick at the end. My car ran very well all day.

"This place is very difficult, how the temperature changes. We made a precise decision today to run the car as if it was going to be sunny, and that helped us a lot. That comes with experience." And Cheever's experience allowed him to experience his greatest triumph in racing—winning the Indianapolis 500.

Greg Ray and Thomas Knapp Motorsports continue to prove that an IRL team doesn't need a huge budget to succeed. Despite battling sponsorship problems, Ray didn't lose sight of his goals. He reeled off four quick laps on Pole Day and qualified second fastest. In the race, he was holding the lead until a gearbox problem forced him out.

Buddy Lazier, 1996 Indy 500 champion, had a shot at victory in 1998, but Eddie Cheever outran him to the checkered. Finishing second, Lazier said, "feels great but bad at the same time."

Eventual winner Eddie Cheever (51), prevented runner-up Buddy Lazier (91) from getting a good run at the lead after the final restart, which came with six laps to go.

For runner-up Buddy Lazier, it was another spectacular run at the Indy 500. He started 11th and drove through the field to take the lead on the 51st lap. After leading for 10 laps, Lazier would lead the race four more times for 10 more laps and was in the lead with 23 laps remaining before finally ending his race in second place.

But being close to victory can sometimes be more disappointing than being out of the hunt. "We're happy with second, but when you can see first place and you know how important it is to win this race, God dang it, it feels great but bad at the same time," said Lazier, who finished 3.191 seconds behind Cheever. "We were so close, but not enough this time. It really is frustrating, and it makes you do things that maybe are not the smartest in the world. I was doing it, trying to bounce off the rumble strips to shake the rear end free a little bit. You start doing things that get you in trouble. We will come back next year, hopefully, and will have enough. It's so hard to be up there near the front, and you really have to savor it."

Few drivers in the history of the Indianapolis 500 have had a three-year ride like Lazier. He won the race with a broken back in 1996, finished fourth in 1997, and ended up second behind Cheever in 1998. (Other strong runs at Indy comparable to Lazier's include Roberto Guerrero's and Rodger Ward's. Guerrero finished second in 1984, third in 1985, fourth in 1986, and second in 1987, but never won the race. Perhaps a better compari-

Eddie Cheever was patient, methodical, and quick as he worked his way into the lead. In the closing laps, Cheever and his Dallara/Oldsmobile Aurora/Goodyear had the acceleration off the corners and straight-line speed his competitors couldn't match.

son may be Ward who won the race in 1959, was second in 1960, third in 1961, won in 1962, was fourth in 1963, and second in 1964.)

"It's awesome, and I'm honored for second place," Lazier said. "[But] it is real sad, it brings tears to your eyes when you are not number one when you are that close. It's just tough to accept. We finished second today and will try to be the quickest next year. We worked awfully hard, and we just about had it. It is so hard to come that close and not get it.

"Ron Dawes [crew chief] and Lee Kunzman [team manager] and my whole crew really brought the car back to me every time. We had a problem at the beginning and had an unscheduled stop. My best shot was to get a run on him, but I would have had a tough time holding him off, even if I had gotten in front of him. At the end, I just didn't have enough. Eddie did a real good job, there is no doubt."

Third-place finisher Steve Knapp commented on his chances of winning the race. "I thought I might have a shot after the last pit stop when we took a little downforce out of the car, but I couldn't go flat though [Turn 1], and that kept me from making a run. It hasn't even sunk in yet. I could have done another 500 miles today, no problem. With 20 laps left, I said, 'This is going to come to an end, and I'm going to have to go back to work.'"

Davey Hamilton was happy to collect fourth but was hoping for better results. "We got caught on a yellow, and I stalled it once in the pits, said

Hamilton. " I told myself last year that I could win this thing if I just didn't make any mistakes. I know you can't make any mistakes in this race, but I did. I screwed up. It was a good day, though. It was pretty steady all day. We had a few sets of tires that weren't too good, and that set us back."

With his crew, the media, and the Indy 500 Queen, Cheever jubilantly celebrates the win he had been waiting for all of his life.

But in the end the race belonged to Eddie Cheever who took the lead for the first time on the 68th lap and led the race at the 200-, 300-, 400-, and 500-mile marks. All the hard work, dedication, and years of waiting paid off. Cheever flew over the row of bricks at the finish line, taking the checkered. The satisfaction of finally getting the big win sunk in as he drove to Victory Circle.

The reaction to the victory was so popular, crew members from all race teams lined up to salute Cheever as he drove into Victory Lane. "I don't know what I'm supposed to say," Cheever said in Victory Lane. "At the start of the race, I turned into Turn 1 . . . and somebody bumped me from behind. I went sideways, but I must have had 15 guardian angels with me because I was able to get through it. . . . It was our day."

OFFICIAL BOX SCORE
PEP BOYS INDY RACING LEAGUE
Indianapolis 500
May 24, 1998

FP	SP	Car	Driver	Car Name	C/E/T	Laps Comp.	Running/ Reason Out	IRL Pts.	Total IRL Pts.	IRL Standings	IRL Awards	Designated Awards	Total Awards
1	17	51 8	Eddie Cheever Jr.	Rachel's Potato Chips	D/A/G	200	145.155 mph	52	78	4	$934,000	$499,000	$1,433,000
2	11	91 5W	Buddy Lazier	Delta Faucet/Coors Light/ Hemelgarn Racing	D/A/G	200	145.118	40	57	9	405,000	78,200	483,200
3	23	55 R	Steve Knapp	Primadonna Resorts/Miller Milling/ ISM Aurora	G/A/G	200	145.076	35	35	21	280,000	58,750	338,750
4	8	6 2	Davey Hamilton	Reebok/Nienhouse Motorsports/ G Force/Aurora	G/A/G	199	Running	32	71	6	273,000	28,650	301,650
5	21	52 R	Robby Unser	Team Cheever	D/A/G	198	Running	30	30	22	187,000	22,400	209,400
6	3	14 1	Kenny Brack	AJ Foyt PowerTeam Racing	D/A/G	198	Running	29	62	7	254,000	56,750	310,750
7	16	81 6	John Paul Jr.	Team Pelfrey	D/A/F	197	Running	26	57	9	171,000	45,350	216,350
8	19	17 R	Andy Michner	Konica/Syan Racing/Dallara	D/A/G	197	Running	24	24	27	164,000	18,050	182,050
9	13	44 R	J. J. Yeley	One Call Communications Quaker State/Menards/SRS	D/A/F	197	Running	22	27	25	158,000	40,550	198,550
10	18	12 2	Buzz Calkins	International Star Registry/ Bradley Food Marts	G/A/G	195	Running	20	58	8	230,000	18,500	248,500
11	26	7 R	Jimmy Kite	Royal Purple Synthetic/ Synertee/Scandia	D/A/G	195	Running	19	45	17	251,000	36,300	287,300
12	22	18 R	Jack Hewitt	Parker Machinery	G/A/G	195	Running	18	18	29	223,000	42,800	265,800
13	27	35 1	Jeff Ward	Team Tabasco/Superflo/Prolong/ ISM Racing Aurora	G/A/G	194	Running	17	90	2	221,000	21,050	242,050
14	14	16 3	Marco Greco	Int. Sports Ltd. Phoenix Racing	G/A/F	183	Engine	16	29	23	142,000	25,800	167,800
15	32	10 4	Mike Groff	Jonathan Byrd's VisionAire Bryant Heating & Cooling	D/A/G	183	Running	15	56	11	215,000	22,600	237,600
16	7	8 3	Scott Sharp	Delphi Automotive Systems	D/A/G	181	Gearbox	14	85	3	212,000	22,800	234,800
17	31	77 3	Stephan Gregoire	Blue Star/Tokheim/Estridge/Miller-Eads	G/A/G	172	Running	13	77	5	210,000	15,300	225,300
18	2	97 1	Greg Ray	Texas Motor Speedway/TNN/ True Value/Dixie Chopper	D/A/F	167	Gearbox	14	38	19	133,000	42,400	175,400
19	30	30 9	Raul Boesel	Beloit/Fast Rod/Team Losi/ TransWorld Diversified	G/A/G	164	Running	11	47	14	206,000	15,300	221,300
20	28	5 13W	Arie Luyendyk	Sprint PCS/Radio Shack/Qualcomm	G/A/F	151	Gearbox	10	40	18	209,000	33,100	242,100
21	15	40 1	Dr. Jack Miller	Crest Racing	D/I/F	128	Running	9	16	30	137,000	22,800	159,800
22	9	21 13	Roberto Guerrero	Pagan Racing Dallara/Oldsmobile	D/A/G	125	Running	8	15	31	125,000	40,300	165,300
23	1	11 1	Billy Boat	Conseco AJ Foyt Racing	D/A/G	111	Drive Line	10	56	11	199,000	165,200	364,200
24	10	4 7	Scott Goodyear	Pennzoil Panther G Force	G/A/G	100	Clutch	6	47	14	198,000	55,300	253,300
25	25	9 2	Johnny Unser	Hemelgarn Racing	D/A/G	98	Engine	5	5	35	121,000	15,300	136,300
26	6	99 1	Sam Schmidt	Best Western Gold Crown Racing Special	D/A/F	48	Accident, T3	4	52	13	195,000	20,300	215,300
27	12	28 2	Mark Dismore	Kelley Automotive	D/A/G	48	Accident, T3	3	47	14	194,000	15,300	209,300
28	29	19 R	Stan Wattles	Metro Racing Systems/NCLD	R/A/G	48	Accident, T3	2	10	32	118,000	20,550	138,550
29	20	53 2	Jim Guthrie	Delco Remy/Goodyear/ ISM Racing Aurora	G/A/G	48	Accident, T3	1	1	37	118,000	15,300	133,300
30	33	33 1	Billy Roe	Royal Purple/ProLink/Scandia	D/A/G	48	Accident, T3	1	1	37	117,000	20,300	137,300
31	5	3 2	Robbie Buhl	Johns Manville/Menards Special	D/A/F	44	Engine	1	29	23	192,000	30,300	222,300
32	24	98 R	Donnie Beechler	Cahill Auto Racing	G/A/F	34	Engine	1	1	37	117,000	15,300	132,300
33	4	1 2	Tony Stewart	Glidden/Menards Special	D/A/F	22	Engine	1	96	1	191,000	29,250	220,250
	NS		Eliseo Salazar	Reebok R&S MK V	R/A/G							10,000	10,000
				Brayton Engineering								2,000	2,000
				Comptech Engines								500	500
				Speedway Engines								500	500
										TOTAL -	$7,100,000	$1,622,150	$8,722,150

Time of Race: 3:26:40.524
Margin of Victory: 3.191 seconds
PPG Pole Winner: Billy Boat
MBNA America Lap Leader: #51 Eddie Cheever Jr.

Average Speed: 145.155 mph
Fastest Lap: #1 Tony Stewart, Lap 19 - 214.746. Fastest Leading Lap: #51 Eddie Cheever Jr., Lap 187 - 213.904
True Value Pole Winning Chief Mechanic: Craig Baranouski/AJ Foyt Enterprises
Coors Pit Stop Challenge Winner: #4 Scott Goodyear/Panther Racing

Chassis Legend: D-Dallara (19); G-G Force (13); R-Riley & Scott (1)   Engine Legend: A-Oldsmobile Aurora (32); I-Nissan Infiniti Indy (1)   Tire Legend: F-Firestone (11); G-Goodyear (22)
Legend: R-Indianapolis 500 Rookie   W-Indianapolis 500 Winner   NS-Non-Starter

The 1998 Indy 500 Winning Crew Chief

Team Cheever's Owen Snyder

by Bruce Martin

The first time Owen Snyder walked into Victory Lane at the Indianapolis 500, he was the chief mechanic for race-winner Al Unser Jr. The year was 1992, and Snyder worked for Galles Racing.

After a four year hiatus, Snyder returned to the fabled track, Indianapolis Motor Speedway. On May 24,1998, Snyder captured his second Indy 500 victory as chief mechanic for Eddie Cheever.

"It was as hard, if not harder, than when Little Al won in 1992," Snyder said of the 1998 win. "It was a small crew, and everybody had to step up and do more. I think we did. Eddie did his fair share, and then some. When Little Al won here in 1992, he was expected to win it, so there was pressure there. It was a busy, shortened schedule this year, but it worked out good."

When Snyder joined Galles Racing, the drivers in CART still included such names as Rick Mears, Al Unser, Johnny Rutherford, and Tom Sneva. As CART accelerated into the 1990s, its names became more international and its focus more global. So when Indianapolis Motor Speedway president Tony George created the Indy Racing League as an open-wheel, oval track series that would race in the United States, Snyder took an interest in the new league.

Eddie Cheever (left) and Owen Snyder (right) were the combination to beat in the 1998 Indy 500. Both used all their years of experience, knowledge, and skill to capture the most lucrative prize in motorsports.

When Snyder and Unser were together through 1993, they were expected to win almost every year. In contrast, Cheever's victory in the 82nd Indianapolis was unexpected, if not dramatic.

"We learned a lot about Indy that day," Snyder recalled. "It's an endurance race and a high-speed endurance race. The first thing is you have to finish, and we learned that in 1992. It's just working with different drivers and engineers and teams and people, you pick up little things here and little things there and keep getting better. Here we are.

"The first day we were in here we unloaded pretty quick and had a real good handle on the race setup. We worked on race setup every day, so we never trimmed out and did the big qualifying run. That is back with the Al Unser Jr. days. He worked on race setup, and that is the one that counts."

To back up Snyder's assertion, Cheever led the race at the 200-, 300-, 400-, and 500-mile marks.

"We had a great race car and had it all day," Snyder said. "We didn't touch a thing on it. He adjusted from the cockpit, we unloaded, and it was ready to race today. This win is special because it was a lot of work. To field Robby Unser as a second driver with a small crew, we all worked together. It was a very demanding month—a short month. It was the same amount of work in half the amount of time. It was very rewarding."

IRL has been able to attract some top-notch crew members to the series away from CART, such as Snyder and Kelley Racing engineer David Cripps.

"They will all be here before it's over," Snyder predicted. "Give this series a couple more years, and there will be a few more top-name mechanics here. I just thought I wanted to make the move as early as I could and understand the cars from the ground up and, hopefully, that is what I'm doing."

"That is exactly why I moved back here [Indianapolis]," Snyder said. "In 1996, I missed the Indy 500 and had to go run the U.S. 500 at Michigan. I liked Eddie Lawson [Galles' team driver for most of the 1996 season] and liked the situation, but not being in Indy during the month of May in 1996 was empty. So I moved back here and guaranteed myself I wasn't going to miss this race again, no matter who is racing.

"Rick Galles got me thinking about it. He was going full-time IRL racing, and things happened. The other reason I wanted to run in the IRL with these guys is I liked what Tony George was trying to do. He has given these good, young open-wheel drivers a chance to move up. I left Galles mainly because he wasn't hiring an American driver. The rest is history."

Communication (verbal and non-verbal) between driver and crew chief must be clear and concise so the team can extract the absolute maximum performance from the car. If the crew chief and the driver gel, typically, the team gels. Cheever explains the behavior of the car so the setup can reach its maximum potential.

#51 Rachel's Potato Chips
Entrant: Rachel's Team Cheever
Team Manager: Dick Caron • Crew Chief: Owen Snyder

EDDIE CHEEVER JR.

DALLARA/OLDSMOBILE AURORA/GOODYEAR

For Eddie Cheever Jr., racing stardom seemed just another finishing position higher, just another race or season away. So many times when Cheever was poised for victory in premier open wheel races, bad luck, mechanical failures, and mistakes prevented him from achieving glory. But Cheever took the loses and setbacks in stride and forged on. Up until his victory in the 82nd Indianapolis 500, Cheever's only major professional formula car victory came at the rain-shortened 1997 IRL Indy 200 at Walt Disney World. After 10 years in Formula One, 6 years in CART, and 2 seasons in IRL, Cheever had earned the reputation as the almost man—blindingly fast on occasion but consistently derailed by problems.

On May 24, 1998, he vanquished any doubts that he could dominate a premier race. In his ninth Indy 500 start, Cheever's calm, patient, and analytical demeanor along with a calculated and aggressive drive was rewarded with a triumphant win in the most prestigious auto race in the world. It gave Cheever something he had been longing for his entire career—an accomplishment that would stand out.

Earlier in his career, however, when Cheever dreamed of winning a race in May, it was often a victory at Monaco, not Indianapolis. "I didn't start my racing career thinking of ovals," Cheever recalled. "My family, although American, was living in Italy, so it was logical for me to think of driving a Formula One car. That is where I went. I started in go-karts and raced in Formula One for 10 years as an American. I thought Monte Carlo and Monza were the two races I had the best chance of winning."

But Cheever's destiny, as it turns out, was to be in his home country, racing Indy cars. When Cheever decided to leave Formula One in 1989, he set his sights on winning at the Brickyard. "What brought me here was the Indianapolis 500," he said.

1998 INDY 500 PERFORMANCE PROFILE

Starting Position:	17
Qualifying Average:	217.334 MPH
Qualifying Speed Rank:	21
Best Practice Speed:	234.381 MPH 5/10
Total Practice Laps:	259
Number Practice Days:	6
Finishing Position:	1
Laps Completed:	200 145.155 MPH
Highest Position 1997 Race:	6
Fastest Race Lap:	187 213.904 MPH
1998 INDY 500 Prize Money:	$ 4,433,000
INDY 500 Career Earnings:	$ 2,961,652
Career INDY 500 Starts:	3
Career Best Finish:	4th 1992

According to Cheever, "When you come to this place, the Indianapolis 500 takes over—it becomes your whole year. Although we have many important events, the Indy 500 is special. There is a lot of history here. I am relieved that finally I have done something in my career that will stick, and a win in the Indy 500 will do that. I came here for the 500."

Cheever's path to the pinnacle of Indy car racing has been long and winding, and his arrival at the top is the result of many years of hard work. For anybody who attempts to demean Cheever's achievement of winning the Indianapolis 500, he has a strong message for them:

"For 10 years, I was an American in Formula One—it's not like I was playing tiddly-winks," Cheever said. "For an American to race in Formula One would be like someone from Europe trying to race NASCAR [Winston Cup]. And I did it for 10 years." Formula One is a unique entity in motorsports. For Americans, it has been particularly hard to break into this unique and ultra high-tech type of formula racing.

The Cheever family was based in Rome, Italy, because Eddie Cheever Sr. was running health clubs in Europe. The younger Cheever's interest in racing began early when his mother bought him and his father go-karts for Christmas one year, sparking a passion that would evolve into a career.

Cheever's racing career began in karts in 1973 when he won the European and Italian championships. He placed second in the 1974

World Karting Championship. In 1977, he finished second in Formula Two and followed that with fourth-place finishes in 1978 and 1979, which earned him his first Formula One ride in 1980 when he drove for the Osella team and qualified for 10 World Championship events. In 1981, he moved to Tyrrell and drove in 14 races, taking home a fourth-place finish in Great Britain and a sixth in Belgium.

In 1982, Cheever drove for Ligier and finished second in the Detroit Grand Prix, third at Las Vegas and Belgium, and sixth in Italy. Cheever's best shot at victory came the following year with access to competitive equipment. He was paired with Alain Prost on the Renault team. The car's turbocharged V-6 proved to be very fast but fragile. When the car didn't break, Cheever only finished out of the points once. He scored a second in Canada, third in France, Italy, and Belgium, fourth in Australia, and sixth in South Africa.

However, Cheever was overshadowed by his teammate, Prost, who would become one of the greatest Grand Prix drivers of all time. In the 1983 season, Prost scored four wins and became the team leader. Cheever moved to the Alfa for a two-year stint. During that time, he started in 31 Grand Prixs with a best finish of 4th in 1984. He drove just one Formula One race in 1986 for the Lola Haas team before moving to Arrows in 1987 where he placed 10th in the standings with a 4th-place finish in Belgium.

Cheever placed sixth in the 1988 Formula One World Championship for Arrows with a third in Italy and a sixth in Mexico. In 1989, his final season in Formula One, he drove for Arrows again and finished third in the Phoenix Grand Prix and fifth in Hungary.

By this time, it was apparent that Cheever wasn't going to get a ride from a front running team with the equipment to win. It was time for a new challenge. It was time to look for a team that was capable of winning races. "I came to the States to run with Chip Ganassi in 1990," Cheever recalled. "The first time I came to this place [Indianapolis Motor Speedway], it terrorized me. I wanted to go home. I didn't understand the speed. Racing in America is totally different than it is in Grand Prix. You go from a dead start and then come flying out of a tunnel at 100 miles per hour. It's a totally different thing to learn. I am still learning ovals. That is why I respect people like Rick Mears and those who were so exceptionally talented at this."

It didn't take long for Cheever to acquaint himself with Indy cars, temporary street courses, or road courses. But ovals were something totally foreign to the American, yet Cheever adapted. In the 1990 Indy 500, he qualified in the middle of the fifth row and finished a very creditable 8th in his first outing. The following year, Cheever returned to the Brickyard with the same team, Target Chip Ganassi Racing, and qualified 10th, but Cheever's race didn't last long. An electrical problem took him out of the running after 17 laps, and he finished 31st. But big things were right around the corner.

After two years at the Indy 500, he showed he was coming to grips with oval racing. Although Cheever couldn't be considered an oval master, he was learning and getting faster. He qualified second fastest at 229.639 miles per hour behind pole-sitter Roberto Guerrero's fastest-ever qualifying speed of 232.482 miles per hour in 1992. In the race, Mario and Michael Andretti bolted in front of Cheever at the start; he hovered between second and third position during the race, waiting to attack in the final laps. Once again, fate wasn't on his side. "I probably could have won in 1992," Cheever recalled. "Michael Andretti was a lot faster, and the two of us had the new Ford engines. Michael was very quick, and I was second most of the race. I was passing cars, and we had a rule we could pass under the yellow. Little Al [Al Unser Jr.] saw it, and he called it in and got me penalized for a lap, which I thought was a very shrewd move."

Cheever was penalized by officials of the United States Auto Club (USAC) for one lap but was reinstated to the lead lap when the official results were posted the following morning at 8 A.M. Cheever was credited with a fourth-place finish, but the complexion of the race had changed. Reinstatement to the lead lap wouldn't give him back the opportunity to win the race. Unser Sr. was third, followed by Cheever. But if Cheever, the faster car on the race track once Andretti dropped out with 11 laps remaining, had been on the lead lap, it's likely he would have been the winner of the 1992 Indianapolis 500.

In 1993, Cheever joined Team Menard to compete in the Indy 500. He qualified 18th and finished 17th, three laps down to the leader at the finish. Cheever's equipment made it difficult to compete at the top level. In 1994, Roger Penske capitalized on a USAC rule change, which said push rod engines didn't have to be production based. Penske had Illmor engineering build push rod race engines specifically for the Indy 500. These incredible engines produced about 1,000 horsepower, which was about 150 more than the competition. Cheever's Menard V-6 powered Lola simply didn't have the horsepower to run with the Marlboro Penske drivers. Starting from the 11th starting position, Cheever rose as high as third but eventually finished eighth.

The opportunity to win an Indy car race presented itself in 1995. Cheever started a lowly 21st in the Bosch Spark Plug Grand Prix held at Nazareth Speedway in Nazareth, Pennsylvania. In this warm-up race to the Indy 500, Cheever's quick, consistent driving brought him to the front of the pack, and finally, he stood on the brink of his breakthrough win. But it wasn't to be; the car's telemetry provided erroneous information on the fuel load. While it looked like he had enough fuel to make it to the checkered flag, two laps from the finish his car sputtered to a halt. A race win that was firmly in his grasp slipped away, but Cheever shook off the bitter disappointment and continued on.

Starting in 1996, Cheever's prospects for victory on the newly formed IRL circuit looked promising. In the 1997 Pennzoil 200 at New Hampshire International Raceway, he sliced his way from 14th place to take an early race lead. Once again, Cheever had firm control of the race when bad luck reared its ugly head. His gearbox packed up, and his day was done. But then the dream came true. On January 25, 1997, Cheever put his car into the lead at the right time in the Indy 200 at Walt Disney World. When the rain came down, the race was stopped with 50 laps to go, and Cheever, the leader at Lap 150, was declared the winner. It was a win, but not a convincing or resounding win. That would come later.

In qualifying for the 1998 Indy 500, Cheever wasn't a part of the shoot-out for the pole but cracked into the top six on the first two days of practice. Drawing the second spot in the qualifying line, Cheever waved off on his first attempt but came back with 55 minutes left in first-day time trials to register a run of 217.334 miles per hour to become the 20th qualifier.

"If I was testing the car, I would have parked it and said: 'fix it,'" Cheever said. "But unfortunately, you can't do that. I don't know [what's wrong], but we're going to find out." A poor qualifying setup, however, wasn't going to deter Cheever's mission for the 82nd edition of the Indy 500. On race day, he found himself with an awesome race setup.

The decisive moment of the race occurred when the green flag waved with six laps remaining and Cheever leading the field to the green flag. "I didn't want to get passed on the final restart," Cheever said. "The restarts are very hard because they want us to start slower, but I kept having these nightmares of doing what Scott Goodyear did by passing the pace car in 1995. I'm sure when he did it, he didn't even know he had done it. It is so easy to get carried away when you are out there and forget about the pace car. I was just trying to find the right gear to do it, and that was all. It is the easiest way in the world to get passed, right after a restart because you are opening the air for everybody else, and the guy behind you can pop out and pass everybody. I've been doing it for years."

Cheever rocketed off the fourth turn and kept Buddy Lazier at bay for the closing, running his car all the way out to the wall. Near the end of the race, Cheever had one more close call but was able to pull it out. With three laps left, he came out of a turn and came dangerously close to brushing the wall. He was able to hold on and drive into Victory Lane. "I wasn't going to finish second," Cheever said. "I was either going to win it or not finish it at all." The reaction to the victory was so popular, crew members from all race teams lined up to salute Cheever as he drove into Victory Lane.

His heads-up drive provided him with the crowning moment of his racing career—winning the biggest race in the world in front of 400,000 fans at the Indianapolis Motor Speedway. He led the race six times for 76 laps and was the leader at the 200-mile, 300-mile, 400-mile, and 500-mile marks.

Despite winning the Indianapolis 500, Cheever admits he still struggles with high-speed racing on the superspeedway ovals. Cheever compares driving technique from Formula One to Indy car oval racing. "When I was taught to drive a racing car, I was taught to downshift, to brake, to turn right, turn left, go fast, go slow," Cheever said. "Those are all things here that are useless. If you downshift here, you should go home. The art of using the gearbox was something that took years and years to develop. So I come to this place and after my first five laps, they tell me to put it in fifth gear and leave it and don't touch the brakes."

On a 2.5-mile oval, the slightest mistakes are amplified and can send one on a trip to the wall. "The wall, they call it the fence, and I looked at the crew and said, 'I guarantee you, that is not a fence. It's a wall.' It has taken me many, many years to deal with that. Just the physics of a car going that fast in such close vicinity to walls all the time takes a different mental training you would have as a Grand Prix driver. I still consider myself a Grand Prix driver. I'll never drive a Grand Prix car again, but that is where my foundation as a racing driver was."

Cheever also learned that the Indianapolis Motor Speedway demands respect. Experience pays huge dividends and is a critical factor for winning the 500-mile sprint race. However, nothing is guaranteed at Indy, not even for veteran drivers. "I remember three years ago a team that had won the Indy 500 the year before came here and could not qualify with two exceptional drivers, Emerson Fittipaldi and Al Unser Jr.," Cheever said.

"This place is a monster. If you don't get it right, it will eat your lunch." Cheever went on to say, "When you race here, you have to beat this track. It's the circuit you have to beat. It's a very hard course to run at."

In addition to battling the challenges of the Brickyard oval, Cheever was also dealing with the challenges of being a team owner. In 1996 he ran the first three races on the IRL schedule with Team Menard. But he left after the 1996 Indianapolis 500 and formed Team Cheever with some help from Menard, who sold him several of his cars and engines. Last year, two of Cheever's partners, Bob Hancher and Gary Sallee, also left at the conclusion of the 1997 IRL season to form ISM Racing. When Team Cheever embarked on the 1998 IRL season, ownership resided solely with Cheever. Dick Caron served as team manager and Owen Snyder as the crew chief. "The whole ownership came about because there was an opportunity, and it was the best opportunity, I felt, to win races," Cheever recalled. "It proved to be correct. At the race track, I'm probably third in the pecking order, and that combination works."

The victory was even more special because Cheever is an owner/driver who came to the Speedway at the beginning of the month without a sponsor. He left with the biggest paycheck of his racing career. "The last eight months have been extremely difficult for us," Cheever said. "We had a verbal commitment from FirstPlus to continue, and they decided to do NASCAR. It's very gratifying right now. I'm still going around left corners trying to avoid obstacles in my head, and it hasn't sunk in yet what we have achieved.

"The driver's side is a lot simpler than the owner's side, and having to do them both at the same time takes a lot of energy. I'm still in a bit of a haze right now. It's a very long race, and you have to keep yourself charged up the whole day to run hard. There were a few times I may have wanted to back off, but I had the momentum going. The last 20 laps for me were the hardest 20 laps I have ever driven. I started those last 20 laps saying I wouldn't give anything; try to use as much road as I could. I had been trying to save those tires because if I had to do more than 24 laps, I wanted to make sure I had enough tire in me. That last run, I used every bit of Goodyear that was in them."

Winning racing's greatest spectacle certainly changes a race driver's life. Cheever can attest to that. For one thing, before the Indianapolis 500, Cheever complained he was having trouble getting a date during the month of May at the Indianapolis Motor Speedway. The articulate world traveler and former Formula One star never had that problem before, but at 40 he was complaining his social status wasn't what it used to be. That all changed when he won the Indy 500. Now, he has more social opportunities than he can handle.

"My life has changed totally," Cheever said. "The happiest part of my day is when I wake up in the morning, the first hour or two, because that is when the telephone doesn't ring. Then the telephone calls start, and it never ends. It's like paying taxes at the end of the year. If you have to pay a lot of taxes at the end of the year, it means you made a lot of money. The response to my victory has exceeded my expectations, 10-fold."

Cheever has received numerous telegrams and phone calls from those who want to congratulate him for his victory in the Indianapolis 500. But, according to Cheever, "the best telephone call of all was to my dad. That was the neatest one of all. I should have taped it. . . ."

Cheever's father has figured largely into the direction his career has taken. When Cheever drove into Victory Lane at the most famous race course in the world, he remembered his father who told him to never lose sight of his racing goals. "My father told me when I was raised in Italy . . . [that] if you win one race in your life, win the Indy 500," Cheever said. "This one is for my dad."

2nd Place

#91 Delta Faucet/Coors/Hemelgarn Racing, Inc.
Entrant: Hemelgarn Racing, Inc.
Team Manager: Lee Kunzman • Crew Chief: Dennis LaCava

BUDDY LAZIER

DALLARA/OLDSMOBILE AURORA/GOODYEAR

As a former Indy 500 champion, Buddy Lazier came to the Speedway already knowing the short way around the 2 1/2-mile oval. He didn't crack the top 10 on the daily speed charts until Day 5, but it was a given that he would be a formidable contender.

In qualifying, Lazier put together four steady laps within a half-mile-per-hour of each other for a 218.288 mile-per-hour average to make his sixth "500" field. "We obviously identified early in the week that we weren't a contender for the pole," he said. "It's just nice to be here and get on with the race."

When the green flag dropped, Lazier came from 11th starting position to take the lead for the first time on Lap 51. In all, he led five times for 20 laps before being overhauled by Eddie Cheever 23 laps from the end, denying a bid for a second Indy 500 triumph by 3.191 seconds.

The runnerup finish, going with fourth place in 1997, and his win in '96, gave him an impressive three-year record. "It's just so hard to come that close and not get it," Lazier said. "We just didn't have enough. We gave it all we had."

1998 INDY 500 PERFORMANCE PROFILE

Starting Position:	11
Qualifying Average:	218.288 MPH
Qualifying Speed Rank:	14
Best Practice Speed:	219.587 MPH 5/14
Total Practice Laps:	205
Number Practice Days:	7
Finishing Position:	2
Laps Completed:	200 145.118 MPH
Highest Position 1998 Race:	1
Fastest Race Lap:	184 213.331 MPH
1998 Prize Money:	$483,200
INDY 500 Career Earnings:	$2,603,180
Career INDY 500 Starts:	6
Career Best Finish:	1st 1996

#55 Primadonna Resorts/Miller Milling/ISM Aurora
Entrant: ISM Racing
Team Manager: L. G. Hancher Jr. • Crew Chief: Gary Armentrout

STEVE KNAPP

G FORCE/OLDSMOBILE AURORA/GOODYEAR

Steve Knapp started his first month of May in Indianapolis in a third car for ISM Racing and steadily worked up to speed. From a lap in the 211-mile-per-hour bracket on the first day, he pushed it up to 216.826 miles per hour on the second day of practice.

In qualifying, he was the fifth driver of the month to complete a run, checking in at 216.445. "I started racing back in 1985 and stopped in 1988 because it got too expensive," Knapp said. "My wife and I sat down and set goals in order to get here. We put together our own business in order to free up my time to be able to race. We've accomplished what we set out to do, and I couldn't be happier."

In the race, he moved steadily from the 23rd starting spot, gaining 10 positions in the first 20 laps. By Lap 30, he was 7th. At the end, he was the top-finishing rookie, just 6.749 seconds behind winner Eddie Cheever. "USA Today had me 1,000-to-1, the last one," Knapp said. "The next day I was 8-to-1. It hasn't even sunk in yet. With 20 laps left, I said, 'This is going to come to an end, and I'm going to have to go back to work.'"

1998 INDY 500 PERFORMANCE PROFILE

Starting Position:	23
Qualifying Average:	216.445 MPH
Qualifying Speed Rank:	31
Best Practice Speed:	217.150 MPH 5/15
Total Practice Laps:	137
Number Practice Days:	6
Finishing Position:	3
Laps Completed:	200 145.076 MPH
Highest Position 1998 Race:	2
Fastest Race Lap:	20 2 12.389 MPH
1998 Prize Money:	$338,750
INDY 500 Career Earnings:	$338,750
Career INDY 500 Starts:	1
Career Best Finish:	3rd 1998

#6 Reebok/Nienhouse Motorsports/G Force/Aurora
Entrant: Nienhouse Motorsports
Team Manager: Jamie Galles • Crew Chief: Darren Russell

DAVEY HAMILTON

G FORCE/OLDSMOBILE AURORA/GOODYEAR

Davey Hamilton came to Indianapolis with a new team (Nienhouse Motorsports) and a veteran crew from Galles Racing. Although he was 7th fastest in Opening Day practice, he didn't reach the 218-mile-per-hour bracket until two days before pole-position qualifying. But he still put the machine in the show with a four-lap average of 219.748 to become the month's 12th qualifier and gain his third 500 starting berth.

"I like going fast, but when it counts," Hamilton said. "We have a lot of downforce in the car, and I didn't want to risk it. The car is consistent." The run was good for eighth starting spot, and he took the lead on Lap 114 for three laps before settling into fourth, his best career 500 finish.

"We got caught on a yellow, and I stalled it once in the pits," Hamilton said. "I told myself last year that I could win this thing if I just didn't make any mistakes, but I did."

1998 INDY 500 PERFORMANCE PROFILE

Starting Position:	8
Qualifying Average:	219.748 MPH
Qualifying Speed Rank:	8
Best Practice Speed:	218.946 MPH 5/14
Total Practice Laps:	342
Number Practice Days:	7
Finishing Position:	4
Laps Completed:	199
Highest Position 1998 Race:	1
Fastest Race Lap:	106 212.029 MPH
1998 Prize Money:	$301,650
INDY 500 Career Earnings:	$699,653
Career INDY 500 Starts:	3
Career Best Finish:	4th 1998

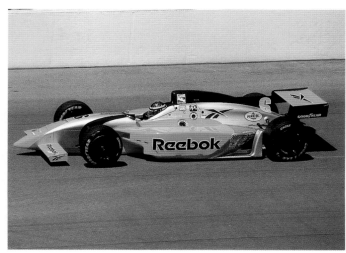

#52 Team Cheever
Entrant: Team Cheever
Team Manager: Dick Caron • Crew Chief: Dane Harte

ROBBY UNSER

DALLARA/OLDSMOBILE AURORA/GOODYEAR

Robby Unser, the son of three-time 500 winner Bobby Unser, got the second seat in the Team Cheever stable for his first month of May in Indianapolis. With it came the Unser legacy at Indy and his family: Uncle Al, cousin Al Jr., cousin Johnny, and father Bobby. Indispensable expert guidance and information, along with a heads-up drive, allowed him to capture fifth place.

He steadily worked up to speed and turned a lap at 217.381 miles per hour the day before pole qualifying. Unser was the month's 10th qualifier, posting a run of 216.534 for the 21st starting position. He secured his spot in Speedway history, becoming the 6th member of the Unser family to qualify for a 500.

"Any time the car moves around that much at 200 miles per hour, it really rocks my nerve," he said. "I think my heart is still hanging out there on the fence in Turn 1. It's one of the harder four laps I've driven this week. I just had to remember what my dad told me, which was that in the worst case scenario, I could go out and try it again."

The run put him 21st in the starting line-up, but he was 7th by Lap 50. At the halfway point, he was 3rd before settling into 5th at the finish. "It's beautiful," Unser said. "It's great. I'm not even sweating. When you love something this much, it just comes."

1998 INDY 500 PERFORMANCE PROFILE

Starting Position:	21
Qualifying Average:	216.534 MPH
Qualifying Speed Rank:	29
Best Practice Speed:	217.381 MPH 5/15
Total Practice Laps:	231
Number Practice Days:	7
Finishing Position:	5
Laps Completed:	198
Highest Position 1998 Race:	3
Fastest Race Lap:	194 213.894 MPH
1998 Prize Money:	$209,400
INDY 500 Career Earnings:	$209,400
Career INDY 500 Starts:	1
Career Best Finish:	5th 1998

KENNY BRACK

DALLARA/OLDSMOBILE AURORA/GOODYEAR

Kenny Brack came back to Indy determined to reverse the fortunes. In the 1997 500, his race was over before it started. In his freshman race, he was involved in a multicar accident as the field formed to take the green flag.

In 1998, however, with A. J. Foyt, the most experienced team owner in IRL in his corner, Brack became Tony Stewart's chief challenger on the speed charts leading up to Pole Day. On three of the practice days, he was second fastest to Stewart.

"Last year I learned how big this event is," Brack said. "You have to focus on what you're doing here. Being with A. J. here is easier because he knows all there is to know."

When Brack's turn came in Pole Day qualifying, Stewart was the fastest at 220.386 miles per hour. But Brack posted a smooth four-lap run of 220.982 to wrest the provisional pole from Stewart as the eighth qualifier of the month. Later qualifying runs by teammates Billy Boat and Greg Ray pushed him to the outside of the front row.

On Race Day, Brack stayed in contention until late, leading three times for 23 laps and finishing sixth, two laps down. "It was the best we could do," Brack said. "We fought a push all day, but I think we could have run with the leaders the whole race. Running out of fuel, we lost a lap, and that really hurt us. But it's the same thing when the driver makes a mistake. Things just happen."

1998 INDY 500 PERFORMANCE PROFILE

Starting Position:	3
Qualifying Average:	220.982 MPH
Qualifying Speed Rank:	3
Best Practice Speed:	223.464 MPH 5/15
Total Practice Laps:	139
Number Practice Days:	6
Finishing Position:	6
Laps Completed:	198
Highest Position 1998 Race:	1
Fastest Race Lap:	182 213.528 MPH
1998 Prize Money:	$310,750
INDY 500 Career Earnings:	$513,000
Career INDY 500 Starts:	2
Career Best Finish:	6th 1998

JOHN PAUL JR.

DALLARA/OLDSMOBILE AURORA/FIRESTONE

John Paul Jr. was rideless through the early part of practice week but wound up in the Team Pelfrey car after Danny Ongais crashed and wasn't cleared to drive. He turned out to be the last driver to get a ride, just two days before Pole Day, and the first to qualify, making the third attempt of the month and registering a run of 217.351 miles per hour.

"I'm ecstatic," Paul said after his run. "It's a great relief. All the variables make it difficult to get in [the race]. It's so hard on your stomach. You may make a mistake, and you don't want to be the one not to hold up your end of the deal." The run was good for the 16th starting spot, but Paul smoothly moved to the front and led at the halfway point. In all, he led twice for 39 laps, second only to winner Eddie Cheever, before a series of setbacks dropped him to 7th at the finish, three laps down.

"I had a big lead when the light [dashboard caution] came on in Turn 4," Paul said. "I slowed down when no one else did. Cheever was coming off of Turn 3, and I was going into Turn 4. I had the whole short chute between us. I had a problem with the clutch overheating. The car was awesome. It's a lot of fun to slice and dice through traffic. It's the only time I've been in the race. It was a blast today. It was an incredible amount of fun. It was a heartbreaker."

1998 INDY 500 PERFORMANCE PROFILE

Starting Position:	16
Qualifying Average:	217.351 MPH
Qualifying Speed Rank:	21
Best Practice Speed:	213.609 MPH 5/15
Total Practice Laps:	108
Number Practice Days:	3
Finishing Position:	7
Laps Completed:	197
Highest Position 1998 Race:	1
Fastest Race Lap:	108 213.655 MPH
1998 Prize Money:	$216,350
INDY 500 Career Earnings:	$1,034,772
Career INDY 500 Starts:	7
Career Best Finish:	7th 1998

ANDY MICHNER

DALLARA/OLDSMOBILE AURORA/GOODYEAR

Although 1998 was Andy Michner's rookie year in the 500, his family has history at the Speedway. His father Joe co-owned a car that started on the front row in 1970 with Johnny Rutherford aboard. Michner began his own Indy experience on Day 3, taking his first practice laps in a car that wasn't ready until the previous night and working his way steadily up to speed to make his first Indianapolis 500 field. On Pole Day, after an early waveoff, Michner recorded a four-lap average of 216.922 miles per hour to earn the 19th starting spot in the race.

"We knew the car had speed in it," Michner said after the run. "I just wanted to get in the show. It's a dream come true. We're happy where we're at. That's the only car we have and the only engine we have. We just wanted to be consistent."

On Race Day, Michner gained eight spots by Lap 70, climbed into the top 10 by late in the race, and finished in eighth place. "We were good in the corners, but there was no straightaway speed due to an electrical problem," Michner said. "I wish we were more in the hunt, but we brought it home in eighth, so I'll take it. I'm satisfied a little, but I wish I had started higher. Maybe we could have done better."

1998 INDY 500 PERFORMANCE PROFILE

Starting Position:	19
Qualifying Average:	216.922 MPH
Qualifying Speed Rank:	26
Best Practice Speed:	217.192 MPH 5/15
Total Practice Laps:	138
Number Practice Days:	5
Finishing Position:	8
Laps Completed:	197
Highest Position 1998 Race:	7
Fastest Race Lap:	194 206.797 MPH
1998 Prize Money:	$182,050
INDY 500 Career Earnings:	$182,050
Career INDY 500 Starts:	1
Career Best Finish:	8th 1998

#44 One Call Communications/Quaker State/Menards/SRS
Entrant: SRS
Team Manager: Joe Kennedy • Crew Chief: Joe Kennedy

J.J. YELEY

DALLARA/OLDSMOBILE AURORA/FIRESTONE

In his first year at the Indy 500, J. J. Yeley was in a Sinden Races Services (SRS) entry (assisted by Team Menard). Commenting on how this sponsorship came about, Yeley had this to say: "Jeff [Sinden of SRS] and John [Menard] have been friends for a long time. There were about 15 or 16 drivers that were vying for this seat. I met with Jeff at Phoenix and got the seat. John Menard is looking for a young driver, and I'm in the number-one slot."

With youthful exuberance, J. J. Yeley came out of the gate fast in a bid to make his first 500 field, finishing 9th fastest on the opening day of practice. On Pole Day, he was the 16th qualifier of the month with a run of 218.044 miles per hour, fastest among the rookies until Jimmy Kite took that honor on the second day of time trials.

On Race Day, Yeley survived a harrowing experience in the first turn on the start with eventual winner Eddie Cheever Jr., which dropped him to the end of the field. He came back to finish 9th. "The first lap was kind of a bummer," Yeley said. "Cheever pinched me down into the grass, but I think he ran into me. It was a lot of fun. We had to come from 33rd in the pack to finish 9th. I guess that will make my first Indy 500 a memorable one."

1998 INDY 500 PERFORMANCE PROFILE

Starting Position:	13
Qualifying Average:	218.044 MPH
Qualifying Speed Rank:	16
Best Practice Speed:	217.307 MPH 5/15
Total Practice Laps:	304
Number Practice Days:	6
Finishing Position:	9
Laps Completed:	197
Highest Position 1998 Race:	9
Fastest Race Lap:	9 211.188 MPH
1998 Prize Money:	$198,550
INDY 500 Career Earnings:	$198,550
Career INDY 500 Starts:	1
Career Best Finish:	9th 1998

#12 International Star Registry/Bradley Food Marts
Entrant: Bradley Motorsports
Team Manager: Mike Collier • Crew Chief: Steve Ritenour

BUZZ CALKINS

G FORCE/OLDSMOBILE AURORA/GOODYEAR

Buzz Calkins had a frustrating week of practice before making his third Indianapolis 500 field. He didn't reach 217 miles per hour until the day before time trials were to begin but put together a steady run of 217.197 miles per hour to nail down the 18th starting spot.

"It's always the longest 2 minutes and 45 seconds of your life here," Calkins said. "It's a relief to be in the field. It's getting slick out there, so we have to be happy, especially considering how we were running 48 hours ago."

In the race, he charged to 10th by the 10th lap and took the lead in Laps 47 to 50 before finishing 10th. "That was a long day," Calkins said. "That was hard work. We fought consistency in the car all day long. It seemed to change, lap to lap, pit stop to pit stop, tire set to tire set. We took downforce out of the car to gain straightaway speed, but we lost grip as a result. It was great to finish the race, but that's only halfway to our goal, which is to win."

1998 INDY 500 PERFORMANCE PROFILE

Starting Position:	18
Qualifying Average:	217.197
Qualifying Speed Rank:	24
Best Practice Speed:	217.276 MPH 5/15
Total Practice Laps:	254
Number Practice Days:	7
Finishing Position:	10
Laps Completed:	195
Highest Position 1998 Race:	1
Fastest Race Lap:	20 208.174 MPH
1998 Prize Money:	$248,500
INDY 500 Career Earnings:	$623,053
Career INDY 500 Starts:	3
Career Best Finish:	10th 1998

#7 Royal Purple Synthetic/"Synerlec"/Scandia
Entrant: Team Scandia
Team Manager: Luke Wethington • Crew Chief: Brad McCanless

JIMMY KITE

DALLARA/OLDSMOBILE AURORA/GOODYEAR

Jimmy Kite was expected to be a contender in his rookie year, but a series of accidents delayed his quest during practice week. Kite hit the Turn 4 wall on the first day of practice, hit the wall again in Turn 4 on Day 5, then hit the Turn 1 wall the morning of Pole Day through a series of mishaps. But when the final day of qualifying came, in a car repaired by Team Scandia, he posted a run of 219.290 miles per hour and became the fastest rookie in the field.

"The team never gave up," Kite said. "Anytime something happened, I got back up. I'm praising the guys every minute. It's been a roller coaster every day. We figured we haven't used any good luck this week, so obviously we had some left. Every year from here on out, I'll always remember this."

He started 26th in the line-up, was 14th by Lap 60, brought out the caution on Lap 96 when he stalled, and wound up 11th at the finish, five laps down. "As the day went on, we got stronger," Kite stated. "Right when the car got perfect, it went back to loose again. Five hundred miles is a whole lot of miles, and when the car is perfect, I can run all day. When you have problems, it wears you out."

1998 INDY 500 PERFORMANCE PROFILE

Starting Position:	26
Qualifying Average:	219.290 MPH
Qualifying Speed Rank:	9
Best Practice Speed:	8.765 MPH 5/10
Total Practice Laps:	276
Number Practice Days:	6
Finishing Position:	11
Laps Completed:	195
Highest Position 1998 Race:	11
Fastest Race Lap:	10 204.769 MPH
1998 Prize Money:	$287,300
INDY 500 Career Earnings:	$287,300
Career INDY 500 Starts:	1
Career Best Finish:	11th 1998

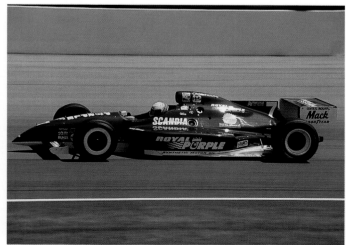

#18 Parker Machinery
Entrant: PDM Racing, Inc.
Team Manager: A. J. Watson • Crew Chief: Paul Murphy

JACK HEWITT

G FORCE/OLDSMOBILE AURORA/GOODYEAR

Jack Hewitt treasured his first voyage to make a bid for a starting spot in the Indianapolis 500. The 46-year-old dirt-track legend hooked up with PDM Racing and Parker Machinery for the adventure and took in every aspect of the month of May.

On the track, it started out shaky as Hewitt hit the Turn 4 wall on the opening day of practice. The PDM crew repaired the machine in three days and got Hewitt back out on Day 4. The next day, he passed the final phase of his driver's test. Hewitt was scheduled to be the first qualifier of the month, but he was waved off after three laps in the 215-mile-per-hour bracket. Later, he became the 22nd qualifier with a four-lap average of 216.540.

"Everybody just stuck behind me," Hewitt said. "I'm indebted to a lot of people. It feels pretty good right now. When you go and have as much trouble as I did this week, it was a long one."

In the race, he dropped from 22nd starting position to 30th but was back up to 17th by Lap 50. He spun and recovered on Lap 180 and continued on to finish 12th.

"It was pretty good just to make the show," Hewitt said. "Now I can say I've finished it. It's unbelievable. I wish Dad could have been here to see it. Now that the whole deal is over with, I know there'll never be another first time. First I got to make it. Then I got to start. Then I got my first lap. Now I can say I finished."

1998 INDY 500 PERFORMANCE PROFILE

Starting Position:	22
Qualifying Average:	216.450 MPH
Qualifying Speed Rank:	30
Best Practice Speed:	214.577 MPH 5/15
Total Practice Laps:	282
Number Practice Days:	5
Finishing Position:	12
Laps Completed:	195
Highest Position 1998 Race:	11
Fastest Race Lap:	155 208.266 MPH
1998 Prize Money:	$265,800
INDY 500 Career Earnings:	$265,800
Career INDY 500 Starts:	1
Career Best Finish:	12th 1998

#35 Team Tabasco/Superflo/Prolong/ISM Racing Aurora
Entrant: ISM Racing
Team Manager: L. G. Hancher Jr. • Crew Chief: Mitch Davis

JEFF WARD

G FORCE/OLDSMOBILE AURORA/GOODYEAR

Jeff Ward was looking to gain two spots from his third-place finish in 1997. It was an incredible performance from the former motocross champion, as he led the race twice and took 1997 Rookie of the Year honors.

He cracked the top 10 in practice once but didn't make a qualifying attempt on Pole Day because the ISM team lost two motors in his machine. On Sunday, though, he was fastest in the morning practice with a lap at 219.149 miles per hour, then became the month's 30th qualifier with a four-lap average of 219.086.

With the run, he was the second-fastest second-day qualifier behind Jimmy Kite. Ward said, "It was easy. The car stuck like glue, so I was real happy with the run. It wasn't a white-knuckle run. There was a lot left in the car." The run left him in 27th starting position, but he came quickly up through the field. He picked up four spots on the first lap and was 14th by Lap 20. After dropping to 30th in a pit-stop incident, he came back through the pack again to finish 13th.

"We had a really good car until I hit Stephan Gregoire exiting my pit," Ward said. "It bent our right front suspension, and the steering wheel remained out of position the rest of the day. Then a wheel nut stripped, and my right rear tire came off. Overall, it was a very rough day."

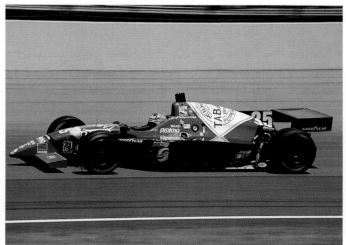

1998 INDY 500 PERFORMANCE PROFILE

Starting Position:	27
Qualifying Average:	219.086 MPH
Qualifying Speed Rank:	10
Best Practice Speed:	218.744 MPH 5/12
Total Practice Laps:	287
Number Practice Days:	7
Finishing Position:	13
Laps Completed:	194
Highest Position 1998 Race:	11
Fastest Race Lap:	18 211.949 MPH
1998 Prize Money:	$242,050
INDY 500 Career Earnings:	$656,300
Career INDY 500 Starts:	2
Career Best Finish:	3rd 1997

14th Place

#16 International Sports Ltd./Phoenix Racing
Entrant: Phoenix Racing
Team Manager: Dick Simon • Crew Chief: Gilbert Lage

MARCO GRECO

Marco Greco came to Indy with his own team and was reunited with longtime engineer and Indianapolis 500 veteran Dick Simon.

After cracking the top 10 on the speed chart on Day 5 of practice, Greco became the next-to-last qualifier on Pole Day with a four-lap average of 217.953 miles per hour. "I'm really pleased," Greco said. "We had a few problems in the morning. We put a new engine in and went straight out to qualifying. We had no practice. It [the engine] is shy 200 revs. Thanks to Dick Simon's experience, we were able to qualify."

In the race, he was bidding to crack the top 10 after starting 14th, but transmission problems slowed his way. "When I shifted from second to third, third to fourth, and then into fifth, it stuck in fifth," Greco said. "I tried to free it up, but I couldn't. After the next pit stop, I had to leave the pits in fifth gear. After another yellow, I pulled hard to try to get it into neutral. I got it to move, but it stayed stuck in fourth. From then on, I was lifting at about the start/finish line so no rev limiter would kick in."

1998 INDY 500 PERFORMANCE PROFILE

Starting Position:	14
Qualifying Average:	217.953 MPH
Qualifying Speed Rank:	18
Best Practice Speed:	220.189 MPH 5/14
Total Practice Laps:	298
Number Practice Days:	7
Finishing Position:	14
Laps Completed:	183
Highest Position 1998 Race:	10
Fastest Race Lap:	19 211.253 MPH
1998 Prize Money:	$167,800
INDY 500 Career Earnings:	$685,865
Career INDY 500 Starts:	4
Career Best Finish:	14th 1998

15th Place

#10 Jonathan Byrd's VisionAire/Bryant Heating & Cooling
Entrant: Jonathan Byrd/Cunningham Racing, LLC
Team Manager: Clayton Cunningham • Crew Chief: Mark Olson

MIKE GROFF

G FORCE/OLDSMOBILE AURORA/FIRESTONE

Mike Groff was first on the track for the month of May in his first Indy 500 foray with Jonathan Byrd/Cunningham Racing. But problems ensued during practice week, and he waved off a qualifying attempt on the first day. After a second waveoff on the final day, he qualified just 37 minutes from the end of the day at 216.704 miles per hour to bump Billy Roe from the field.

"We had a rough week," Groff said. "It came down to the wire. The guys rose to the occasion. There's some work to do; we didn't get to run with full tanks, and it doesn't look like we're going to get to do it. It's going to be hard."

On Race Day, after starting 32nd, he moved up, gaining 16th position by Lap 50 and finishing 15th. "Starting 32nd, I was really being cautious on the start," Groff said. "We were dodging race cars and parts all day. We started with an engine miss. I really wasn't competitive all day. Our 15th shows just about where we were all month."

1998 INDY 500 PERFORMANCE PROFILE

Starting Position:	32
Qualifying Average:	216.704 MPH
Qualifying Speed Rank:	20
Best Practice Speed:	217.234 MPH 5/13
Total Practice Laps:	382
Number Practice Days:	7
Finishing Position:	15
Laps Completed:	183
Highest Position 1998 Race:	15
Fastest Race Lap:	31 206.006 MPH
1998 Prize Money:	$237,600
INDY 500 Career Earnings:	$890,505
Career INDY 500 Starts:	5
Career Best Finish:	12th 1997

69

16th Place

#8 Delphi Automotive Systems
Entrant: Kelley Racing
Team Manager: David Cripps • Crew Chief: Mike Horvath

SCOTT SHARP

DALLARA/OLDSMOBILE AURORA/GOODYEAR

Scott Sharp, the 1996 Indy Racing League co-champion, and Kelley Racing came to Indianapolis with high hopes of a victory.

He made a lot of noise near the top of the daily practice speed charts, moving into the top three on all but two days during the week. After a waveoff in the original qualifying line, Sharp came back to register a four-lap average of 219.910 miles per hour late in Pole Day to claim the seventh starting spot.

"It felt great on the first lap," Sharp said. "I thought I had 221s, but I got a big push. Lots of drama for the team, so it's good to be in the show now."

On Race Day, he moved to fourth position by Lap 60 and regained the spot by Lap 180 after dropping back. But a gearbox problem sent him to the sidelines in 16th.

"Went to shift up to second gear," Sharp said. "No gears."

1998 INDY 500 PERFORMANCE PROFILE

Qualifying Average:	219.910 MPH
Qualifying Speed Rank:	7
Best Practice Speed:	222.107 MPH 5/11
Total Practice Laps:	265
Number Practice Days:	7
Finishing Position:	16
Laps Completed:	181
Highest Position 1998 Race:	3
Fastest Race Lap:	100 211.590 MPH
1998 Prize Money:	$234,800
INDY 500 Career Earnings:	$756,519
Career INDY 500 Starts:	4
Career Best Finish:	10th 1996

#77 Blue Star/Tokheim/Estridge/Miller-Eads
Entrant: Chastain Motorsports
Team Manager: Pat Chastain • Crew Chief: Darrell Soppe

STEPHAN GREGOIRE

G FORCE/OLDSMOBILE AURORA/GOODYEAR

Stephan Gregoire and the Chastain Motorsports team were frustrated early in practice week and didn't make a qualifying attempt on Pole Day. But with Bubble Day winding down, Gregoire found the magic and reeled off a four-lap run of 217.036 miles per hour.

"We've been struggling," Gregoire said. "The first lap was the best. The push started on the second lap. We lost time with the engine. It was our fault, not the engine builder's. The Calkins helped us out last night. We'll banzai to the front. It's not 200 miles like Phoenix, so we'll take it a little slower."

After starting 31st, Gregoire steadily moved through the pack to 10th by Lap 50 and 8th by Lap 70. But a pit road clash with Jeff Ward hampered his effort, and he brushed the wall on Lap 176. Still, he continued to 17th.

"The handling of the car was very bad," Gregoire said. "We touched someone in the pits earlier. I don't know if that's the problem."

1998 INDY 500 PERFORMANCE PROFILE

Starting Position:	31
Qualifying Average:	217.036 MPH
Qualifying Speed Rank:	25
Best Practice Speed:	217.365 MPH 5/11
Total Practice Laps:	272
Number Practice Days:	6
Finishing Position:	17
Laps Completed:	172
Highest Position 1998 Race:	4
Fastest Race Lap:	73 209.035 MPH
1998 Prize Money:	$225,300
INDY 500 Career Earnings:	$720,006
Career INDY 500 Starts:	4
Career Best Finish:	17th 1998

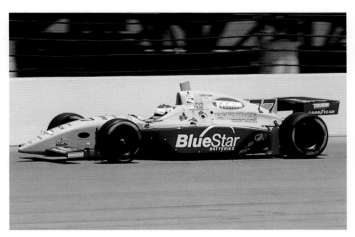

#97 Texas Motor Speedway/TNN/True Value/Dixie Chopper
Entrant: Thomas Knapp Motorsports/Genoa Racing
Team Manager: Marshall Pruett • Crew Chief: Jon Ennik

GREG RAY

DALLARA/OLDSMOBILE AURORA/FIRESTONE

Greg Ray and Thomas Knapp Motorsports came to Indianapolis on a wing and a prayer. After a sponsor failed to fulfill a commitment, the team was forced to rethink its mission. But people stepped up to help them out. They managed the Cinderella story of the month.

The money problem limited their practice time, and they didn't get on the track until Day 3 (when Ray had the fifth-fastest speed). Still, he continued to hover in the top six the rest of the week.

With Billy Boat's pole speed as a target and 45 minutes left in Pole Day qualifying, Ray recorded a run of 221.125 miles per hour, good for a spot in the middle of the front row. "Earlier in the day I thought it was too hot, and we had some handling problems," Ray said. "The car was pretty loose. I'm so happy for this small team. Every boy dreams of running the Indy 500. I'd like to see the checkered flag."

On Race Day, he proved to be a contender, taking the lead from Boat on Lap 13 and leading 18 laps in all. But while leading on Lap 32, he slowed on the backstretch with gearbox problems. He returned to the track, but the gearbox woes finally put him out in 18th place. "I'm disappointed," Ray said. "We didn't have a very good payday. Winning is first; money is second. We made a hell of an impression out there today. I just hope it generates enough interest that someone will want to get involved."

1998 INDY 500 PERFORMANCE PROFILE

Starting Position:	2
Qualifying Average:	221.125 MPH
Qualifying Speed Rank:	2
Best Practice Speed:	222.717 MPH 5/14
Total Practice Laps:	129
Number Practice Days:	5
Finishing Position:	18
Laps Completed:	167
Highest Position 1998 Race:	1
Fastest Race Lap:	91 213.154 MPH
1998 Prize Money:	$175,400
INDY 500 Career Earnings:	$346,650
Career INDY 500 Starts:	2
Career Best Finish:	18th 1998

19th Place

#30 Beloit/Fast Rod/Team Losi/TransWorld Diversified
Entrant: McCormack Motorsports
Team Manager: Dennis McCormack • Crew Chief: Phil McRobert

RAUL BOESEL

G FORCE/OLDSMOBILE AURORA/GOODYEAR

Raul Boesel hooked up with the McCormack Motorsports team and came back to the Speedway after a two-year absence. "This place is very special," Boesel said about his return. "The emotions are quite different. The fans and the history and the other races they did here all add up[here]."

After postponing a qualifying attempt until the final day, he turned a lap at 218.781 in the morning practice. Then, as the first qualifier on the final day, he posted a run of 217.303 miles per hour. "I'm so pleased we qualified," Boesel said. "It's been a very long week. We struggled quite a bit and had major problems almost day-to-day. We dropped a little bit of speed from the first laps. In Turn 4 the car started to react differently, and I lost a lot of grip."

On Race Day, the problems continued. He pulled to pit road on the second pace lap, dropping to last place on the scoring pylon early. "I noticed a problem as soon as it started to run," Boesel said. "I think we have a fuel pickup problem." After that, he returned to the track and completed 164 laps for 19th place.

1998 INDY 500 PERFORMANCE PROFILE

Starting Position:	30
Qualifying Average:	217.303 MPH
Qualifying Speed Rank:	23
Best Practice Speed:	216.534 MPH 5/11
Total Practice Laps:	191
Number Practice Days:	7
Finishing Position:	19
Laps Completed:	164
Highest Position 1998 Race:	19
Fastest Race Lap:	68 207.991 MPH
1998 Prize Money:	$221,300
INDY 500 Career Earnings:	$1,642,980
Career INDY 500 Starts:	10
Career Best Finish:	3rd 1989

ARIE LUYENDYK

G FORCE/OLDSMOBILE AURORA/FIRESTONE

Arie Luyendyk returned to Indianapolis to defend his second 500 win but found rough going in the effort. He started out fast, second quickest to Tony Stewart on Opening Day. But problems persisted during the week, and he waved off his only Pole Day attempt.

"Yesterday, the moment I went out of the pits to practice, the motor wouldn't run," Luyendyk said. "The day was a complete loss for us. The second motor wouldn't run in afternoon qualifying, either. For sure we'd look stupid, not making the show after winning it last year."

On the final day, he qualified at 218.935 miles per hour and would start 28th in the line-up in G Force chassis No. 001, the first G Force ever built and the same car in which he won the 1997 edition of the 500.

By Lap 50 of the race, Luyendyk had gained 20 positions, moving up to 8th. Continuing to move up through contenders, he took the lead for the first time on Lap 85 and again on Lap 147. But he stalled on Lap 153 to bring out a caution and was sidelined by gearbox problems in 20th place. "On the first pit stop, we had a clutch problem," Luyendyk said. "Up until then, it was going real well. It was hard without a clutch. The car was plenty good. It's hard to get upset. We ran a good race."

1998 INDY 500 PERFORMANCE PROFILE

Starting Position:	28
Qualifying Average:	218.935 MPH
Qualifying Speed Rank:	11
Best Practice Speed:	220.464 MPH 5/13
Total Practice Laps:	338
Number Practice Days:	7
Finishing Position:	20
Laps Completed:	151
Highest Position 1998 Race:	1
Fastest Race Lap:	30 214.480 MPH
1998 Prize Money:	$242,100
INDY 500 Career Earnings:	$5,269,429
Career INDY 500 Starts:	14
Career Best Finish:	1st 1990, 1997

#40 Crest Racing
Entrant: Crest Racing/SRS
Team Manager: Jeff Sinden • Crew Chief: Ken Brooks

DR. JACK MILLER

DALLARA/NISSAN INFINITI/FIRESTONE

Dr. Jack Miller and the Crest Racing team came to Indianapolis as the only group to employ the Nissan Infiniti Indy engine. The car reached 217.328 miles per hour the day before pole qualifying, and, after an early waveoff on Pole Day, he was the day's final qualifier with 4 minutes remaining at 217.800. His last three laps were his fastest three of the month.

"Nissan has stuck with us, and we stuck with them, and it paid off today," Miller said. "It's been a struggle. I knew all along that Nissan was going to work. We have to have some reliability. I definitely think it'll make it."

On Race Day, after starting 15th, Miller drove a steady pace but had to pit for his crew to change a header and alternator, putting him behind in the race. "We finished, and that's all that matters," Miller said. "This is the first IRL race we've finished. We were not going to give up. We were going to take the checkered flag."

1998 INDY 500 PERFORMANCE PROFILE

Starting Position:	15
Qualifying Average:	217.800 MPH
Qualifying Speed Rank:	19
Best Practice Speed:	217.328 MPH 5/15
Total Practice Laps:	204
Number Practice Days:	6
Finishing Position:	21
Laps Completed:	128
Highest Position 1998 Race:	14
Fastest Race Lap:	14 210.177 MPH
1998 Prize Money:	$159,800
INDY 500 Career Earnings:	$331,050
Career INDY 500 Starts:	2
Career Best Finish:	20th 1997

ROBERTO GUERRERO

DALLARA/OLDSMOBILE AURORA/GOODYEAR

Roberto Guerrero and Pagan Racing suffered through a tough practice week before finding speed the day before qualifying was to begin. After an early wave-off on Pole Day, Guerrero registered a four-lap run of 218.900 miles an hour, good for the ninth starting spot. Before that, his best practice lap for the week was 218.701.

"The team worked so very hard," he said. "We're just happy that we're finally in the race. In the middle of the week, I was worrying about that. I was looking at the speeds on my dash with the corner of my eye. Every time, I said, "'One more lap, one more lap.'"

In the race, he was hovering in the top 10 when he was involved in a multicar tangle in Turn 3. After surveying the damage, he brought the car to pit road where his crew made adjustments and repairs. He was running at the end, finishing 22nd.

"I'm disappointed," Guerrero said. "I don't seem to get any breaks here. We'll keep trying, though. We'll be back here next year to do it all over again.

"It [the accident] was a long chain reaction by the time it got to me," he added. "I hit pretty hard, but when I got out of the car [in the pits], I looked at it and said to myself, 'There's nothing wrong with it.' So I got back in and got some more laps."

1998 INDY 500 PERFORMANCE PROFILE

Starting Position:	9
Qualifying Average:	218.900 MPH
Qualifying Speed Rank:	12
Best Practice Speed:	218.701 MPH 5/11
Total Practice Laps:	352
Number Practice Days:	7
Finishing Position:	22
Laps Completed:	125
Highest Position 1998 Race:	5
Fastest Race Lap:	32 209.395 MPH
1998 Prize Money:	$165,300
INDY 500 Career Earnings:	$2,504,063
Career INDY 500 Starts:	14
Career Best Finish:	2nd 1984, 1987

BILLY BOAT

DALLARA/OLDSMOBILE AURORA/GOODYEAR

Billy Boat came to Indianapolis with a full-time ride from AJ Foyt Enterprises and was looking to win. When practice opened, Boat was on the sidelines. But when Foyt unleashed his troops on Day 2, Boat and Kenny Brack quickly moved to the top four and continued to be factors at the top of the speed chart throughout the week.

Boat suffered a setback the day before qualifications began when he hit the wall in Turn 3, relegating him to his backup. In the morning practice on Pole Day, Boat turned a lap at 223.836 miles per hour, the fastest lap recorded at Indy for the two-year-old Pep Boys Indy Racing League formula.

With Tony Stewart holding the fastest four-lap average in qualifying, Boat posted a run of 223.503 miles per hour, with a fastest lap of 224.573 to take his first Indy pole. "When we went out this morning, I knew we could run 224 today," he said. "The only problem I had was in Turn 1 with the wind. My goal was to go out and do the best I could. I didn't know what to expect. I just knew I had to hold up my end of the bargain."

In the race, he led the first 12 laps before turning the point over to Greg Ray; however, mechanical malfunctions plagued him. He slowed on the backstretch on Lap 51, smoking. "The car was stuck in second gear on the restart," Boat said. "Then it locked up completely." After the car was pushed to Gasoline Alley for a gearbox change, he returned to the track, but driveline problems ended his day in 23rd.

1998 INDY 500 PERFORMANCE PROFILE

Starting Position:	1
Qualifying Average:	223.503 MPH
Qualifying Speed Rank:	1
Best Practice Speed:	222.008 MPH 5/11
Total Practice Laps:	206
Number Practice Days:	6
Finishing Position:	23
Laps Completed:	111
Highest Position 1998 Race:	1
Fastest Race Lap:	9 213.523 MPH
1998 Prize Money:	$364,200
INDY 500 Career Earnings:	$633,900
Career INDY 500 Starts:	2
Career Best Finish:	7th 1997

#4 Pennzoil Panther G Force
Entrant: Panther Racing, LLC
Team Manager: John Barnes • Crew Chief: Kevin Blanch

SCOTT GOODYEAR

G FORCE/OLDSMOBILE AURORA/GOODYEAR

Scott Goodyear came to Indy with a new team, Panther Racing, formed by a group that includes NFL quarterback Jim Harbaugh.

Goodyear was quiet during practice week as the team worked its way up to speed. On Pole Day, he became the month's 11th qualifier with a steady four-lap run of 218.357 miles per hour. "We found a consistent race car today, and also the limit for the G Force, which is a 218 or 219," Goodyear said. "I had a little push on the first lap, but I used the weight jacker to make adjustments. The wind made things really tricky. The car seems to be good with or without fuel, so that's a really good sign for Race Day."

After starting 10th, Goodyear quickly moved to the front, gaining four spots in the first 10 laps. However, he pulled in on the 25th circuit with a clutch problem. Although he returned, he was out at the halfway point with a 24th-place finish. "We lost the clutch for some reason," Goodyear said. "I'm not really sure how or why. I'm disappointed. We had a great car. Our goal was to get it up to the front within 50 laps, and we were there."

1998 INDY 500 PERFORMANCE PROFILE

Starting Position:	10
Qualifying Average:	218.357 MPH
Qualifying Speed Rank:	13
Best Practice Speed:	220.604 MPH 5/11
Total Practice Laps:	480
Number Practice Days:	7
Finishing Position:	24
Laps Completed:	100
Highest Position 1998 Race:	4
Fastest Race Lap:	71 213.093 MPH
1998 Prize Money:	$253,300
INDY 500 Career Earnings:	$2,266,362
Career INDY 500 Starts:	8
Career Best Finish:	2nd 1992, 1997

#9 Hemelgarn Racing
Entrant: Hemelgarn Racing, Inc.
Team Manager: Lee Kunzman • Crew Chief: Dennis LaCava

JOHNNY UNSER

DALLARA/OLDSMOBILE AURORA/GOODYEAR

Johnny Unser stepped into a backup Hemelgarn Racing entry for the second straight year at Indy. He didn't get on the track until the day before qualifying was to begin but quickly turned a best lap of 216.539 miles per hour.

In qualifying, he was the first to return after the original qualifying line, ran three laps in the 217 bracket, and ran out of fuel. Less than an hour later, he put the car in the show at a four-lap average of 216.316. "We just had a miscalculation and ran out of gas," Unser said of his first attempt, adding he didn't feel very good about his second completed run. "We tried to duplicate exactly what we had. Same tires on it, but they just didn't come up quite the way that the first run did. It's just unfortunate. I had to lift. It was either that or hit the wall, so I had to sacrifice a little speed."

After starting 25th, he moved to 12th by Lap 50. But by Lap 100, he was smoking on the backstretch, out with an engine problem in 25th place. "We started the race with the wrong setup," Unser said. "After the first stop, it got better. After the second stop, it got very good."

1998 INDY 500 PERFORMANCE PROFILE

Starting Position:	25
Qualifying Average:	216.316 MPH
Qualifying Speed Rank:	33
Best Practice Speed:	216.539 MPH 5/15
Total Practice Laps:	90
Number Practice Days:	1
Finishing Position:	25
Laps Completed:	98
Highest Position 1998 Race:	5
Fastest Race Lap:	84 209.785 MPH
1998 Prize Money:	$136,300
INDY 500 Career Earnings:	$438,253
Career INDY 500 Starts:	3
Career Best Finish:	18th 1997

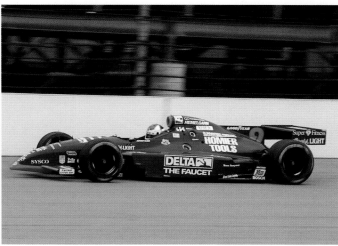

26th Place

#99 Best Western Gold Crown Racing Special
Entrant: LP Racing, Inc./PCI
Team Manager: Larry Nash • Crew Chief: Todd Tapply

SAM SCHMIDT

DALLARA/OLDSMOBILE AURORA/FIRESTONE

Sam Schmidt went into his second Indy 500 aligned with LP Racing for the first time. He was a surprising fifth-fastest on Day 2 of practice and became the second qualifier of the month with an impressive four-lap average of 219.982 miles per hour. "We struggled with a lack of motors all week," Schmidt said. "We ran in various conditions all week. Today, the car really stuck to the ground. I think we should have no problem running all day at 215 or 216. I think the track conditions and lack of a tow like you have in practice contributed to the slower speeds, and the car is a little bit loose as well."

The run was good for the 6th starting spot in the field. In the race, Schmidt circulated in the top eight steadily until a multicar tangle in Turn 3 put him on the sidelines in 26th place. "We were just riding it out," Schmidt said. "It's just a racing deal. We were staying away from the dicing, but in this case it was either go in the grass or hit Davey Hamilton. I thought we had a top-five car. It's pretty disappointing."

1998 INDY 500 PERFORMANCE PROFILE

Starting Position:	6
Qualifying Average:	219.982 MPH
Qualifying Speed Rank:	6
Best Practice Speed:	221.588 MPH 5/11
Total Practice Laps:	207
Number Practice Days:	6
Finishing Position:	26
Laps Completed:	48
Highest Position 1998 Race:	4
Fastest Race Lap:	9 211.094 MPH
1998 Prize Money:	$215,300
INDY 500 Career Earnings:	$365,550
Career INDY 500 Starts:	2
Career Best Finish:	26th 1998

MARK DISMORE

DALLARA/OLDSMOBILE AURORA/GOODYEAR

Indy 500 veteran Mark Dismore returned to Indy for a second consecutive year with Kelley Racing. Dismore and teammate Scott Sharp immediately began a speed competition with AJ Foyt Enterprises and Team Menard. Dismore was in the top 10 in practice on every day but one leading up to pole-position qualifying. When his turn in line rolled around, he put his backup machine in the show at a four-lap average of 218.096 miles per hour to become the month's eighth qualifier.

"The car was a really good car, and I thought we could do 220s," Dismore said. "But on the first lap, I looked down and saw [2]19.4. I knew I was in trouble because the car was pushing. This is the best ride I've ever had and I hope I'm here until I retire from racing."

After starting 12th, he moved into the top 10 before being eliminated in a multicar tangle in Turn 3. "We really made some good decisions today and were very competitive," Dismore said. "I know we'll do well here some day. The track problem was a situation where I got by [Sam] Schmidt, and he and Davey Hamilton got together. Then I rolled out of the throttle, and someone drove over me from behind."

1998 INDY 500 PERFORMANCE PROFILE

Starting Position:	12
Qualifying Average:	218.096 MPH
Qualifying Speed Rank:	15
Best Practice Speed:	219.909 MPH 5/15
Total Practice Laps:	249
Number Practice Days:	7
Finishing Position:	27
Laps Completed:	48
Highest Position 1998 Race:	7
Fastest Race Lap:	42 208.035 MPH
1998 Prize Money:	$209,300
INDY 500 Career Earnings:	$529,553
Career INDY 500 Starts:	3
Career Best Finish:	19th 1996

STAN WATTLES

RILEY & SCOTT/OLDSMOBILE AURORA/GOODYEAR

Stan Wattles and his Metro Racing Systems came to Indy with an all-American effort, a Riley & Scott chassis, an Aurora Indy V-8 engine, and Goodyear tires, to compete in the "Greatest Spectacle" in racing for the first time.

He had only reached a speed of 212.329 miles per hour in practice, and his outlook wasn't rosy going into time trials. He waved off on his first attempt on Pole Day. "We got up to 216.6, which is our fastest speed here yet," Wattles said. "But I think we're going to need more to stay in the field."

On the final day, he recorded a run of 217.477 miles per hour. "It's quite a relief," Wattles said. "We've worked very hard at assembling this team, getting the Riley & Scott up to speed, myself up to speed. That's the way to do it, have the 217 in qualifying, not in practice. It's a real thrill."

He started 29th in the race and had charged to 15th by Lap 40, only to be eliminated in the multicar tangle on Lap 49 in Turn 3. "I was between Roberto [Guerrero] and the wall," Wattles said. "I kept watching Roberto, and the accident happened, and I ran into the back of [Mark] Dismore. My car was very fast and especially easy to drive. I feel bad, especially for my crew."

1998 INDY 500 PERFORMANCE PROFILE

Starting Position:	29
Qualifying Average:	217.477 MPH
Qualifying Speed Rank:	20
Best Practice Speed:	212.329 MPH 5/11
Total Practice Laps:	224
Number Practice Days:	6
Finishing Position:	28
Laps Completed:	48
Highest Position 1998 Race:	6
Fastest Race Lap:	14 210.133 MPH
1998 Prize Money:	$138,550
INDY 500 Career Earnings:	$138,550
Career INDY 500 Starts:	1
Career Best Finish:	28th 1998

29th Place

#53 Delco Remy/ISM Racing/Goodyear
Entrant: ISM Racing
Team Manager: L. G. Hancher Jr. • Crew Chief: Mike McGuire

JIM GUTHRIE

G FORCE/OLDSMOBILE AURORA/GOODYEAR

Jim Guthrie joined ISM Racing for 1998 to concentrate on driving rather than co-ownership of his machine.

He got into the top 10 on the Day 2 speed charts, but that was his only trip to the front during practice. After a waveoff on Pole Day, he qualified at 216.604 miles per hour. "We'd like to be further up, but now we can start the race and have a chance to finish," Guthrie said. "The first run we started . . . it was too hot. The car was sliding all around. Turn 1 is a nemesis. They have a patch there that's a little darker, a little hotter, and a lot slicker. We took out some downforce and found a couple of miles per hour."

The run put him in 20th spot in the line-up, and he had moved to 13th by Lap 40 before being sidelined by a multicar crash in Turn 3. He was taken to Methodist Hospital with a broken right arm and a small cut on his right leg.

1998 INDY 500 PERFORMANCE PROFILE

Starting Position:	20
Qualifying Average:	216.604 MPH
Qualifying Speed Rank:	28
Best Practice Speed:	218.946 MPH 5/11
Total Practice Laps:	149
Number Practice Days:	5
Finishing Position:	29
Laps Completed:	48
Highest Position 1998 Race:	11
Fastest Race Lap:	29 209.795 MPH
1998 Prize Money:	$133,300
INDY 500 Career Earnings:	$466,253
Career INDY 500 Starts:	3
Career Best Finish:	18th 1996

BILLY ROE

DALLARA/OLDSMOBILE AURORA/GOODYEAR

Billy Roe faced an uphill battle to make his second Indianapolis field, joining Team Scandia for the first time.

Roe completed his first qualifying attempt on Pole Day, putting together a smooth four-lap average of 215.781 miles per hour. But as things wound down on the second day of time trials, his run appeared in jeopardy. With 37 minutes remaining, Mike Groff bumped him from the field. Roe then returned in his other machine 13 minutes later to post a run of 217.835 to bump Eliseo Salazar.

"We went out and qualified the backup car [Saturday]," Roe said. "Everybody thought a [2]15.8 would be good enough, so we just took it. It made for some exciting drama today. Eddie Cheever asked me, "'Are you on Quaaludes? How can you stand there like this and smile when you're about to get bumped from the Indy 500.'"

The run left Roe 33rd in the starting line-up, but he gained seven positions in the first 20 laps and six more by Lap 30. While continuing his charge to the front, he was sidelined in a multicar accident in Turn 3 on Lap 49. "I saw it coming," Roe said. "It's the biggest mess I've seen. I headed for the grass, but there was nowhere to go. I'm very disappointed now."

1998 INDY 500 PERFORMANCE PROFILE

Starting Position:	33
Qualifying Average:	217.835 MPH
Qualifying Speed Rank:	18
Best Practice Speed:	215.502 MPH 5/15
Total Practice Laps:	344
Number Practice Days:	7
Finishing Position:	30
Laps Completed:	48
Highest Position 1998 Race:	15
Fastest Race Lap:	31 209.707 MPH
1998 Prize Money:	$137,300
INDY 500 Career Earnings:	$287,550
Career INDY 500 Starts:	2
Career Best Finish:	22nd 1997

#3 Johns Manville/Menards Special
Entrant: Team Menard, Inc.
Team Manager: Larry Curry • Crew Chief: John O'Gara

ROBBIE BUHL

DALLARA/OLDSMOBILE AURORA/FIRESTONE

Robbie Buhl figured this might be his year at Indianapolis, his second with Team Menard. He was fastest in practice on Day 1 with a lap at 219.325 miles per hour and was in the top 10 on every day but one leading up to time trials. He became the third qualifier of the month with a run of 220.236, which was good enough for the pole. "Every lap was on the rev limiter," he said. "We lost our qualifying motor yesterday, so we're pretty happy."

But the glory was short-lived; the fourth qualifier, teammate Tony Stewart, eclipsed Buhl's average.

Buhl's run was good for the fifth starting spot, however, and he stayed in the top five through 40 laps. On the 45th circuit, his engine expired on the inside of the backstretch, and he was done for the day. "The race car was great," he said. "We were just biding our time. I'm really disappointed. They've changed a bunch of motors this month. It's just too bad."

1998 INDY 500 PERFORMANCE PROFILE

Starting Position:	5
Qualifying Average:	220.236 MPH
Qualifying Speed Rank:	5
Best Practice Speed:	220.399 MPH 5/14
Total Practice Laps:	349
Number Practice Days:	7
Finishing Position:	31
Laps Completed:	44
Highest Position 1998 Race:	2
Fastest Race Lap:	29 213.619 MPH
1998 Prize Money:	$222,300
INDY 500 Career Earnings:	$652,903
Career INDY 500 Starts:	3
Career Best Finish:	8th 1997

DONNIE BEECHLER

G FORCE/OLDSMOBILE AURORA/FIRESTONE

Donnie Beechler joined forces with sprint car team owner Larry Cahill to take on Indy for the first time. Beechler reflected on his decision to race the Indy 500: "I raced with Ken Schrader and saw him getting stock car rides, so I thought that was the only way for me to go. But when Larry Cahill gave me the opportunity [to come to Indy], I jumped at it."

Beechler spent a practice week working up to speed and reached his fastest practice lap (215.879 miles per hour) on the day of qualifying. When it started, he became the sixth qualifier of the month with a four-lap run of 216.357. "All week, I fought a push in the car," he said. "We made some adjustments and ran a 216.8. Then this morning, we ran a 217.5 so we didn't change a thing."

The run gave Beechler the 24th starting spot, and he moved up to 18th by Lap 30. But on Lap 34, a blown engine ended his day. "A blown engine is just racing luck," he said. "We had a hodgepodge crew, a couple of guys from Texas, a couple of guys from here and there. Overall, we didn't have a great week. I just tried to be smooth."

1998 INDY 500 PERFORMANCE PROFILE

Starting Position:	24
Qualifying Average:	216.357 MPH
Qualifying Speed Rank:	32
Best Practice Speed:	215.879 MPH 5/15
Total Practice Laps:	252
Number Practice Days:	7
Finishing Position:	32
Laps Completed:	34
Highest Position 1998 Race:	15
Fastest Race Lap:	33 210.931 MPH
1998 Prize Money:	$132,300
INDY 500 Career Earnings:	$132,300
Career INDY 500 Starts:	1
Career Best Finish:	32nd 1998

TONY STEWART

DALLARA/OLDSMOBILE AURORA/FIRESTONE

Tony Stewart qualified second fastest and finished fifth in the 1997 edition of the Indy 500. For 1998, he had sights on Victory Lane.

He was back for a third season with Team Menard, and he set a fast pace from Opening Day forward, taking the top spot on the speed chart on four of the six days of practice. His top practice lap came on Day 6 at 223.797 miles per hour. On Pole Day, he was fourth out to qualify and registered a run of 220.386, which wound up putting him fourth on the grid.

For Stewart, it was disappointing.

"Well, what can I do now?" he asked as others took their turns. "There's nothing left for me to do now but just wait. I wish we could've run a [2]22 like we did this morning. But as warm as it got from the time we practiced this morning until now and knowing how much I had to get off the gas . . ."

On Race Day, he stayed with the leaders, turning the race's fastest lap on the 19th circuit with 214.746. On Lap 21, he took the lead. But on Lap 22, he stopped on the side of the track in Turn 1 with engine failure. "It just broke," he told his crew on the radio. "It popped."

1998 INDY 500 PERFORMANCE PROFILE

Starting Position:	4
Qualifying Average:	220.386 MPH
Qualifying Speed Rank:	4
Best Practice Speed:	223.797 MPH 5/15
Total Practice Laps:	264
Number Practice Days:	6
Finishing Position:	33
Laps Completed:	22
Highest Position 1998 Race:	1
Fastest Race Lap:	19 214.746 MPH
1998 Prize Money:	$220,250
INDY 500 Career Earnings:	$787,353
Career INDY 500 Starts:	3
Career Best Finish:	5th 1997

: Team owner
acing legend
Foyt watches
e of his dri-
Billy Boat,
stands furious
el-to-wheel rac
win the True
500K. This
it was for
s!

A Texas-Style Duel to the Wire

BOAT HOLDS OFF RAY TO SCORE FIRST VICTORY

by Bruce Martin

The memory of last year's controversy at Texas Motor Speedway (TMS) has haunted Billy Boat for a year. After taking the checkered flag in the 1997 True Value 500 and basking in the glory of the winner's circle, apparently victorious, the win was taken away. When the timing and scoring equipment failed during the first nighttime race in modern Indy car racing history, the United States Auto Club (USAC) lost track of the correct running order. Arie Luyendyk had been the fastest driver and had completed more laps but was not declared the official winner until the next morning. Boat was subsequently demoted to second place.

The demotion was difficult for Boat to accept, as the 1997 True Value 500 would have been his first career IRL win. But on June 6, 1998, Boat was able to put those bitter memories to rest with a victory in the 1998 True Value 500. This time, no timing or scoring equipment would hamper the event; no Victory Circle arguments would erupt between drivers and team owners. This time, Boat

Billy Boat celebrates his first IRL career win with his AJ Foyt Conseco team. Boat and Greg Ray diced for the lead with Ray driving over the infield grass to get around Boat. But Boat was able to repass Ray and pull away for the win.

The midsummer Texas heat was nothing compared to the red-hot racing action on the repaved Texas Motor Speedway. Six drivers swapped the lead 22 times during the battle under the lights.

Racing almost within sight of his Plano, Texas, home, Greg Ray fiercely battled with winner Billy Boat through the race's final laps before being relegated to a runner-up finish.

Scott Sharp pitted during a caution period, one of the few times he wasn't on the gas. The brightly colored IRL cars appear even more colorful when viewed under the lights—especially at speed.

would stand alone as the undisputed champion of the True Value 500 and be rewarded with his first Indy car win (as well as winnings of $130,250).

"We wanted this more than anyone else tonight," Boat said. "I left this race here last year a winner and woke up a second-place finisher. I wasn't going to let that happen tonight. The car was absolutely perfect all night long. We didn't make any changes to it all weekend. Tonight was our night."

On this Saturday night in June, under the lights at TMS and in front of over 90,000 fans, an intense battle developed between Boat and Greg Ray in the closing laps of a thrilling Indy car race. With eight laps remaining and Boat in the lead, Ray passed Boat for the lead in Turn 3, but one lap later Boat was able to nudge ahead of Ray for the race-winning pass.

The two cars raced inches apart with Ray even trying to pass in the grass before Boat was able to pull away in the closing laps for the win. "I knew I had a good race car . . . even when Greg got by me, I didn't panic," Boat said. "I knew I could get back by him."

Boat just refused to be denied. "We really wanted to win this race bad," Boat said. "We never, ever gave up all night long. I had a great race car and was flat-out all night long. I knew I had a good race car. I just had to set the traffic right. This is a great victory for us."

Making the victory even sweeter was the fact that team owner A. J. Foyt was able to score an Indy car win in his home state of Texas. "I wish this could be two wins straight, but this was our day," Foyt said. "I thought we won this race last year, but we didn't get it. Nobody could take this away from us today."

Laughingly, Foyt said, "Hell, I thought last year was more fun," referring to his altercation with Luyendyk in Victory Circle. "We've been there before on different occasions," he went on to say. "We've been there happy, and we've been there sad. All in all, it's great. Any time you win, it's wonderful. I'm so proud of Billy and Kenny Brack. Both drove a hell of a race. It looked like it was Billy's day today."

Runner-up Greg Ray was quite satisfied with his final standing as well. Ray, who is from nearby Plano, Texas, drove his car with fearless abandon, giving the hometown fans more thrills than they could probably stand. His second-place finish was the best of his Indy car career. "This is almost like a victory for us," he said. "It has been a Cinderella story for us. This has been a great success for a small team. This is very exciting for us."

Commenting on the race itself, Ray had this to say about his battle with Boat: "I actually thought I hit him in Turn 1. We were going through traffic, and I wouldn't be surprised if there wasn't a mark on the nose of my car. I really thought I got that

Starting from the inside of Row 2 gave Robbie Buhl a boost in confidence heading into the Texas race. He finished sixth, giving him two straight top-10 finishes.

close to him. Three times I got in the grass. Billy was making his car pretty wide, and he was pushing me there on the inside. I knew I could probably clip at least a foot of that grass. We did it three laps in a row. My crew chief got on the radio and said, Easy Hoss.'"

But Boat survived the struggle for the lead and came away with his first Indy car victory giving him wins at every level of his career. "One thing about winning, I've won at most every level and to win races, you have to stay after it," Boat said. "No matter how hard you try, you have to make it happen. Once you get that victory and everybody on the team knows what it is like, that is the only thing you will accept. Hopefully, this team has a taste of it, and we will be looking for more of these this year."

When qualifying for the True Value 500, it was Tony Stewart, not Billy Boat, who had the edge. Stewart's pole-winning lap was so easy, he thought about what he was going to have for lunch during his run. Stewart won the pole the day before the 312-mile (500-kilometer) IRL race when he ran a 224.448-mile per hour lap in his Team Menard Dallara/Oldsmobile Aurora/Firestone Indy car. That was faster than Boat's lap of 223.547 miles per hour in A. J. Foyt's Dallara/Aurora/Goodyear.

"We were worried about what both of Foyt's cars would do, but I was locked in on what I was doing with my car and was pretty confident," Stewart said. "It was so easy here, I was thinking about what I wanted to eat for lunch after I got done qualifying. It's a tribute to how good of a job

they did here on this race track. It's so easy and so much fun to run around here, you lose focus. It's almost bad in a way because it is so comfortable to drive around, you have to force yourself to focus on what you need to do."

Stewart's teammate Robbie Buhl qualified third with 223.104 miles per hour, followed by defending winner Arie Luyendyk and Marco Greco. Stewart's lap was the second fastest lap in the new IRL cars, just a tick slower than Boat's lap of 224.573 miles per hour during his pole-winning run in the 82nd Indianapolis 500.

Winning the pole helped make up for the misgivings Stewart and his crew had after dropping out of the Indianapolis 500. "It's more so for the

A fish-eye lens distorts the shape of Davey Hamilton's car (foreground), but offers a good wide-angle view of the massive garage area at the Texas Motor Speedway.

guys on the crew than me," Stewart said, "because I know we can run quick. After the performance we had at Indy, it makes the guys feel like we are back on track. This pole has helped put that behind us."

Six caution flags flew during the race for a total of 45 of the 208 laps. The first one appeared on Lap 1. As the field took the green flag to start the race, Billy Roe spun out coming off the fourth turn. Ahead in the field, defending Indianapolis 500 winner Eddie Cheever, entering his first turn, had to lock up his brakes to avoid a collision.

The race was restarted on the fourth lap, and Buddy Lazier, who started 23rd, sliced his way through the field before the next caution flag appeared on the fifth lap because of a major accident involving several cars. The crash began when Roberto Guerrero was loose in the second turn, which started a chain reaction, causing Raul Boesel to spin on the backstretch. Rookie Donnie Beechler tried to avoid the crash and ran into the back of Stephan Gregoire, forcing both cars into Cheever's path. Those three cars crashed into the inside wall on the backstretch with Beechler's car landing upside-down. Rookie J. J. Yeley was also involved in the massive crash, but fortunately none of the drivers involved were injured.

"It was all my fault," Guerrero said. "I got loose out of Turn 2 and lost it and caused all the confusion. I had a clutch problem, but unfortunately we can't use that as an excuse. I'm the one that created it. I don't know what happened. I got all the other guys in trouble. I just got loose. It happens."

In some of the best racing of the season, Tony Stewart, who was the favorite to win, passed Boat

on the backstretch of Lap 158 to take the lead. But by the time both cars got to the start/finish line, Boat passed Stewart, regaining the lead and bringing the huge crowd to its feet. Boat and Stewart both pitted on the 168th lap, but Stewart was slow to get back up to speed because of a gearbox problem. His engine began losing coolant, bringing out another caution flag and forcing him to drop out of the race on Lap 176. Apparently, the radiator in Stewart's car exploded during the race, which caused all the water to leak out.

Before his mechanical troubles, Stewart ran a very fast race. He soared around the 1.5-mile oval on Lap 86 at 228.012 miles per hour, 3.564 miles per hour faster than the 224.448 that he turned Friday while winning the pole. He also led seven times for a total of 57 laps. "I'm not happy that we dropped out, but I'm happy we're back on track," Stewart said, "We're running well again. We had as good a shot as anybody. The car was great. Anytime you run around a track wide open, and you get some cars you can get a tow off of, you're going to run quicker than you qualified. That wasn't unexpected on our part. We ran faster in the race last year than we qualified, so I think we expected all that and everybody else did too."

Stewart has been a major story in every race ever run in the Indy Racing League. But once again, instead of enjoying a victory, he was left to deal with disappointment. "I don't know what caused the overheating problem, but I think part of it was

that I stayed behind Billy Boat as long as I did," Stewart said. "It's just part of racing . . . I guess."

The green flag flew on the 180th lap with fantastic racing as A. J. Foyt teammates Boat and Brack went side-by-side entering the first turn. Ray rocketed into the two cars and passed Brack for second place as the cars went three-wide in the third turn before they zigzagged down the frontstretch, narrowly averting disaster. "That's what the fans want to see," Boat said. "Racing is racing, and I've been running inches apart banging wheels all of my life; only in this deal, you don't want to be banging any wheels."

As the race came to its dramatic conclusion, Boat was able to keep the lead ahead of Greg Ray, teammate Kenny Brack, Scott Goodyear, and Scott Sharp (the eventual second through fifth place finishers), giving a Saturday night crowd in Texas a chance to see open-wheel racing at its best. Passing Ray just seven laps from the finish, Boat regained the lead, crossing the finish line a mere 0.928 of a second ahead of Ray. Over the course of the 208-lap race, Boat led for 108 laps, averaging 145.388 miles per hour a lap.

According to Foyt, the type of competitiveness seen at the True Value 500 is exactly what the IRL needs: "I'm awful proud of this series because you are getting a lot of these boys who know how to drive race cars and race on ovals come up through the ranks. When you look back at it, that is the type of racing I came from, along with drivers like Jim Hurtubise and Parnelli Jones. Then, all the close racing fell apart in the recent years. This is showing the talent of a lot of the young drivers who never had a chance, and they are standing on the gas."

"The racing tonight was unbelievable. If anybody thinks they can come over here and blow these boys off, they have another thing coming to them. These guys are used to running wheel-to-wheel and inches apart. That is what the fans really want to see. The series is very competitive and every race we have had this year has been a hell of a race to the bitter end."

OFFICIAL BOX SCORE
PEP BOYS INDY RACING LEAGUE
True Value 500 at Texas Motor Speedway
Saturday, June 6, 1998

FP	SP	Car	Driver	Car Name	C/E/T	Laps Comp.	Running/ Reason Out	IRL Pts.	Total IRL Pts.	IRL Standings	IRL Awards	Designated Awards	Total Awards
1	2	11	Billy Boat	Conseco AJ Foyt Racing	D/A/G	208	Running	54	110	3	$102,900	$27,350	$130,250
2	14	97	Greg Ray	AT&T Wireless Services	D/A/F	208	Running	40	78	10	84,900	15,650	100,550
3	11	14	Kenny Brack	AJ Foyt PowerTeam Racing	D/A/G	208	Running	35	97	6	71,800	1,500	73,300
4	7	4	Scott Goodyear	Pennzoil Panther G Force	G/A/G	208	Running	32	79	9	58,800	0	58,800
5	9	8	Scott Sharp	Delphi Automotive Systems	D/A/G	208	Running	30	115	2	54,000	3,600	57,600
6	3	3	Robbie Buhl	Johns Manville/Menards Special	D/A/F	207	Running	29	58	15	26,100	0	26,100
7	15	6	Davey Hamilton	Reebok/Nienhouse Motorsports	G/A/G	207	Running	26	97	5	46,900	0	46,900
8	5	16	Marco Greco	Int. Sports Ltd.-	G/A/F	205	Running	24	53	20	23,700	750	24,450
9	27	52 R	Robby Unser	Team Cheever/ADT Automotive	G/A/G	204	Running	22	52	21	23,700	0	23,700
10	26	19	Stan Wattles	Metro Racing Systems/NCLD	R/A/G	198	Running	20	30	27	22,500	0	22,500
11	23	91	Buddy Lazier	Hemelgarn Racing/Delta Faucet/Coors	D/A/G	194	Wheel Bearing	19	76	11	43,400	0	43,400
12	28	81	Tyce Carlson	Team Pelfrey	D/A/F	191	Running	18	54	19	20,200	0	20,200
13	4	5	Arie Luyendyk	Sprint PCS/RadioShack/QUALCOMM	G/A/F	178	Running	17	57	16	41,000	0	41,000
14	1	1	Tony Stewart	Glidden/Menards Special	D/A/F	176	Radiator tank split	19	115	1	39,800	54,500	94,300
15	10	12	Buzz Calkins	Bradley Food Marts/Sav-O-Mat	G/A/G	172	Running	15	73	12	38,600	0	38,600
16	12	10	John Paul Jr.	Jonathan Byrdis VisionAire Bryant Heating & Cooling	G/A/F	169	Running	14	71	13	37,400	0	37,400
17	13	35	Jeff Ward	ISM Racing	G/A/G	165	Engine	13	103	4	36,200	0	36,200
18	24	99	Sam Schmidt	Best Western Gold Crown Racing Special	D/A/F	163	Running	12	64	14	36,200	0	36,200
19	22	44 R	J. J. Yeley	Quaker State/Menards/SRS	D/I/F	162	Running	11	38	24	13,000	5,250	18,250
20	25	27	Billy Roe	Blueprint/Klipsch/Overhead Door	D/I/F	108	Running	10	11	33	11,900	0	11,900
21	6	28	Mark Dismore	Kelley Automotive	D/A/G	70	Accident	9	56	18	32,700	0	32,700
22	21	40	Dr. Jack Miller	Crest Racing	D/I/F	38	Engine	8	24	30	10,100	0	10,100
23	18	15	Eliseo Salazar	Reebok R&S MK V	R/A/G	32	Engine	7	32	26	9,700	0	9,700
24	8	21	Roberto Guerrero	Pagan Racing Dallara/Oldsmobile	D/A/G	4	Accident	6	21	31	9,700	0	9,700
25	16	77	Stephan Gregoire	Blue Star Batteries/Chastain Mtrspts.	G/A/G	4	Accident	5	82	8	31,700	0	31,700
26	20	51	Eddie Cheever Jr.	Team Cheever/Rache's	D/A/G	4	Accident	4	82	7	31,700	0	31,700
27	17	98 R	Donnie Beechler	Cahill Auto Racing/G Force/ Firestone/Oldsmobile Special	G/A/F	4	Accident	3	4	37	9,700	0	9,700
28	19	30	Raul Boesel	TransWorld Diversified Services/ Beloit/McCormack Mtrspts.	G/A/G	4	Accident	2	49	22	31,700	0	31,700
			Katech Engines									600	600
			Brayton Engineering									800	800
										TOTAL -	$1,000,000	$110,000	$1,110,000

Time of Race: 2:08:45.543
Margin of Victory: 0.928 seconds
Fastest Leading Lap: #11 Billy Boat (Lap 142, 227.273)
True Value Pole Winning Chief Mechanic: Bill Martin/Team Menard Inc.

Average Speed: 145.388
Fastest Lap: #1 Tony Stewart (Lap 86, 228.012)
PPG Pole Winner: Tony Stewart
MBNA America Lap Leader: #11 Billy Boat

Legend: R-Indy Racing League Rookie   Chassis Legend: D- Dallara; G- G Force; R- Riley & Scott   Engine Legend: A- Oldsmobile Aurora; I- Nissan Infiniti   Tire Legend: F- Firestone; G- Goodyear

Inset: The thrill of victory returned to Team Menard in sunny New Hampshire after Tony Stewart held off Scott Goodyear for the team's second win in four 1998 races.

Team Menard Scores Revenge

TONY STEWART'S CALCULATED CRUISE TO VICTORY

by Bruce Martin

Two years ago, Tony Stewart dominated this race with a two-lap lead and only 18 laps to go, when disaster struck—his engine expired. Stewart had an outstanding debt to collect, and he was going to collect it this year. Before 20,000 fans at the 1998 New England 200, the Team Menard driver got his revenge, winning the race by 1.788 seconds over the hard-charging Scott Goodyear. Stewart started in sixth position and steadily worked his way up the order and into the lead. In a well-balanced car with a lot of grip in the corners, Stewart averaged 113.861 miles per hour around the 1.058-mile New Hampshire International Speedway. The victory earned him $122,950. Kelley Racing's Scott Sharp was third, followed by Davey Hamilton in fourth and Arie Luyendyk in fifth.

It was Stewart's second IRL victory of the season and the third of his career. And it came at just the right time. The competition was starting to apply the pressure. Scott Sharp came to the race tied in championship points with Stewart. When

Determined, Tony Stewart rebounded from his huge disappointment at Indianapolis and Texas Motor Speedway to win the New England 200 by 1.788 seconds over Scott Goodyear and increase his points lead.

95

Arie Luyendyk enjoyed considerable improvement over his showing at Indy, qualifying seventh and finishing fifth at New Hampshire. Still, for a former champion, there are no moral victories.

Sharp finished third, Stewart opened up a 17 point lead in the championship. "I felt like I was owed a victory here last year from 1996," Stewart said. "You don't so much feel like the track owes you one, you feel like you really want to get one back. When you let one get away that way, you really want to make sure you come back and tackle this place. It's like the big fish that got away; you always go back to the pond the next time looking for that big fish."

In last year's race, Stewart was a non-factor and finished 14th when a malfunctioning shock absorber upset the handling of his race car. This time, Stewart's G Force/Oldsmobile Aurora on Firestone tires was dialed into the track conditions and able to pass on the high side of the race track. "Our car was well balanced," Stewart said. "We made changes to help the car stick in the corners. I tend to think when we get to the one-mile ovals, I get to show my abilities."

Lap speeds during qualifying predicted a good race. Jeff Ward had broken the track record and was sitting on pole position. But the track kept getting better as time wore on. As the next-to-last driver to make a qualification attempt, Boat blew away the competition with a record lap of 162.146 miles per hour. "I think it's an advantage to know what you are up against," said Boat, who drives a Dallara/Oldsmobile Aurora/Goodyear combination for team owner A. J. Foyt. "I knew where everybody was and how fast they went, and I knew what we had to do. When I saw that speed on the first lap, I stepped it up a bit."

Boat's second qualification lap was almost 4 miles per hour faster than his first, which led competing teams to believe something sneaky was going on. His first lap was 158.443 miles per hour and his second increased to 162.146 miles per hour. "It never surprises me when Foyt's cars come up to speed that quickly," said Ward. "They seem to do it all the time."

The start of the race was equally dramatic, though not from speed. Kenny Brack backed his car into the fourth turn wall at the completion of the first lap. Then John Paul Jr.'s engine caught fire, bringing out the first of six caution flags. Jeff Ward had worked his way into the lead passing Boat, the pole sitter, in the second turn of the first lap and retained the lead when the green flag waved on the 12th lap. Two laps later, another caution flag flew when rookie Jack Hewitt crashed in the fourth turn.

The green flag dropped again on the 20th lap, and Scott Sharp got a great jump on the restart to take the lead away from Ward. Eight laps later, Ward was back in front after Sharp pitted during a caution period. Ward was still in the lead at Lap 56, when an engine fire took him out of the race. This put Goodyear in front for the next 20 laps before Davey Hamilton took the lead when he beat the field out of the pits during a caution period.

The worst luck of the day belonged to Billy Boat. On Lap 32, he spun coming out of Turn 2 and ended up on the infield grass on the back straight. He was towed back to the pits, fueled and fitted with new tires, and reentered the race. He should have stayed down. On the 95th lap, he was involved in a multi-car crash, again in Turn 2. Rookie J. J. Yeley spun out and fellow rookie Donnie Beechler

It's all business in the pits; the place where races can be won or lost. The Panther Racing Team quickly services Scott Goodyear's G-Force/Oldsmobile Aurora. Smoking the tires out of the pit box, Goodyear rejoined the fight and secured a second-place finish.

grazed Yeley's car. Boat, with nowhere to go, plowed into the back of Yeley's car. Boat's car careened to the outside wall, slid back across the track to the inside, and was T-boned by Raul Boesel's car.

Boat had to be extricated from his car and put on a stretcher. He was transported to Concord Hospital with a broken left thigh. Boesel said of the crash: "I saw the incident in front of me, and I went low to avoid everyone. I thought I had passed everyone, and then all of a sudden, Billy Boat came right down on me and unfortunately ended our

day. It's really too bad because the car kept getting better and better."

Stewart, who had taken the lead for the first time on the 92nd lap, avoided the crash and stayed in front until he made his final pit stop on Lap 158. After the pit stop cycle was complete, Stewart was back in front on the 163rd lap. He led by over 11 seconds on the 182nd lap before Sharp made his charge to cut the lead to 1 second. "I was aware that he was coming," Stewart said. "We caught some bad breaks in traffic, and I probably let the gap close up a little more, making sure I didn't catch a lapped car in the wrong spot. So instead of giving up 2 seconds on one given lap, I gave up 1 second."

During the early and middle stages of the race, Goodyear was on a tear and spent 44 laps in the lead. "It was after a pit stop on fresh tires, we had a good race car, and we were catching up mainly in traffic," Goodyear said. "That was our opportunity to catch [Stewart]. If there was an opportunity to pass him, it would have been in a gaggle of traffic, but it didn't happen." Goodyear put in a brilliant charge late in the race and had Stewart in his sights. Goodyear had a fast car, but it was far from perfect.

"The car jumped out of fifth gear in the very beginning and we had to go to sixth gear, which we ran when we were leading the race," Goodyear said. "Unfortunately, we could not get fifth and sixth

gear after one of our pit stops, and we could only use fourth gear. When Tony went past me, I was only in fourth. I had to run fourth all day long, and the car was on the rev-limiter halfway down the straight, and that cost us close to 1 second a lap. Not taking anything away from Tony, but when we were running with fifth and sixth gear, we were strong and felt we could have won the race."

With 15 laps to go, Goodyear had a lurid slide in Turn 2. He chose to back off and hold second place rather than throw the car away in an attempt to take the win. "It was called overdriving the car for the speed that it wanted to go," Goodyear said. "The thing just did a big tank-slapper coming out, and that's when I was catching Tony."

The New England 200 was the first time Sharp had raced at New Hampshire International Speedway since he won this event in 1996. He was unable to compete in last year's race because of a head injury he had suffered at Pikes Peak International Raceway that left him parked for the season. By finishing third, Sharp had successfully returned to the tight 1.058-mile oval.

Sharp made the best of his car, putting in a solid performance with less than the ideal race set-up. "I never moved my weight jack as much before," he said. "The conditions changed a lot during the race, and the car loosened up after the first few laps. Then, it tightened up as the sun came out. I'm happy with third, and I want to concentrate on being consistent. I like tracks where it's not all flat-out. . . . You need a little more finesse at tracks like this."

Robbie Buhl leads an IRL freight train. Scott Goodyear, Davey Hamilton, and Buhl's team-mate (and eventual race winner) Tony Stewart all want what Buhl's got—the lead.

The New England 200 was one of the season's most-competitive races, with six drivers swapping the lead 10 times. Buddy Lazier (91) finished seventh, one lap off the pace.

Sharp had to work hard to keep ahead of Davey Hamilton as the laps counted down. Sharp kept his car wide enough to prevent Hamilton from coming by. But other cars on the track were giving him fits. "Robbie Buhl wouldn't get out of the way," complained Sharp. "When someone's slowing you down a second a lap, it's not too hard for the fourth place guy to come running right up on your tail. I think it was pretty obvious, once I could get by traffic, I could pull back away. I was getting pretty frustrated for awhile. I kept seeing the orange car [of Hamilton] getting real close." Sharp had problems getting past both Buhl and the Reebok car driven by Eliseo Salazar.

Davey Hamilton was arguably the fastest car on the track up to the middle stages of the race. Starting from the 22nd qualifying position, he sliced his way through the field and displayed amaz-ing speed through the turns. And he probably had the quickest car in the first half of the race. On Lap 77, however, he broke the pit lane speed limit during a routine pitstop, which dropped him down the order and out of contention for the win.

"That killed me," Hamilton said, "that green flag, I mean, you're losing serious time. I was on the rev-limiter [in the pits] the whole time, we really don't know. We can't explain it. I mean, it was on there. Maybe it shut off just a little bit early. At that point of the pits, you feel you're out of the pits. I don't shut it off, it just shuts off automatically. I've got to go look at all our telemetry and stuff, just to find out exactly what the deal was."

The flying Dutchman, Arie Luyendyk, finished in fifth position in his Treadway Racing G Force. He was on the pace early in the day but faded as the race progressed. Luyendyk was disappointed when the team's changes to the car didn't go their way. "After the first set [of tires], I was getting loose, he said. "I told them to take two turns of wing out. Then it turned out the stagger had grown quite a bit—way too much. On the second set, I had a big push. That was okay, but then the last 30 laps, the voltage went out. It was misfiring through the turns, and I just had to hope I could finish the race for once. [It was] my first real finish without incidents, fifth place. I probably could have stayed on the lead lap if it wasn't for the misfire, making the first adjustment cost us."

Nothing could stop Stewart and Team Menard, however, and he was able to claim another victory. It was the second-straight win for Team Menard in this event. Robbie Buhl won this race last year. "I wasn't going to act like I had won the race until I knew I could coast to the checkered flag," Stewart said. "After what has happened to me before here, I wasn't counting anything in the bag yet."

The IRL drivers dealt with a slippery race track from all the rubber "marbles" (balled up chunks of rubber from racing tires) that were put down in the NASCAR Modified series race, which was held before the New England 200. "It's the same thing as we always [have] here," Stewart said. "I look forward to coming here from the standpoint that when we run with the NASCAR modifieds and we start our race, the track is totally different from when we practice and qualify. The marbles really make it slippery.

"When we started the race, with all [the] modified rubber that was on the track, the safety crews work in between the races to get as much rubber off the track as they could. It always seems to take 50 laps for our cars to take their rubber off and get our own rubber down to get a good bite. The first half of the race, we were really sliding around, but the last half of the race was much better."

For Team Menard owner, John Menard, it was a special moment that deserved reflection. It took 18 years for the team to win its first Indy car race. Less than 12 months later, he has now won four IRL races. "It's what I'm doing this for," Menard said. "It's all important. You become greedy after awhile when you do win and when you don't win, you feel worse about it than before. We have a great team right now and a great driver with Tony. Everything has come together and we've had some stability for the last couple of years."

With the win, Stewart moved into a tie as the all-time victory leader in the IRL with three wins. Arie Luyendyk also accumulated three IRL victories.

Boat, who had gone to Concord Hospital with a broken thigh bone, was airlifted to Methodist Hospital in Indianapolis for surgery the following day. He would return to racing in the August 16 Radisson 200 at Pikes Peak International Raceway.

OFFICIAL BOX SCORE
PEP BOYS INDY RACING LEAGUE
New England 200 at New Hampshire International Speedway
Sunday, June 28, 1998

FP	SP	Car	Driver	Car Name	C/E/T	Laps Comp.	Running/ Reason Out	IRL Pts.	Total IRL Pts.	IRL Standings	IRL Awards	Designated Awards	Total Awards
1	6	1	Tony Stewart	Glidden/Menards Special	D/A/F	200	running	52	167	1	$94,600	$28,350	$122,950
2	5	4	Scott Goodyear	Pennzoil Panther G Force	G/A/G	200	running	40	119	5	79,000	12,250	91,250
3	4	8	Scott Sharp	Delphi Automotive Systems	D/A/G	200	running	35	150	2	67,200	3,650	70,850
4	22	6	Davey Hamilton	Reebok/Nienhouse Motorsports	G/A/G	200	running	32	129	3	55,300	4,250	59,550
5	7	5	Arie Luyendyk	Sprint PCS/Radio Shack/Qualcomm	G/A/F	199	running	30	87	12	51,000	1,000	52,000
6	17	15	Eliseo Salazar	Reebok R&S MK V	R/A/G	199	running	28	60	20	23,700	0	23,700
7	3	91	Buddy Lazier	Hemelgarn Racing/Delta Faucet	D/A/G	199	running	27	103	9	44,500	0	44,500
8	13	28	Mark Dismore	Kelley Automotive	D/A/G	199	running	24	80	14	43,500	750	44,250
9	11	51	Eddie Cheever Jr.	Rachel's Potato Chips/ Team Cheever	D/A/G	198	running	22	104	8	43,500	0	43,500
10	12	3	Robbie Buhl	Johns Manville/Menards Special	D/A/F	198	running	20	78	15	42,500	600	43,100
11	18	52 R	Robby Unser	The Children's Beverage Group/ Team Cheever	D/A/G	198	running	19	71	18	41,300	0	41,300
12	24	99	Sam Schmidt	Best Western Gold Crown Racing Special	D/A/F	196	running	18	82	13	40,300	0	40,300
13	14	16	Marco Greco	Int. Sports Ltd.	G/A/F	191	running	17	70	19	39,200	250	39,450
14	25	81 R	Brian Tyler	Team Pelfrey	D/A/F	190	running	16	40	27	16,100	0	16,100
15	23	12	Buzz Calkins	Bradley Food Marts/Sav-O-Mat	G/A/G	183	running	15	88	10	37,100	0	37,100
16	19	40	Dr. Jack Miller	Crest Racing	D/I/F	168	running	14	38	28	14,000	5,000	19,000
17	26	19	Stan Wattles	Metro Racing Systems/NCLD	R/A/G	127	handling	13	43	26	12,900	0	12,900
18	8	14	Kenny Brack	AJ Foyt PowerTeam Racing	D/A/G	98	handling	12	109	7	34,900	0	34,900
19	9	30	Raul Boesel	TransWorld Diversified Services/ Beloit/McCormack Mtrspts.	G/A/G	94	accident	11	60	20	33,800	0	33,800
20	15	98 R	Donnie Beechler	Cahill Auto Racing	G/A/F	93	accident	10	14	33	10,800	0	10,800
21	1	11	Billy Boat	Conseco AJ Foyt Racing	D/A/G	91	accident	12	122	4	32,800	22,500	55,300
22	2	35	Jeff Ward	ISM Racing/Prolong/Team Tabasco	G/A/G	56	engine	10	113	6	32,800	0	32,800
23	21	44 R	J. J. Yeley	Sinden Racing Service/Menards	D/I/F	38	accident	7	45	24	10,800	0	10,800
24	16	77	Stephan Gregoire	Chastain Motorsports	D/A/G	22	engine	6	88	10	32,800	0	32,800
25	20	18 R	Jack Hewitt	Parker Machinery	G/A/G	11	accident	5	23	31	32,800	0	32,800
26	10	10	John Paul Jr.	Jonathan Byrd's VisionAire Bryant Heating & Cooling	G/A/F	2	accident	4	75	17	32,800	0	32,800
				Menard Engines								1,000	1,000
			Brayton Engineering								400	400	
										TOTAL -	$1,000,000	$80,000	$1,080,000

Time of Race: 1:51:30.262
Margin of Victory: 1.788 seconds
Fastest Leading Lap: #1 Tony Stewart (Lap 187, 157.362)
True Value Pole Winning Chief Mechanic: Craig Baranouski/AJ Foyt Enterprises

Average Speed: 113.861
Fastest Lap: #6 Davey Hamilton (Lap 141, 158.252)
PPG Pole Winner: Billy Boat

Legend: R-Indy Racing League Rookie   Chassis Legend: D- Dallara; G- G Force; R- Riley&Scott   Engine Legend: A- Oldsmobile Aurora; I- Nissan Infiniti   Tire Legend: F- Firestone; G- Goodyear

Race winner Scott Sharp (left) provides the crowd with a champagne shower while third-place finisher Marco Greco clutches his trophy, and the Pep Boys—Manny, Moe, and Jack—contently stay dry.

IRL Cars Put on a Wild Show at Dover

SCOTT SHARP CONQUERS THE MONSTER

by Bruce Martin

SUNDAY, JULY 19, 1998

The number-one axiom of racing (to finish first, first you must finish) held special meaning at the Pep Boys 400K, which took place on the third weekend in July at Dover Downs International Speedway. Winning on the bump-infested track required a sound race strategy, quick pit stops, consistent lap times, and most importantly, reliability.

Drivers discovered that Dover's reputation as "The Monster Mile" was well earned, as a large part of the field was claimed from the extremely rough conditions. The track presented a daunting challenge to the front runners as well. Tony Stewart, the IRL points leader heading into the race, led early and had a shot at victory in the middle stages of the race. But fate intervened, and a broken suspension took him out of contention. This allowed Kelley Racing's Scott Sharp to seize the lead and take the win. Buddy Lazier finished a scant 0.689 seconds behind the winner.

Two wins in five races helped Scott Sharp reclaim the points lead from Tony Stewart. Sharp outlasted Buddy Lazier to win the grueling inaugural IRL race at Dover Downs International Speedway.

101

In the end, Sharp's victory earned him $128,550 and vaulted him into the points lead in the Pep Boys Indy Racing League championship standings with 202 points. Stewart dropped to second with 194 points after entering the race with a 20-point lead over Sharp in the standings. The 99 caution laps dropped Sharp's average speed for the race to 99.318 miles per hour.

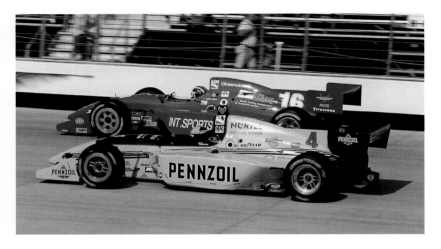

Marco Greco (16), seen here passing Scott Goodyear (4), started 21st but charged to a third-place finish, his fourth straight top-15 finish in the 1998 season, putting him 12th in points.

Sharp ran only as fast as he needed to win and did his best to not tangle with any cars on his way to the winner's circle. "Tony [Stewart] had a little faster car than we did today," Sharp said. "In his draft, I think we were almost as fast as him. When he was behind me, I think it would be a different story. You never want to see anybody have bad luck, but they've been real fast but sort of unreliable. I felt like he was our number one competition, after that we sort of switched our sights to Buddy [Lazier] and Arie [Luyendyk]."

It was a race for survival as much as it was a race for victory and championship points. The Dover track put the cars through grueling punishment, but Sharp had a combination of speed and longevity that no one was able to beat. "I figured out it was 'The Monster Mile' after about 40 laps," said Sharp, who won his second IRL race of the season and the third of his career. "I knew it was going to be a race of attrition. It says a lot for the IRL, how these cars held up in the wrecks and also the ones that made it through the race. I had a few close calls, but I was fortunate enough to stay away from the mess. There were so many times I ran through debris and was waiting for something to take us out. It was a strenuous test on the motors and cars. Everything went our way today, and thank God for that."

Buddy Lazier added his own element of drama to the race. As Sharp headed to the checkered flag and dramatically slowed near the finish line, Lazier tried to capitalize on the opportunity and nearly ran into the back of Sharp's car at the checkered flag. "At the end

Few drivers escape the "Monster Mile" unscathed. Jeff Ward's car left the track on the hook after his crash on Lap 21. The costly accident dropped Ward from sixth to seventh in the points chase.

of the race, Scott [Sharp] slowed down a little bit," Lazier said. "I don't know if he was just being conservative or was really slowing. At the end of the race, I didn't slow down until after I had passed the start/finish line, and then I couldn't lift when I went over the line. I thought, 'Uh-oh, this won't be good. I'm going to finish and collect both first and second.' It was a hopeless attempt to get by, but you just never know."

Lazier faced an uphill battle throughout the entire race due to an ill-handling car. But Lazier hung tough and took advantage of several yellow-flag periods and remained on the lead lap for the duration of the race. In fact, Lazier had his stint in the lead. He took over when Sharp ducked into the pits during a caution period late in the race, but Sharp had a quicker car underneath him and retook the lead when the course returned to green-flag racing.

A testimonial to the rough-and-tumble reputation of the track was the fact that only 10 of the 22 cars that started the race were running at the finish. Sharp and Lazier were the only two competitors to finish on the lead lap. Third-place Marco Greco and fourth-place Davey Hamilton were both 2 laps in back of the winner. Stephan Gregoire finished fifth, 4 laps down, and sixth-place finisher Scott Goodyear was 6 laps down. Seventh-place finisher Jim Guthrie was 19 laps down, followed by Tony Stewart who was 28 laps down. Brian Tyler was credited as the last car running at the end of the race, finishing 12th behind two cars that had dropped out of the 248-lap race on the 203rd and 197th laps respectively.

Eight drivers were taken out of the race by crashes, with rookie Robby Unser suffering the most serious injury, a minor fracture to his left foot, which was placed in a splint. Indianapolis 500 Rookie of the Year Steve Knapp was treated and released for a minor concussion. Jack Miller, Jeff Ward, Sam Schmidt, Greg Ray, Eddie Cheever, and Arie Luyendyk were all involved in separate incidents and were treated and released from the infield care center.

The Indy Racing League was making its first-ever appearance at the 1.0-mile track, and it was the

Despite winning the pole and leading 85 laps, Tony Stewart (1) couldn't overcome handling problems on the demanding 1-mile oval. Forced to pit frequently, he finished eighth. Srewart battles with Marco Greco (16).

first time an Indy car race had been held at Dover since 1969. Dover is a high-banked, concrete oval that is famous for NASCAR Winston Cup racing. With 107,000 seats, it is jammed with fans for its two Winston Cup races a season. A crowd estimated at 40,000 came out to see the sleeker, faster, open-wheel, open-cockpit cars run 248 circuits around the track. As attested to above, it turned out to be an exciting show—a wild ride for spectators, teams, and drivers alike.

The first 21 laps of the race were green-flag racing until a crash by Ward into the fourth-turn wall. A right front A-arm broke, which sent his car into the wall, shearing off the right-hand side. Miller and Goodyear spun out on the front straight trying to avoid the debris with Goodyear sustaining damage to his car. Miller collected some of the debris and was finished for the day. However, Goodyear's crew replaced the nose on his race car, and he rejoined the race.

Stewart was setting the pace early in the race and led for 74 of the first 85 laps before two of the most severe crashes of the race. Sam Schmidt slammed hard into the fourth-turn wall and slid down the front stretch and didn't stop sliding until he was well into the first turn. The impact was hard enough to destroy one of the video cameras mounted on the wall.

The green flag waved on the 104th lap

with Sharp in the lead followed by Stewart, Hamilton, Ray, and Cheever. But one lap later, Ray and Cheever locked wheels and took a ride to the outside of Turn 2, and each driver blamed the other for the mishap. "It would have been a move someone with more experience could have made," Cheever said of Ray. "He panicked. It was a very stupid move. He should get an idea of what he should do. I got hit from behind. I'm particularly angry. It was very dangerous."

Ray placed responsibility on Cheever and said the reigning Indianapolis 500 champion came down the race track and pinched him off in the second turn, which caused the crash. "I remember when he hit me, he still had a lot of room on the outside," Ray said. "He just didn't give me any room. He is the one, unfortunately, that caused the incident. If that would have been the last lap, I could probably live with this. But we weren't even halfway; it was uncalled for."

Buddy Lazier (91) could be excused if he had driven to the pit of Dr. Jack Miller. After all, runner-up Lazier said the rough Dover Downs track knocked at least two fillings loose in his mouth.

Buddy Lazier's late-race charge fell just short. Scott Sharp beat Lazier to the line by 0.689 seconds. Buddy is congratulated for his fine performance by wife Kara.

Marco Greco and G Force/Aurora were quick and consistent. He was able to cope with the bumps and finished two laps behind Scott Sharp and Buddy Lazier.

The rough track began to take its toll on equipment as well. The dashboard on Stewart's race car actually broke off its mounting bracket, landed in his lap during the race, and was later reattached with duct tape. Stewart led the race three times for 85 laps, but his shot at victory ended on Lap 170 when his right rear suspension failed (broken CV joint). His Team Menard crew replaced the complete suspension assembly and sent him back on the race track after a lengthy stay in the pits.

Others suffering misfortune included Steve Knapp and Robby Unser. Knapp's day abruptly ended when he slammed into the second turn wall on Lap 152. Unser had been in the top five for most of the race and was running third before he crashed on the 184th lap.

When the race was restarted on the 201st lap following Unser's crash, Stephan Gregoire held up the leaders at the start/finish line. Sharp made a bold move going three-wide into the first turn trying to take the lead away from Lazier. Sharp's brave pass and near miss paid off, and he stayed in front for the rest of the race.

Even though he went on to victory, high-speed racing on the high banks of the bumpy concrete oval at Dover provided many challenges for Sharp, as well as for all the other drivers. According to Sharp,

"You don't want to ever give up track position because it is tough to pass around here, but when you run through all the debris you think something must have cut your tire. I was trusting God a lot today because I could have sworn a couple of times I had cut the tire. The whole idea of coming here is it's a different track than we race on. It's another variable the whole garage area has to try to tackle. I like different challenges, and trying to run around 'The Monster Mile' is certainly a major challenge."

Buddy Lazier also had more than his fair share of bumps and jolts. "This place is demanding," Lazier said. "I'm hurting bad. The vibration didn't bother my eyesight, but I actually lost some fillings in my teeth. I even have a few loose teeth from it. It's a violent ride. I can't imagine if this place was smooth because it is very fast with the bumps. That's just a characteristic of this place."

According to Denis McGlynn, president and CEO of Dover Downs International Speedway, Corporation, he was pleased with the performance and the turnout for the race and looks forward to the IRL's return next season. "I thought it was a great show; these guys have a great product; we

would like to have them back, and I think they are willing to come," he said.

Leo Mehl, the executive director of the Indy Racing League, said he was very proud of the effort made by the teams and the drivers throughout the grueling and demanding race. "This was a long afternoon," Mehl said. "They worked hard. I thought the suspensions in general did a heck of a job. We had the problem on Saturday with Eliseo Salazar's crash[that caused serious injury], but I thought the suspensions in general held up."

Mehl was with Goodyear in 1969 and was not part of the last Indy car race at Dover. "I've heard a lot of stories from Al Unser and Johnny Rutherford, and they had a lot of problems here in 1969," Mehl said. "What is different now is what they have done to the race track to accommodate our cars. If we have a problem, we can get down on the runoff area at the bottom. They did a great job with the bumps, but the concrete pits gave us a lot of grip."

Next year's IRL race at Dover may be altered slightly, either with a different race date or a shorter race distance. "We would like to shorten the race down a little bit," Mehl said. "I don't know if fatigue was a situation today, but we did have a number of accidents. Just talking to the fans when they were leaving, they sure enjoyed watching the guys run, but we might want to shorten it to 200 miles next year."

Several Indy Racing League drivers were thrilled to race at Dover Downs International Speedway because they are big NASCAR Winston Cup fans. "Our sponsors had a great time here," said Lazier. "I can't speak for all the other drivers, but I can speak for a lot of them. I know I always watch Winston Cup

when we aren't racing, and I'm a big fan of Winston Cup. Watching them race here for a number of years, it's really nice to race here in an Indy car. And obviously, Indy cars are not Winston Cup [cars]. This is a different type of racing, but it is good racing too."

The Doctor is in: Using what appears to be dentist's equipment (from Dr. Jack Miller's tool box perhaps?), this crew member attends to a set of pipes to ensure their proper fit and function.

OFFICIAL BOX SCORE
PEP BOYS INDY RACING LEAGUE
Pep Boys 400K at Dover Downs International Speedway
Sunday, July 19, 1998

FP	SP	Car	Driver	Car Name	C/E/T	Laps Comp.	Running/ Reason Out	IRL Pts.	Total IRL Pts.	IRL Standings	IRL Awards	Designated Awards	Total Awards
1	4	8	Scott Sharp	Delphi Automotive Systems	D/A/G	248	running	52	202	1	$103,700	$24,850	$128,550
2	14	91	Buddy Lazier	Hemelgarn Racing/Delta Faucet/ Coors Light	D/A/G	248	running	40	143	5	86,200	17,000	103,200
3	21	16	Marco Greco	Int. Sports Ltd./Mexmil	G/A/F	246	running	35	105	12	72,900	10,000	82,900
4	2	6	Davey Hamilton	Reebok/Nienhouse Motorsports/ G Force/Aurora	G/A/G	246	running	34	163	3	59,500	1,750	61,250
5	11	77	Stephan Gregoire	Chastain Motorsports	G/A/G	244	running	30	118	9	54,600	250	54,850
6	6	4	Scott Goodyear	Pennzoil Panther G Force	G/A/G	242	running	28	147	4	48,700	0	48,700
7	20	23	Jim Guthrie	CBR Cobb Racing/G Force/Aurora	G/A/F	229	running	26	27	30	25,400	0	25,400
8	1	1	Tony Stewart	Glidden/Menards Special	G/A/F	220	running	27	194	2	46,200	22,500	68,700
9	10	5	Arie Luyendyk	Sprint PCS/RadioShack/Qualcomm	G/A/F	203	accident	22	109	11	46,200	0	46,200
10	12	14	Kenny Brack	AJ Foyt PowerTeam Racing	D/A/G	197	running	20	129	6	45,000	0	45,000
11	16	52 R	Robby Unser	The Children's Beverage Group/ Team Cheever	G/A/G	183	accident	19	90	16	43,800	0	43,800
12	19	81 R	Brian Tyler	Team Pelfrey/Enginetics	D/A/F	162	running	18	58	22	42,600	0	42,600
13	5	18 R	Steve Knapp	Earl's Performance Products/ Parker Machinery	G/A/G	146	accident	17	52	25	19,400	250	19,650
14	9	30	Raul Boesel	TransWorld Diversified Services/ Beloit/McCormack Mtrspts.	G/A/G	123	engine	16	76	20	40,100	0	40,100
15	7	11	Greg Ray	Conseco AJ Foyt Racing	D/A/G	104	accident	15	93	14	39,000	2,000	41,000
16	17	51	Eddie Cheever Jr.	Rachel's Potato Chips/ Team Cheever	D/A/G	104	accident	14	118	9	37,800	0	37,800
17	18	99	Sam Schmidt	Best Western Gold Crown Racing Special	D/A/F	85	accident	13	95	13	36,500	0	36,500
18	3	28	Mark Dismore	Kelley Automotive	D/A/G	43	engine	13	93	14	36,500	0	36,500
19	8	35	Jeff Ward	ISM Racing/Prolong/Superflo/Tabasco	G/A/G	21	accident	11	124	7	35,300	0	35,300
20	15	40	Dr. Jack Miller	Crest Racing	D/I/F	20	accident	10	48	26	12,200	5,000	17,200
21	13	10	John Paul Jr.	Jonathan Byrd's VisionAire Bryant Heating & Cooling	G/A/F	6	engine	9	84	18	34,200	0	34,200
22	22	15	Scott Harrington	Reebok R&S MK V	R/A/G	0	handling	8	8	37	34,200	0	34,200
			Speedway Engines									400	400
			Roush Engineering									400	400
			Brayton Engineering									600	600
										TOTAL -	$1,000,000	$85,000	$1,085,000

Time of Race: 2:29:49.262
Margin of Victory: 0.689 seconds
Fastest Leading Lap: #1 Tony Stewart (Lap 56, 183.439)
True Value Pole Winning Chief Mechanic: John OiGara/Team Menard Inc.

Average Speed: 99.318
Fastest Lap: #11 Greg Ray (Lap 73, 183.468)
PPG Pole Winner: Tony Stewart

Legend: R-Indy Racing League Rookie   Chassis Legend: D- Dallara; G- G Force; R- Riley&Scott   Engine Legend: A- Oldsmobile Aurora; I- Nissan Infiniti   Tire Legend: F- Firestone; G- Goodyear

Inset: Kenny Brack celebrates with team owner A. J. Foyt after Brack's first-ever IRL victory. "It's just great to see that No. 14 car back in Victory Lane again," Foyt said.

A.J. Foyt's Charlotte Power Play

KENNY BRACK BLITZES THE IRL FIELD

by Jonathan Ingram

SATURDAY, JULY 25, 1998

It may come as a surprise to people, but driver Kenny Brack is in the habit of sending "love notes" to team owner A. J. Foyt. At least that's the way the ornery Texan and four-time winner of the Indy 500 describes Brack's habit of putting all his thoughts down on paper about how the A. J. Foyt Enterprises team and its cars are working.

Brack, who hails from Karlstad, Sweden, speaks English well. Racing in the United States en route to the 1993 Zerex Barber Saab Series championship gave him the opportunity to practice the language. But just as driving on ovals in the Indy Racing League requires special concentration for the driver who earned his spurs as a road racer, explaining his point of view in English requires careful consideration. For the sake of clarity and concision, Brack puts his thoughts down on paper and then hands them over to Foyt.

"I always write a report after qualifying and races," said Brack. "I write down what I think is

Kenny Brack missed his pit box during a pit stop and went to the back of the pack. He was so fast he sliced through the field, retook the lead, and claimed the win.

107

missing, what is good, bad, or whatever. I give that to A. J. and then we talk about it. That's the way we work."

In their first season together, the dedication, honesty, and hard work reflected by Brack's written reports helped cement the bond between the low-key, blond Swede and the high-profile Texan—that plus Brack's ability to consistently run at the front of the field after some coaching by one of America's greatest oval drivers.

"To learn from him is invaluable for a driver," said the 33-year-old Brack who started in the IRL in 1997 with the Galles International team after three seasons in the Formula 3000 series in Europe, the stepping stone to Formula 1. "I have 17 years in road racing, but on ovals I'm not experienced. To be with A. J. is fantastic. It has made me a more complete driver as well."

Through the season's first six races, Brack had finished no higher than third due to a variety of problems that were, no doubt, well documented in his race reports. At the Charlotte Motor Speedway everything finally fell into place for what would appear to be one of the IRL's most unlikely duos. After all, Foyt is hardly known for his reading habits when it comes to how to set up a car or run a race team. In the VisionAire 500, Brack led 76 of 208 laps and brought home his first IRL victory in a car carrying Foyt's famed number 14.

There was a major problem in this race; one that was hardly confined to Brack's point of view from the cockpit. With 25 laps remaining and Brack in the lead during a caution period, the Swede missed the entrance to pit road for his final

pit stop—because he was busy concentrating on his conversation with Foyt on the two-way radio since there's hardly time for written missives during a race. "It is difficult to talk to him on the radio during the race," acknowledged Brack.

This seemingly victory-killing error took place on a night when Foyt's famed temper had already exploded earlier in the race due to a snafu by the crew of his Conseco entry driven by Greg Ray. "I've never seen a crew make so many mistakes," growled

Scott Goodyear posted his fifth top-six finish in the season's seven IRL races with his third place at Charlotte. He was Mr. Consistency, having finished third at Charlotte in 1997, as well.

With 35 laps to go, Jeff Ward had the lead and the speed to win. But a combination of tire wear and a daring Kenny Brack pass relegated Ward to second place.

Arie Luyendyk qualified a disappointing 15th, but showed much better speed when the sun went down, coming on to take fourth. It was a considerable improvement over his 21st-place 1997 Charlotte finish.

Foyt, who subsequently elected to "devote all [his] time to Kenny's team."

Once Brack missed his pit stop, he lost his lead when he pitted on the following lap and then had to restart at the rear of the field. Since Foyt had chewed out his team publicly during the race in a live pit road interview, it was assumed Brack might be hearing something similar on his radio.

"I told him we might have just blown the race," confessed Foyt. But there are more tools in the team owner's motivational arsenal than anger. The Texan concentrated on helping to settle down his driver and coach him during the final 31 laps of green. In an impressive display of rapid-fire overtaking, Brack overtook all 10 cars ahead of him in 20 laps, including front runners Jeff Ward and Scott Goodyear, the only other two drivers on the lead lap. "I think A. J. was driving the car harder than Kenny," said team manager Tommy LaMance.

Foyt figured he owed Brack a favor. During testing at Charlotte, the Power Team entry had blown an engine, causing Brack to crash heavily into the wall. And Brack figured he owed a race victory to Foyt, because it was the team owner who had decided to make a crucial change in the rear springs after the final practice on Friday night. That change enabled Brack to get over the notorious bumps in Charlotte's harrowing Turns 3 and 4 better than any other driver during the race. "I decided to make a change," said Foyt. "When we came in [on race day], he sent me a little love note about it, and everything was fine."

Fortunately for Brack, who qualified his Dallara-Aurora third on Goodyear tires, traffic was relatively light as the IRL continued its assault on high-banked, NASCAR-style tracks. There was lit-tle attrition in the grandstands. Despite a 1-hour rain delay at the start of the race, an estimated 50,000 fans stayed until midnight as Brack sliced and diced his way to the front at speeds up to 218 miles per hour under the lights.

With his speed 3 to 5 miles per hour faster than leader Ward and second-place Goodyear, Brack

screamed through lapped traffic, catching Goodyear 10 laps after the final restart by nipping past at the edge of the grass on the front straight, one of many close passes that evening. "I just had to go for it," said Brack, who had the crowd on its feet. "I always drive hard, but I really wanted to win this one bad."

Up ahead, Ward led by 2.072 seconds, but that margin diminished rapidly, and Brack caught the leader after seven laps. But his first abortive attempt to retake the lead on the backstraight became a typical maneuver during what Brack described as a "wild night of passing." The two drivers simultaneously

Two-time USAC Midget National Champion Stevie Reeves (21) made his IRL debut and posted a 10th-place finish. Reeves, shown passing Jim Guthrie (23) in practice, started from the 20th position.

John Paul Jr., qualified only 13th-best. But he had his finest race of the season, moving up to take sixth. It was his second top-10 finish of 1998.

Scott Goodyear was all smiles after the Saturday night Charlotte race, having started seventh and raced for the lead before ending up third, less than a half-minute behind winner Kenny Brack.

overtook Tyce Carlson's machine at the entrance to Turn 3 with one flying high (Brack) and one diving low (Ward).

Ward retained the lead, but Brack's decisive pass came on the following lap, and this time traffic played to his advantage. Marco Greco inadvertently blocked Ward at the exit of Turn 2 as Brack careened around the high side. Former motocross champion Ward, who recorded his best finish in the IRL after leading 56 laps aboard the G Force-Aurora of ISM Racing, later conceded it would have been tough to fend off Brack's charge.

"I picked up a vibration because there was a problem with one of the wheels," said Ward. "I didn't give up, but I couldn't have held him off." Likewise, Goodyear, who finished third in the Pennzoil G Force, faded with a vibration in his drivetrain so severe he couldn't read the dashboard.

At the finish, Brack led Ward by 5.602 seconds. "Winning feels great," he said. "I hadn't won a race since Formula 3 in Europe in 1996, and I'm used to winning much more often than that." A healthy field of 24 cars did start the race, something which had been in doubt. After a crash-fest at Dover, Delaware, six days earlier, many people were concerned about the number of starting cars, including CMS president and famed promoter H. A. "Humpy" Wheeler. Then he found a garage full of teams preparing cars at his track two days after the Dover event.

"I saw a bunch of guys working in the garage area, and it looked like the reconstruction scene of an aircraft accident," said Wheeler. "I haven't seen that in 20 years, guys on the road trading parts, engines, and suspension struts. It's the spirit they have, and it's a total positive attitude, and that can't do anything but win in buttressing this whole thing and the Indianapolis 500."

But the demands of the 1.5-mile Charlotte track, which features a dog-leg bend on the front straight and tight corners on either end of the oval, took a toll on the IRL field once again. The "Humpy bumps" in Turns 3 and 4, not so affectionately named after the track president, were exacerbated by the summer heat and gave all drivers fits—but none more than Scott Sharp.

Running third on the 105th lap, a rude bump (recorded by the team's shock absorber telemetry) launched Sharp's Dallara into a spin and the Turn 4 wall. "We were fighting the car all night," said Sharp, who led 25 laps. "It was sliding around all over the place." In a tough night for Kelley Racing, hard-luck teammate Mark Dismore blew his second engine in six days after leading 21 laps.

Sharp's crash eliminated the chance for the points leader to pad his margin over Tony Stewart, who started on the pole with a record lap of 220.498 miles per hour. Alas, his Team Menard entry broke an oil line, which destroyed the engine in his Dallara-Aurora. "I wish I knew what I was doing to make the Lord mad," said Stewart, who led once for 19 circuits on his Firestone tires before retiring after just 54 laps. "It must be something."

A penitent Greg Ray, who led the first four laps from his front row starting position, apologized for joining his crew in a mistake-ridden night aboard his Foyt entry while substituting for injured Billy Boat. Ray missed his pit stall once, spun once on pit road, and missed two shifts on restarts before his gearbox jammed. That left it up to Brack to salvage the evening.

"I told Kenny I felt like I was running the car harder than he was," acknowledged Foyt, who watched the track and a TV monitor mounted on the team's pit wagon. "Everything was on Kenny to win, and he made us look like champions."

This time the written race report/love letter waited while Brack and the Foyt team celebrated with champagne ordered by team manager LaMance, A. J.'s nephew, who is a veteran of such celebrations. But before celebrating, Brack needed to make one phone call back home to Sweden. "It's 7 A.M. there," he said, "so I'm going to give them the good news."

Like all IRL crews, the SRS crew works hard to find the perfect race set-up for the 1.5-mile Charlotte track. Ever-changing temperatures in a nighttime race compound the challenge.

OFFICIAL BOX SCORE
PEP BOYS INDY RACING LEAGUE
VisionAire 500K at Charlotte Motor Speedway
Saturday, July 25, 1998

FP	SP	Car	Driver	Car Name	C/E/T	Laps Comp.	Running/ Reason Out	IRL Pts.	Total IRL Pts.	IRL Standings	IRL Awards	Designated Awards	Total Awards
1	3	14	Kenny Brack	AJ Foyt PowerTeam Racing	D/A/G	208	running	53	182	4	$111,100	$28,750	$139,850
2	10	35	Jeff Ward	ISM Racing/Prolong/Superflo/Tabasco	G/A/G	208	running	40	164	6	91,400	7,850	99,250
3	7	4	Scott Goodyear	Pennzoil Panther G Force	G/A/G	208	running	35	182	4	77,000	10,500	87,500
4	15	5	Arie Luyendyk	Sprint PCS/RadioShack/Qualcomm	G/A/F	206	running	32	141	9	62,600	1,000	63,600
5	5	16	Marco Greco	Int. Sports Ltd./Mexmil	G/A/F	205	running	30	135	10	57,400	1,000	58,400
6	13	10	John Paul Jr.	Jonathan Byrd's VisionAire Bryant Heating & Cooling	G/A/F	203	running	28	112	13	50,800	0	50,800
7	8	6	Davey Hamilton	Reebok/Nienhouse Motorsports	D/A/G	202	running	26	189	3	49,500	0	49,500
8	18	77	Stephan Gregoire	Chastain Motorsports	D/A/G	201	running	24	142	8	48,200	5,000	53,200
9	17	40	Dr. Jack Miller	Crest Racing	D/I/F	194	running	22	70	23	26,200	6,000	32,200
10	20	21 R	Stevie Reeves	Pagan Racing Dallara/Olds	D/A/G	184	tripod	20	20	35	24,900	0	24,900
11	19	18	Tyce Carlson	Earl's Performance Team/Sailfish/ Parker Machine	G/A/G	184	running	19	73	21	23,600	750	24,350
12	16	15 R	Andy Michner	Reebok R&S MK V	R/A/G	174	running	18	42	30	22,300	0	22,300
13	14	91	Buddy Lazier	Hemelgarn Racing/Delta Faucet/ Coors Light	D/A/G	171	running	17	160	7	42,900	0	42,900
14	22	99	Sam Schmidt	Best Western Gold Crown Racing Special	D/A/F	147	electrical	16	111	14	41,600	0	41,600
15	4	28	Mark Dismore	Kelley Automotive	D/A/G	144	engine	15	108	15	40,300	250	40,550
16	11	81 R	Brian Tyler	Team Pelfrey/Enginetics	D/A/F	144	electrical	14	72	22	39,000	0	39,000
17	2	11	Greg Ray	Conseco AJ Foyt Racing	D/A/G	122	transmission	15	108	15	37,700	0	37,700
18	6	8	Scott Sharp	Delphi Automotive Systems	D/A/G	104	accident	12	214	1	37,700	0	37,700
19	24	98 R	Donnie Beechler	Cahill Racing/Amerapress/Voxcom/ Firestone/Olds.Spl.	D/A/F	102	accident	11	25	32	14,400	0	14,400
20	12	51	Eddie Cheever Jr.	Rachel's Potato Chips/ TCBG/Team Cheever	D/A/G	71	engine	10	128	11	35,100	0	35,100
21	1	1	Tony Stewart	Glidden/Menards Special	D/A/F	54	engine	12	206	2	33,800	32,500	66,300
22	21	23	Jim Guthrie	CBR G Force/Aurora/Firestone	G/A/F	49	handling	8	35	31	11,100	0	11,100
23	23	44	Jimmy Kite	SRS/Royal Purple/Menards	D/I/F	29	handling	7	52	26	10,700	0	10,700
24	9	30	Raul Boesel	TransWorld Racing/BeloitT/ McCormack Mtrspts.	G/A/G	5	engine	6	82	19	10,700	0	10,700
				Roush Engineering								400	400
				Computech Engines								1000	1000
										TOTAL -	$1,000,000	$95,000	$1,095,000

Time of Race: 1:58:10.555   Average Speed: 158.408 mph   Margin of Victory: 5.602 seconds   Fastest Lap: #14 Kenny Brack (Lap 40, 218.314 mph)
Fastest Leading Lap #14 Kenny Brack (Lap 40, 218.314 mph)   PPG Pole Winner: Tony Stewart   True Value Pole Winning Chief Mechanic: John O'Gara/Team Menard Inc.
MBNA America Lap Leader: Kenny Brack   MBNA Charge through the Field: Stephan Gregoire

Lap Leaders
Lap-Lap	Driver				
1-4	#11 Greg Ray	33-34	#15 Andy Michner	111-145	#35 Jeff Ward	196-206	#14 Kenny Brack
5-23	#1 Tony Stewart	35-39	#8 Scott Sharp	146	#14 Kenny Brack		
24-30	#28 Mark Dismore	40-76	#14 Kenny Brack	147-150	#4 Scott Goodyear	Caution Flags	
31	#14 Kenny Brack	77-96	#8 Scott Sharp	151-172	#14 Kenny Brack	Laps	Reason/Incident
32	#28 Mark Dismore	97-107	#28 Mark Dismore	173	#4 Scott Goodyear	10-13	#30 Boesel, Stall
		108	#14 Kenny Brack	174	#14 Kenny Brack	30-34	#1 Stewart, Smoke
		109-110	#28 Mark Dismore	175-195	#35 Jeff Ward	72-80	#51 Cheever, Smoke

Legend: R-Indy Racing League Rookie   Chassis Legend: D- Dallara; G- G Force; R- Riley & Scott   Engine Legend: A- Oldsmobile Aurora; I- Nissan Infiniti   Tire Legend: F- Firestone; G- Goodyear

A.J. Foyt Copilots a Mile-High Triumph

KENNY BRACK RACKS UP SECOND CONSECUTIVE WIN

by Bruce Martin

Inset: Kenny Brack's performance at Pikes Peak International Raceway demonstrated considerable maturity, discipline, and speed, and his team's strategy worked to perfection.

SATURDAY, JULY 25, 1998

Deft precision driving and copiloting from A. J. Foyt earned Kenny Brack his second-straight win this season at the Pep Boys Indy Racing League's Radisson 200 at Pikes Peak International Raceway. Brack wasn't the fastest driver overall, but he was the most efficient, conserving vital fuel to take him to the checkered flag.

With five laps remaining, Brack was running third behind leaders Robbie Buhl and Tony Stewart. First, Buhl ran out of fuel, but he made it back to his pits, received a splash of gas and returned to the race. Stewart took over the lead while Brack hounded him in second, but Stewart was in the same boat as his teammate. Starving for fuel, he dashed into the pits with three laps remaining and gave up any chance of taking the win.

When Brack inherited the lead with three decisive laps to go, the team hoped to stretch his fuel mileage to the absolute maximum and make it to the finish. With more than 40 years of profes-

He wasn't necessarily the fastest, but Kenny Brack was the best fuel manager, which helped him avoid a late-race pit stop and win at Pikes Peak, his second-straight IRL victory.

Tony Stewart (1) and teammate Robbie Buhl (3) fell victim to copious fuel consumption, forcing them to pit late for fuel and give up the lead to eventual winner Kenny Brack.

sional racing experience behind him, A. J. Foyt, the team owner, helped his driver to run as fast as possible while conserving just enough fuel to make it to the end.

"On the last pit stop, we were lean on fuel, in sixth gear running half-throttle," Brack said. "I was looking at the fuel numbers, trying to calculate how much fuel the car used per lap, then tried to pace myself. It wasn't easy. It came down to strategy at the end. I wasn't over 9,500 revs the last 10 laps, and these engines rev at 10,500. I was cutting back and looking at the fuel numbers all the time."

finishing . . . under no circumstances did we want to run out of fuel."

By finishing third, Stewart regained the lead in the Pep Boys Indy Racing League standings, at least it appeared that way. In the original results table, Stewart led Scott Sharp by 9 points and Brack by 10. But five days after the race, the Indy Racing League assessed penalties against Team Menard drivers Buhl and Stewart for running illegal rear wings. Buhl and Stewart were docked 15 points each, and the team was fined $25,000 for the rules infraction. The points reduction demot-

After starting eighth, Scott Sharp (8) slipped back to an 11th-place finish, costing him the points lead after eight races. Tony Stewart regained the top spot in points with his third-place finish.

Brack finished 7.542 seconds ahead of Buhl, followed by Stewart in third; Stephan Gregoire of France held down fourth, and Davey Hamilton rounded out the top five. Brack averaged 133.515 miles per hour in a Dallara/Oldsmobile Aurora in front of 32,537 fans. He collected $112,950 for his fine performance. "It was pretty close, but close is good enough," said Brack, who last pitted for fuel on the 120th lap. "I knew I was close on fuel, so we leaned it out and ran sixth gear for the last five laps. We were lucky and made it."

Third-place Stewart also provided some perspective on his race performance. "We are pretty happy," he said. "By no means did we have the dominant car, but there were times during the race when we had the best car. And there were times during the race when we had to back off quite a bit and let the tires catch up."

The crowd at Pikes Peak International Raceway saw 11 lead changes and only three caution periods in the quickest race in IRL history, a 1-hour, 29-minute, 52.649-second contest.

Stewart went on to say, "The race was pretty uneventful. We just kind of slid around for 200 laps today. The car was pretty good on new tires, but that only lasted for 10 laps, and then the car just skated around. We just kept doing the best we could inside the car to make changes. We just missed it a little bit today. I didn't want to risk not

the start/finish line. Ten laps later, Ward passed Stewart to regain the lead.

The first caution period came on the 24th lap when Buzz Calkins' engine blew up. The race was restarted on the 35th lap with Ward in front of Stewart and Buhl. Shortly after the green flag waved, a thrilling duel between Stewart and Ward developed. Neither driver seemed to have an advantage over the other as they traded the lead four times over the first 58 laps.

For the next 50 laps Ward set the pace and looked like the man to beat. He passed Stewart to take the lead on the 59th lap and held it until Lap 118. "Jeff would have been very difficult to catch," Stewart said. "I had a good run with him the first half of the race, and it was fun. I wasn't even that disappointed when he got back by me. I really didn't want to see him out because I wanted to finish what we started. He had a really strong car."

But Ward's day came to a premature end on Lap 118 in Turn 2. He had gone high in the fourth turn, brushed the wall, and tried to get back into the low groove. When he got into the first turn, the car broke loose, and Ward's shot at his first career victory ended abruptly at the second-turn wall. Ward was uninjured in the crash.

"It's pretty disappointing because we had such a good car today," Ward said. "The team did a great job on the car, especially on the pit stop. I believe we cut a tire. We went up into Turn 4 and barely

Billy Boat (11) won the pole but never led a lap. He was in fourth place when he ran out of fuel on Lap 198, leading to a ninth-place finish.

ed Stewart from championship points leader to second position.

"After such a great race at Pikes Peak International Raceway last Sunday, it's very disappointing that this had to happen," said IRL Director of Racing Operations Brian Barnhart.

Team Menard Racing Director Larry Curry stated, "I have no reaction. There was nothing they haven't seen before."

Following the readjustment in points, Kelley Racing's Scott Sharp led the championship with 233 points, followed by Brack of AJ Foyt Power Team Racing 1 point behind and Team Menard's Tony Stewart in third with 227 points.

At the start of the race, Boat; driving for the first time since breaking his leg in a crash at the New England 200 on June 28; was on the pole but was shifting slowly, which dropped him from first to fifth on Lap 1. Jeff Ward took the lead and held it until the 13th lap when Stewart passed him at

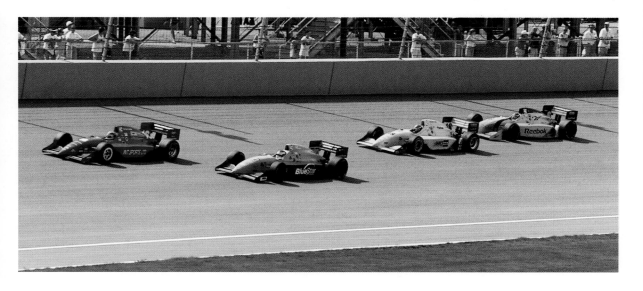

The racing was nose-to-tail as sixth-place finisher Marco Greco (16) leads a pack that includes fourth-place finisher Stephan Gregoire (77), Steve Knapp (18) and fifth-place Davey Hamilton (6).

Davey Hamilton anticipated victory as he led Laps 127–164, but his car was overhauled down the stretch, and he remained winless in IRL action. He finished fifth, good for fourth in points.

Stephan Gregoire not only improved on his 18th-place starting position to finish fourth, he also climbed to eighth in the points race. It was his third-straight top-10 finish.

It was Buhl's first race back since team owner John Menard parked him for the two races at Dover and Charlotte. "The last 25 laps were really fun; that is what you love in racing," Buhl said. "The car was fun; it was balanced. The guys were doing a great job in the pits. For me, we had missed the last two races. It's a nice way to come back. . . . [We've had] these sabbaticals with previous races and come back and had a good race. That is what happened when we won at New Hampshire last year."

Buddy Lazier, who hails from Vail, Colorado, had a shot at the win before a home crowd. At one point in the race, Lazier was running second to Ward but was nearly a half-lap behind the leader. "You have to pace yourself," Lazier said. "It's a long

made it through. It just took off on the straightaway and didn't feel good at all. By the time I got to Turn 2, it just went straight to the wall."

When the race restarted on the 130th lap, Davey Hamilton was in front and led for the next 35 laps. Brack took the lead on Lap 165 as the top four cars ran nose-to-tail. Before Hamilton could get into the first turn, Brack's teammate Billy Boat passed Hamilton, demoting him to third place. With 11 laps remaining, Buhl shot past Brack to take the lead in the third turn and began to drive away from the field. But on Lap 195, Buhl's crew called him into the pits for refueling.

Buhl said, "That previous yellow, we knew what our fuel window was, and we were trying to stay out as long as we could. We knew what we had to have in the tank to go the distance. We came up probably two laps short of that; that was too bad, but we were playing that game. With five laps to go I was reading what I had on my dash, and I was giving it to the guys. Then they said, 'Pit, pit, pit,' but I was too far through Turns 3 and 4 to pit. At the start/finish line, it burbled a little bit, but I was able to get back to the pits, so we were lucky from that standpoint."

race. And the race track was changing out there, so you are making adjustments with the weight jacker and the sway bars. We were just pacing ourselves. We were really pushing, and my guys did a great job. They got us in sequence in the pits. We had a good shot of winning this one."

Lazier's hopes were dashed by a suspension problem late in the race. "I had no fuel concerns at all," Lazier said. "With 20 laps to go, we were really fast on the end of the tank of fuel. We were catching the leaders. I could see the two Menard cars, but going into Turn 3, I heard a loud pop. My car jumped really loose, and I had a huge vibration from there on out. We were just trying to bring it home. Whatever it was that went, I would get halfway through the corner and the car would jump loose two or three times, so we were just hanging on for the last 20 laps."

Roberto Guerrero reclaimed an IRL ride, running as high as third place before finishing 21st. The fact that his car proved competitive buoyed the spirits of the Infinity engine team.

Stewart knew the finish would come down to fuel. "Kenny [and I] were running half throttle for the last 20 laps," he said. "There was no way we could make it on fuel. We had to stop. We came in here trying to get back in the points race, and that is what we did. We are looking down the road on this points battle, and we needed to make sure we finished. We did what we had to do today."

Brack had to win his second-straight IRL race in a totally different fashion from his first race. Rather than charging through the field as the last car in line on the final restart as he did at Charlotte, Brack had to baby the car and sparingly apply the throttle to make it to the end. His car ran out of fuel in the fourth turn of the final lap and coasted to the checkered flag. "The Charlotte race was much, much tougher for me physically and mentally because you had to be flat-out all the time," Brack

said. "Here, you had to drive accordingly.

"We've had two very good races, and hopefully, we will continue like that for the rest of the year," Brack said. With two wins in a row, the driver from Karlstad, Sweden, was asked if he was beginning to feel like an American racing hero. "No, not yet," Brack said. "It takes more wins than that. A. J. Foyt has 67 wins, and he is an American racing hero. So I have 65 more to go."

Tony Stewart (1) fell victim to a fuel shortage while Buddy Lazier (91) lost ground late in the race because of a suspension problem. Lazier pressed on and took seventh.

OFFICIAL BOX SCORE
PEP BOYS INDY RACING LEAGUE
Radisson 200 at Pikes Peak International Raceway
Sunday, August 16, 1998

FP	SP	Car	Driver	Car Name	C/E/T	Laps Comp.	Running/ Reason Out	IRL Pts.	Total IRL Pts.	IRL Standings	IRL Awards	Designated Awards	Total Awards
1	5	14	Kenny Brack	AJ Foyt Power Team Racing	D/A/G	200	running	50	232	2	$96,200	$16,750	$112,950
2	6	3	Robbie Buhl	Johns Manville/Menards/Special	D/A/F	200	running	25	103	18	58,100	5,850	63,950
3	3	1	Tony Stewart	Glidden/Menards Special	D/A/F	200	running	21	227	3	68,100	2,500	70,600
4	18	77	Stephan Gregoire	Blue Star Batteries/ Chastain Motorsports	G/A/G	199	running	32	174	8	56,000	15,000	71,000
5	7	6	Davey Hamilton	Reebok/Nienhouse Motorsports	G/A/G	199	running	30	219	4	51,500	0	51,500
6	9	16	Marco Greco	International Sports Limited/Mexmil	G/A/F	199	running	28	163	9	46,100	2,000	48,100
7	17	91	Buddy Lazier	Hemelgarn Racing/Delta Faucet/ Coors Light	D/A/G	199	running	26	186	6	45,000	0	45,000
8	16	51	Eddie Cheever Jr.	Rachel's Potato Chips/ Team Cheever	D/A/G	199	running	24	152	10	43,900	0	43,900
9	1	11	Billy Boat	Conseco AJ Foyt Racing	D/A/G	198	running	25	147	12	43,900	22,500	66,400
10	21	98 R	Donnie Beechler	Cahill Racing/Amerapress/Voxcom/ Firestone/Olds. Spl.	D/A/F	197	running	20	45	29	20,900	0	20,900
11	8	8	Scott Sharp	Delphi Automotive Systems	D/A/G	196	running	19	233	1	41,700	1,000	42,700
12	23	52 R	Robby Unser	The Children's Beverage Group/ Team Cheever	G/A/G	196	running	18	108	16	40,600	0	40,600
13	19	99	Sam Schmidt	Best Western Gold Crown Racing Special	D/A/F	195	running	17	128	13	39,600	0	39,600
14	14	18 R	Steve Knapp	Earl's Performance Products	G/A/G	195	running	16	68	24	38,400	750	39,150
15	13	10	John Paul Jr.	Jonathan Byrd's VisionAire Bryant Heating & Cooling	G/A/F	195	running	15	127	14	37,400	0	37,400
16	24	81 R	Brian Tyler	Team Pelfrey/Enginetics	D/A/F	186	running	14	86	21	36,300	0	36,300
17	20	15 R	Andy Michner	Reebok R&S MK V	R/A/G	180	running	13	55	27	35,100	0	35,100
18	11	4	Scott Goodyear	Pennzoil Panther G Force	G/A/G	174	running	12	194	5	35,100	0	35,100
19	4	28	Mark Dismore	Kelley Automotive	D/A/G	133	running	11	119	15	34,100	250	34,350
20	2	35	Jeff Ward	ISM Racing/Superflo/Prolong	G/A/G	117	accident	14	178	7	33,000	12,000	45,000
21	10	23	Roberto Guerrero	CBR G Force/Infiniti/Firestone	G/I/F	106	ignition	9	30	33	11,000	5,000	16,000
22	22	5	Arie Luyendyk	Sprint PCS/RadioShack/QUALCOMM	G/A/F	73	engine	8	149	11	33,000	0	33,000
23	25	40	Dr. Jack Miller	Crest Racing	D/I/F	35	clutch	7	77	22	11,000	0	11,000
24	15	12	Buzz Calkins	Bradley Food Marts/Sav-O-Mat	G/A/G	23	engine	6	94	19	33,000	0	33,000
25	12	30	Raul Boesel	TransWorld Racing/Beloit/ McCormack Motorsports	G/A/G	23	engine	5	87	20	11,000	0	11,000
			Menard Engines								1,400	1,400	
										TOTAL -	$1,000,000	$85,000	$1,085,000

Time of Race: 1:29:52:649   Average Spd: 133.515 mph   Margin of Victory: 7.542 seconds   Fastest Lap: #35 Jeff Ward (Lap 3, 170.020 mph)
Fastest Leading Lap #35 Jeff Ward (Lap 3, 170.020 mph)   PPG Pole Winner: Billy Boat   True Value Pole Winning Chief Mechanic: Craig Baranouski/AJ Foyt Enterprises
MBNA America Lap Leader: Kenny Brack   MBNA Charge through the Field: Stephan Gregoire

Lap Leaders				Caution Flags		Accident
Lap-Lap	Driver	51-59	#1 Tony Stewart	165-188	#14 Kenny Brack	3 Caution Flags, 28 Laps
1-11	#35 Jeff Ward	60-117	#35 Jeff Ward	189-196	#3 Robbie Buhl	24-34	#12 Calkins, #30 Boesel, Engine
12-22	#1 Tony Stewart	118-125	#91 Buddy Lazier	197-200	#14 Kenny Brack	75-79	#5 Luyendyk, Engine
23-50	#35 Jeff Ward	126	#1 Tony Stewart			118-129	#35 Jeff Ward,
		127-164	#6 Davey Hamilton			

Legend: R-Indy Racing League Rookie   Chassis Legend: D- Dallara; G- G Force; R- Riley & Scott   Engine Legend: A- Oldsmobile Aurora; I- Nissan Infiniti   Tire Legend: F- Firestone; G- Goodyear

Inset: Winners for the third-straight race, team owner A. J. Foyt and driver Kenny Brack celebrate their narrow win at Atlanta—a win that gave them the lead in the points

The Brack Factor

AJ FOYT'S POWER TEAM CLAIMS THIRD WIN IN A ROW

by Jonathan Ingram

SATURDAY, AUGUST 29, 1998

During the first night race held at the Atlanta Motor Speedway, some lights atop the grandstand in Turn 4 went out at the 50-lap mark, leaving the exit of the corner in the dark which is where Kenny Brack left his competition. With enough speed to come back after losing a lap midway in the race, Kenny Brack was gone with the wind by the finish, easily winning his third-straight race in the AJ Foyt Power Team Dallara-Aurora. For the first time in his career the Swede took the lead in the Pep Boys IRL series, and it proved to be a truly dark night for championship contenders Tony Stewart and Scott Sharp.

After beating runner-up Davey Hamilton by nearly a second, Brack left the Atlanta track looking like a million bucks or possibly two million. His second victory in a Saturday night race put him in position to win a $1-million bonus offered by MCI to any driver sweeping the three night races at Charlotte, Atlanta, and the season finale

Cars blurring past the grandstands at 220-plus miles per hour thrill the crowd at the Atlanta Motor Speedway. The IRL generates excitement with every one of its Saturday night races, and Atlanta is no exception.

The first driver to win three consecutive IRL races, Kenny Brack "decided to go for it" and took the lead on Lap 195, then held off Davey Hamilton to win the 208-lap race by less than a second.

Shown here in practice at Atlanta, Indy 500 winner Eddie Cheever, qualified a disappointing 11th, but came on to finish third, his best showing since winning at Indianapolis.

in Las Vegas. Plus, Brack's commanding lead in the points gave him a leg up on the $1 million bonus offered by the Pep Boys to the league's championship driver and team.

The typically laconic, cool Swede had this assessment of his hot streak and the potential payday that loomed large in Vegas. "I know A. J. has got a good team, but there are other people who can win races, too. So you have to race with them . . . you have to take home the trophies one at a time."

In the IRL's first appearance at AMS, in front of an estimated 50,000 fans who saw average lap speeds of 222 miles per hour on the 1.54-mile, high-banked track, former points leaders Scott Sharp and Tony Stewart faltered. And it wasn't due to their own shortcomings. Sharp's Kelley Racing Dallara broke an input shaft on its gearbox after entering the pits in second position on the 135th lap and retired with an 18th-place finish.

Despite turning laps of 228 miles per hour when testing at night earlier in the year, Stewart qualified a lowly 25th at 213 miles per hour on the sultry Friday evening before the MCI Atlanta 500 Classic, because his Team Menard-built Aurora engines failed miserably. "We came in thinking we could dominate the front row," said Menard teammate Robbie Buhl, who qualified 21st in his Dallara. "Coming off the corner, the engine was flat. The rpms wouldn't come up."

For the race, the Menard team resorted to engines that had been rebuilt after the previous event at Pikes Peak, a 1-mile flat track that places considerably different demands on engines than the 28-degree high banks in Atlanta. While Buhl experienced problems in the race due to decreasing rpms (which turned out to be a bigger problem during the race than during qualifying), Stewart drafted brilliantly through the field in his Dallara, and even led once for 12 laps. But Stewart slipped to fifth at race's end after losing the draft of "dancing partner" Eddie Cheever, who finished third and scored his best finish since winning the Indy 500.

"There's nothing we did tonight that couldn't have been cured by 40 more horsepower," said Menard team manager Larry Curry. Stewart, meanwhile, considered himself lucky to leave AMS with

After finishing last in three of the previous four races, Raul Boesel rebounded nicely at Atlanta, qualifying 15th and moving up to finish 10th. It was only his second top-10 finish of the season.

a fifth-place finish and was shocked to have been able to lead through drafting and good pit stops. "We didn't have enough horsepower to hold them off," he said.

Driving the Dallara-Aurora of Nienhouse Motorsports, Davey Hamilton came charging through the points table into second place ahead of Stewart and Sharp. Still looking for his first victory, Hamilton drove one of his best races. His Reebok-sponsored entry led 19 of the 208 laps before succumbing to Brack's oncoming Dallara-Aurora 14 laps from the finish. His career-best sec-

ond place gave him six straight races in the top five. "We had a great race," he said. "Hopefully, a win is right around the corner."

Brack took the lead from Hamilton 63 laps after he regained his lost lap. He lost the lap shortly before the halfway mark when a cut tire sent Greg Ray spinning down the back straight just as Brack entered the pits. The ensuing caution and pace car came out before Brack could exit the pits. On the restart, he was ahead of the leaders, who had pitted during the yellow, but he was almost a full lap down. Brack made up that lap with the help

Nighttime practice and qualifying sessions let teams set-up their cars in conditions similar to those of the race. Scott Goodyear's crew made numerous adjustments, front and rear, during this practice.

Davey Hamilton was fast in practice (shown here), qualified 10th, and made an all-out run at race leader Kenny Brack in the final laps. He fell .944-seconds short and finished second.

For the second-straight race, Jeff Ward (shown here in practice) started second. His sixth-place finish at Atlanta, where he led 38 laps, moved him up to sixth in points.

of the subsequent caution for Stephan Gregoire's spin in Turn 4, because he was fast enough to stay ahead of leader Scott Goodyear for 26 laps.

"I'm learning how to drive faster after getting slowed down in the pits," joked Brack, whose first victory resulted from a charge from the back of the pack in Charlotte after the driver missed the pit entrance during a yellow. Until Brack got his lap back, the G Forces of Scott Goodyear, who led 93 laps in the Pennzoil Panther Racing entry, and Jeff Ward, who led 64 circuits in the Thermo Tech entry of ISM Racing, were the dominant cars for most of the evening.

Excellent drivers both, their G Forces had not been the strongest challengers against the Dallaras on the faster courses earlier in the year. Their respective teams had not been able to find consistency with the chassis over the course of races, a problem that again raised its head at the end of this one. Both encountered handling difficulties, which dropped Goodyear to fourth and Ward to sixth. Ward set the fastest lap of the race on the fourth circuit. Arie Luyendyk, who finished a lap down in eighth, also had words of encouragement for the G Force brigade. "I think we had a car that could have

won in the end," he said, "but we lost too much time [sorting out the handling] at the beginning."

The G Force showed strongly in qualifying, however. Billy Boat, driving A. J. Foyt's Conseco Dallara-Aurora, may have earned his second straight pole since recovering from a broken leg and pelvis suffered in an accident at the New Hampshire International Speedway, but he had to pip Ward and his newly sponsored Thermo Tech entry by 0.019 seconds to do it.

How strong were the Foyt team's Aurora engines built by Katech? After losing time prior to qualifications replacing an alternator, Boat left the pits for his two flying laps without any post-practice gear ratio changes. On his pole-winning lap, Boat hit the rev limiter down the backstraight and was still fast enough to win his third pole of the season, turning a lap of 224.145 miles per hour. "With the problems we had, we're please to be up front," he said.

Not pleased was teammate Brack, who qualified sixth. "The problem in qualifying's search for one perfect lap," said Foyt, "is driving technique. An oval track driver in midgets most of his career, Boat was more gentle with the wheel at the entrance to the track's high-speed corners. Road racers like Brack, tend to go into the corners a little deeper and that binds the car up." In the race, Boat also made up a lost lap. At the start, a problem with tire stagger affected the handling of his Dallara and dropped him back through the field. This was followed by a subsequent stall in the pits, which put him a lap down.

After making up his lap with the aid of a caution flag Boat might have been a contender, but a collision with Marco Greco at the exit of Turn 2

John Paul Jr. (10) and Scott Sharp (8) ran hard here in practice but were disappointed by finishing 23rd and 18th, respectively, in the race. Sharp fell to fourth in points with two races left.

ruined his prospects. That accident also collected Robby Unser and Steve Knapp, whose G Force nearly flipped after hitting the wall on the back-straight. The accident flipped Unser's lid and

brought on some heated words between Greco and Unser after the two climbed from their cars.

Foyt had a few words for Greco as well. "He's three or four laps down, and I don't know what he's racing for," said the Texan. Actually Greco was two laps behind and had led three laps before a pit road accident. Foyt was more on target when he chewed out his nephew and team manager Tommy LaMance, who didn't send Brack through the pits when the yellow fell on Lap 95 and instead elected to service the car, which temporarily cost Brack a lap. But all's well that ends well, which was becoming a theme for the Foyt team. "If it's meant to be, we'll win the championship," said Brack, who was still taking races one at a time even after winning three in a row.

Raul Boesel's crew gained confidence by helping him move up to a 10th-place finish at Atlanta. It was the team's best finish since taking eighth at Phoenix back in March.

OFFICIAL BOX SCORE
PEP BOYS INDY RACING LEAGUE
Atlanta 500 Classic Presented by MCI at Atlanta Motor Speedway
Saturday, August 29, 1998

FP	SP	Car	Driver	Car Name	C/E/T	Laps Comp.	Running/ Reason Out	IRL Pts.	Total IRL Pts.	IRL Standings	IRL Awards	Designated Awards	Total Awards
1	6	14	Kenny Brack	AJ Foyt PowerTeam Racing	D/A/G	208	running	50	282	1	$94,200	$66,750	$160,950
2	10	6	Davey Hamilton	Reebok/Nienhouse Motorsports	D/A/G	208	running	40	259	2	78,200	14,250	92,450
3	11	51	Eddie Cheever Jr.	Rachel's Potato Chips/ Team Cheever	D/A/G	208	running	35	187	8	66,600	3,100	69,700
4	4	4	Scott Goodyear	Pennzoil Panther G Force	G/A/G	208	running	34	228	5	54,900	10,000	64,900
5	25	1	Tony Stewart	Glidden/Menards Special	D/A/F	208	running	30	257	3	50,700	6,000	56,700
6	2	35	Jeff Ward	Thermo Tech Prolong Superflo Racing	G/A/G	208	running	30	208	6	45,300	2,000	47,300
7	5	28	Mark Dismore	Kelley Automotive	D/A/G	208	running	26	145	13	44,300	1,000	45,300
8	9	5	Arie Luyendyk	Sprint PCS/RadioShack/Qualcomm	G/A/F	207	running	24	173	11	43,200	0	43,200
9	14	15 R	Andy Michner	Reebok R&S MK V	R/A/G	206	running	22	77	24	43,200	0	43,200
10	15	30	Raul Boesel	TransWorld Racing/Beloit/ McCormack Motorsports	G/A/G	202	running	20	107	19	20,200	0	20,200
11	21	3	Robbie Buhl	Johns Manville/Menards Special	D/A/F	185	clutch	19	122	16	41,100	0	41,100
12	1	11	Billy Boat	Conseco AJ Foyt Racing	D/A/G	169	accident	21	168	12	40,000	34,500	74,500
13	7	16	Marco Greco	International Sports Limited/Mexmil	G/A/F	167	accident	17	180	10	39,000	0	39,000
14	19	18 R	Steve Knapp	Earl's Performance Products/ Hyper-Stop	G/A/G	167	accident	16	84	22	37,900	750	38,650
15	22	99	Sam Schmidt	Best Western Gold Crown Racing Special	D/A/F	158	engine	15	143	14	36,900	0	36,900
16	13	52 R	Robby Unser	The Children's Beverage Group/ Team Cheever	G/A/G	143	accident	14	122	16	35,800	0	35,800
17	18	91	Buddy Lazier	Hemelgarn Racing/Delta Faucet/ Coors Light	D/A/G	136	engine	13	199	7	34,700	0	34,700
18	3	8	Scott Sharp	Delphi Automotive Systems	D/A/G	135	gearbox	13	246	4	34,700	250	34,950
19	28	23	Roberto Guerrero	CBR G Force/Infiniti/Firestone	G/I/F	133	clutch	11	41	32	11,700	5,000	16,700
20	8	77	Stephan Gregoire	Blue Star Batteries/ Chastain Motorsports	D/A/G	131	accident	10	184	9	32,600	0	32,600
21	23	81 R	Brian Tyler	Team Pelfrey/Enginetics	D/A/F	123	engine	9	95	21	31,600	0	31,600
22	24	98 R	Donnie Beechler	Cahill Racing/Amerapress/Voxcom/ Firestone/Olds. Spl.	D/A/F	110	engine	8	53	28	9,000	0	9,000
23	17	10	John Paul Jr.	Jonathan Byrd's VisionAire Bryant Heating & Cooling	G/A/F	96	accident	7	134	15	30,700	0	30,700
24	16	97	Greg Ray	TKM/Genoa/Firestone	D/A/F	94	accident	6	114	18	8,700	0	8,700
25	26	44 R	J. J. Yeley	Sinden Racing Service	D/I/F	58	engine	5	50	30	8,700	0	8,700
26	20	19	Stan Wattles	Metro Racing Systems/NCLD	R/A/G	29	engine	4	47	31	8,700	0	8,700
27	27	40	Dr. Jack Miller	Crest Racing	D/I/F	15	handling	3	80	23	8,700	0	8,700
28	12	12	Buzz Calkins	Bradley Food Marts/Sav-O-Mat	D/A/G	2	brakes	2	96	20	8,700	0	8,700
				Brayton Engineering								1,000	1,000
				Menard Engines								400	400
										TOTAL -	$1,000,000	$145,000	$1,145,000

Atlanta 500 Classic   Time of Race: 2:17:15.289   Average Speed: 140.026 mph   Margin of Victory: 0.944 seconds   Fastest Lap: #11 Billy Boat (Lap 109, 224.163 mph)   Fastest

Leading Lap: #35 Jeff Ward (Lap 4, 223.018 mph)   PPG Pole Winner: Billy Boat

True Value Pole Winning Chief Mechanic: Craig Baranouski/AJ Foyt Enterprises   MBNA America Lap Leader : Scott Goodyear   MBNA Charge through the Field: Tony Stewart

Caution Flags:		63-71	#44 Yeley, engine	133-140	#77 Gregoire, Accident T3		#52 Unser Jr, Accident
		95-107	#97 Ray Accident	164-168	#99 Schmidt, Engine		Backstretch
Laps	Reason/Incident		Backstretch,	170-184	#16 Greco, #18 Knapp,	6 caution flags, 56 laps
54-59	Track Lights went off T4		#10 Paul Jr, Accident T2		#11 Boat, Marco Greco	

Legend: R-Indy Racing League Rookie   Chassis Legend: D- Dallara; G- G Force; R- Riley & Scott   Engine Legend: A- Oldsmobile Aurora; I- Nissan Infiniti   Tire Legend: F- Firestone; G- Goodyear

et: John Paul Jr.
euphoric with
Texas win.
day was just
some. We
dn't do any-
g wrong," he
d. Despite track
peratures of
degrees, he
med to be
sh as a daisy"
"ready to go
ther 300 laps."

John Paul Jr. Shines Through

THE JONATHAN BYRD TEAM SURVIVES AND WINS

by Bruce Martin

TEXAS MOTOR SPEEDWAY
SEPTEMBER 20, 1998

In one of the most improbable comebacks in motorsports history, John Paul Jr. won the tumultuous and drama-filled Lone Star 500, the second Pep Boys Indy Racing League race to be held at Texas Motor Speedway this season. Paul's triumph over adversity and perseverance to rebuild a shattered career is absolutely astonishing. During his career he has gone from the top of U.S. open-wheel racing down to being an unemployed bystander back up again to the top of U.S. open-wheel racing.

In this incident-mired race, Paul held off a determined Robby Unser by 1.577 seconds to claim his first Indy car victory in 15 years. Aboard his G Force/Oldsmobile Aurora/Firestone, he motored around the 1.5-mile Texas Motor Speedway quad oval at an average speed of 131.931 miles per hour to capture the checkered flag and $122,550. A crowd of 81,049 race fans endured the 100-degree tempera-

Eventual winner John Paul Jr. (10) dove under rookie Dave Steele (43) in Turn 4 at Texas Motor Speedway. Paul led for a total of 31 laps en route to his first IRL win. His Cinderella-story race took him back to the winner's circle 15 years after his last major open-wheel victory.

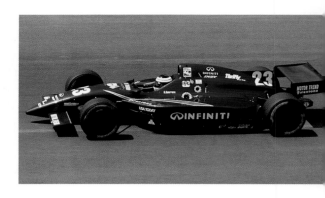

tures and were treated to a thrilling and thoroughly memorable race.

Paul became the sixth different winner in 10 IRL races run this season. He finished ahead of Robby Unser, Jeff Ward, and Roberto Guerrero—the only four cars on the lead lap at the finish.

For fifth-place finisher Kenny Brack and other Goodyear drivers, the Lone Star 500 was a story of tires and Texas heat as much as it was about the rise of a former champion. While the Firestone drivers faired well, most of the Goodyear men struggled with tires ill-equipped to handle the intense track temperatures and battled just to finish. But despite these problems suffered throughout the race, three of the top-five drivers—Unser, Ward, and Brack—were on Goodyears.

Forced to drive a conservative race because of tire concerns, Kenny Brack saw his three-race winning streak come to an end. His fifth-place finish, however, was enough to earn him valuable points and further his points lead in the championship race to 31. Even if second-place runner Davey Hamilton were to win the season finale at Las Vegas, Brack needed only to finish eighth or higher to wrap up the championship. After the penultimate round, Brack, Hamilton, and reigning champ Tony Stewart were the only three drivers who remained in mathematical contention for the championship.

Prior to the race, during pole qualifying (which was held on Friday rather than Saturday), Billy Boat continued to set the pace. His competitors were bewildered and accused his team of foul play. Boat responded to the claim by stating the secret to his success—tire management. He used that strategy to perfection when he turned a lap at 225.979 miles per hour—the fastest lap in Pep Boys Indy Racing League history.

It was the third pole in a row, the fourth of the season, and the fifth of his career for the Phoenix, Arizona, native. Boat's speed in team owner A. J. Foyt's Dallara/Oldsmobile Aurora/Goodyear combination broke the previous IRL qualification record of 224.448 miles per hour, set by Tony Stewart in the True Value 500 at Texas Motor Speedway in June.

At the start of the race itself, Boat was slow to shift heading to the green flag, allowing Stewart to rocket into the lead entering the first turn. Stewart's karting mentor, Mark Dismore, wasn't going to let Stewart get away without a battle. The two cars went side by side through the high-banked first and second turns before continuing their high-speed duel on the backstretch. Stewart, however, was able to extract more horsepower from his Oldsmobile Aurora engine and took the lead. At the end of the first lap, Stewart led Dismore by just 0.037 seconds as the raucous Texas Motor Speedway crowd roared its approval.

As Boat dropped back to sixth place, Stewart grabbed the lead, setting a series record by leading at least one lap in all 10 IRL races during the 1998 season. Stewart has also led all three IRL races at Texas Motor Speedway. He stayed in front as Dismore continued the pressure but stretched out his lead in the early laps, leaving Dismore to contend with a fast-approaching Jeff Ward, teammate Scott Sharp, and Davey Hamilton.

The first sign of tire problems came on the 15th lap when Hamilton had a right rear tire deflate. He entered the race 23 points behind Brack and desperately needed to add to his points in the championship chase.

Five laps later, Stephan Gregoire crashed coming out of the second turn to bring out the first yellow flag of the race. As Boat tried to avoid the crash, Greg Ray ran into the back of his car. Ray, from Plano, Texas, had his hopes for a home-state win quickly extinguished. It was a disappointment for the driver who thrilled the 95,000 fans with his second-place finish in the True Value 500 at Texas Motor Speedway on June 6, 1998.

The race was restarted on the 28th lap with Stewart in the lead, but he missed a shift and dropped back to fourth as Dismore sped into the lead. Dismore's teammate, Sharp, also took advantage of Stewart's missed shift to take over second place as Stewart hustled to get back with the leaders. Two laps later Dismore led by 0.630 seconds over Sharp. Meanwhile, Brack was running up through the field and was in fifth place by the 35th lap. By that time, Dismore and Sharp were engaged in a close duel near the front of the field as Ward, Brack, Stewart, and

Buddy Lazier continued a spirited fight for positions three through six.

On the 40th lap, Dave Steele's right rear Goodyear tire exploded on the front straight. The car went sliding and came to rest between the first and second turns, and luckily for the rookie driver from Tampa, Florida, he was uninjured. The yellow flag came out, and three laps later, the pits were open as Stewart, Brack, Marco Greco, Paul, Hamilton, Andy Michner, Scott Goodyear, Unser, Sharp, Dismore, Lazier, Guerrero, and Ward all came to the pits. That put former CART veteran Raul Boesel into the lead and

Donnie Beechler in second when the green flag waved on the 49th lap. Both Boesel and Beechler made their pit stops during the first caution on the 21st lap.

As the race continued, the Goodyear drivers struggled with their tires. Two laps after he took the lead away from Boesel, Sharp's right rear Goodyear deflated on Lap 53, but he was fortunate enough to make it back to the pits for a change of tires and returned to the race. Stewart resumed the lead when he passed Sharp in the third turn on Lap 52.

At this point of the race, Stewart was the leading candidate for victory, barring some unforeseen disaster. Ward was also a contender for his first career win as he had one of the fastest cars on the race track followed by Paul and Lazier. On Lap 65, Stewart was in front of Ward, Paul, and Lazier, and Boesel had moved back into the top five followed by Brack.

Hamilton had another tire problem that sent him into the pits on the 67th lap. Sharp wasn't as lucky. One of his tires exploded in the third turn, sending his car into the wall to bring out another caution flag on the 70th lap. Fortunately, Sharp was uninjured in the crash. Stewart, Ward, Paul, Lazier, and Brack all pitted on the 75th lap when the pits were opened, and the two Foyt cars—Brack and Boat—both pitted on Lap 76. Ward was in front when the race was restarted on the 78th lap followed by Paul, Boesel, Michner, Unser, and Stewart.

Stewart was forced to drop out of the race with a blown engine on the 80th lap, giving Paul the oppor-

tunity to grab the lead for the first time on Lap 81. On Lap 104, Boesel continued his day of surprises, taking the top position. He was followed by another big surprise—Guerrero. Guerrero and the CBR Cobb Racing G Force/Infiniti/ Firestone machine were running in second and looked to have race-winning speed. To add to the improbable mix, rookie Andy Michner was third, followed by Ward, Lazier, and another rookie, Beechler.

Boat crashed into the wall on the 107th lap when another Goodyear tire failed, which angered Foyt. "Goodyear brought the hard compound tire," Foyt said. "I told them not to bring it. They did any way, and now we're paying for it."

Lazier led when the green flag waved on the 117th lap and was in front until he pitted on Lap 131. A four-car crash in the second turn involving Marco Greco, Beechler, Steve Knapp, and Boesel on the 134th lap brought out another caution period.

After that crash, Robby Unser took the green flag on the 153rd lap, followed by Paul. Lazier and Ward, who both fell back one lap by making pit stops under green, were able to get back on the lead lap by passing Unser. Seven laps later, another yellow flag waved when the engine on Michner's car spewed oil on the track. Unser, Paul, and Brack all pitted during the caution, so Guerrero took over the lead when the green flag waved on the 165th lap. Ward was able to close in on Guerrero and seized the lead with a pass on the front straight on Lap 185. One by one the leaders stopped for service. Guerrero pitted on Lap 191, Lazier pitted on Lap 192, and Ward pitted on Lap 193. This allowed Paul to assume the lead.

As pit strategy played itself out, Paul found himself in a comfortable position, well in front of his pursuers. Hamilton had another tire explode on the front straight on the 197th lap, sending his car spinning across the track in front of Paul, who was leading the race. Paul was able to avoid collecting the spinning car as Hamilton went into the quad-oval grass. Hamilton's crew was able to rescue the car, push it to the pits, and change the blown tire in time to get him back onto the track.

"When David Steele's tire started to shred, I had a little more track at that point to get around him [on Lap 40]," Paul recalled. "It was narrower where Davey's tire took place. I was afraid he was going to come across me on a snap-spin, but the car stayed to the right, and I was able to get underneath him. As soon as I saw stuff flying, I got down by the

Billy Boat won his third straight pole and fifth of the season with a track-record run of 225.979 miles per hour. On race day, however, he couldn't recapture his front-running speed. He never led a lap and finished 14th.

Team Cheever's Robby Unser had John Paul Jr. in his sights, but in the end, he couldn't chase him down. He finished 1.577 seconds behind Paul and scored a career-best second place.

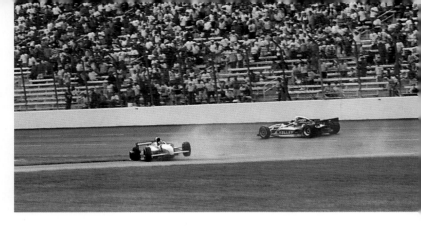

Davey Hamilton (left) slid into the grass after his right rear tire gave out on the front straight. His crew pushed the car to its pit, changed tires, and sent him back out to a big roar from the Texas crowd.

grass. It could have gone either way. It really could."

The field was given the green flag on Lap 202, six laps from the checkered flag with Paul in front of Unser, Guerrero, Ward, Brack, Lazier, Robbie Buhl, and Stan Wattles. Paul and Unser were the only cars on the lead lap on Lap 203, but Ward passed Paul one lap later to get back on the lead

Stan Wattles charged through the field from his 26th starting position and finished 8th. "It was a good run. Texas has been good to us," he said. "Hopefully, this is part of an upward swing for the team."

Buddy Lazier (91) pressured John Paul Jr. (10) on the front straight. Lazier led 14 laps of the 208-lap race, but in the end, Paul pulled away for the win, and Lazier came home sixth. It was a triumphant moment for Paul, who has worked so hard to regain top racing form.

lap. Ward thought the pass was for the lead, but Paul was actually 1.100 seconds ahead of Unser. The lead increased to 1.479 seconds when the white flag waved at the end of Lap 207.

Paul was now racing away from his bitter past and wasn't going to deny himself from once again reaching the pinnacle. He stretched his lead on the final lap to finish 1.577 seconds ahead of Unser. It was his first-ever victory in the IRL and his first Indy car win since taking the checkered flag in the 1983 Michigan 500 on the CART circuit.

"That win was a long time ago," Paul recalled. "That day, we were very competitive, and I was able to pass Rick Mears in the final corner of the final lap. This is very gratifying for me to win another Indy car race. All of the ingredients are here to win a race. It was a matter of getting the variables to all fall into place, and today was our day. It's taken me a while to get back here, but I'm very, very thrilled to win again.

"I'm very relieved to win my first IRL race," Paul continued. "I think the series is just fantastic, and I'm very proud to be associated with the series. To be with a race team like Jonathan [Byrd] is very rewarding. We have been competitive everywhere we went. We just never managed to put it all together on any given day. We all knew we had a car capable of winning races, and today we showed them. It's a very special moment for the team."

With the help of his team, Paul managed to overcome the fact that he had to drive much of the race

without a right-side mirror. "When that tire exploded on David Steele's car, it ripped the right-side mirror completely off of the car," Byrd said. "John Paul drove the whole race with no right-side mirror except for my spotter, my oldest son, Jonathan II. He was the right-side mirror. He became the world's first 280-pound right-side mirror."

Robby Unser's second-place finish moved the rookie driver closer to adding his name to the Indy car race winners column and putting it alongside the illustrious members of his family. "I think it's very important," Unser said. We have a series that is going to go down to the last race for winning the championship. We have six different winners in this thing. I think the rules are great; the drivers are great. There was more than one time where I found myself two wide, inches away from a guy. You just don't see that everywhere in open-wheel cars."

Jeff Ward's third-place finish came as a surprise to the driver. He thought he had actually won the

race but was in fact one lap down. "We went down a lap and got it back, but at the end there, I didn't know where we were," Ward said. "Whoever was in front of me, I was going to pass them. I thought today was the day. For Brack and other Goodyear proponents, tires were the "hot" topic at Texas Motor Speedway. When the 500-kilometer, 312-mile race started, the air temperature was 98 degrees with the track temperature 32 degrees hotter. Because of this the Goodyears built up extreme tire pressure, causing some of them to explode.

"It's not a proud day for us," said Scott Walter, a Goodyear tire engineer. "We put a heat resistant compound on, and the problem was it wouldn't blister off to cool the tire off. The temperature played a big role in

it. The tire we brought here was similar to the tire we ran here in June." Of course, the previous IRL race held at Texas Motor Speedway—the June 6 True Value 500—was a night race with much cooler track conditions, whereas the Lone Star 500 was run on a bright, sunny, hot day with a track temperature of 130 degrees.

Next, all the teams turned to testing, preparing, and strategizing for the final race. Although Kenny Brack had to finish only as high as eighth to secure the championship, anything can happen in racing. If bad luck, an accident, or mechanical gremlins intervened on Brack's race, Stewart and Hamilton would have the opportunity to steal the IRL Drivers' Points Championship.

It was on to the nail-biting showdown in Las Vegas.

OFFICIAL BOX SCORE
PEP BOYS INDY RACING LEAGUE
Lone Star 500 at Texas Motor Speedway
Sunday, September 20, 1998

FP	SP	Car	Driver	Car Name	C/E/T	Laps Comp.	Running/ Reason Out	IRL Pts.	Total IRL Pts.	IRL Standings	IRL Awards	Designated Awards	Total Awards
1	14	10	John Paul Jr.	Jonathan Byrd's VisionAire Bryant Heating & Cooling	G/A/F	208	running	50	184	12	$94,200	$28,350	$122,550
2	17	52 R	Robby Unser	The Children's Beverage Group/ Team Cheever	G/A/G	208	running	40	162	15	78,200	9,250	87,450
3	5	35	Jeff Ward	Thermo Tech/Prolong/Superflo/ G Force	G/A/G	208	running	35	243	5	66,600	6,500	73,100
4	18	23	Roberto Guerrero	Cobb Racing/G Force/Infiniti/Firestone	G/I/F	208	running	32	73	25	32,900	5,000	37,900
5	10	14	Kenny Brack	AJ Foyt PowerTeam Racing	D/A/G	207	running	30	312	1	50,700	50,000	100,700
6	19	91	Buddy Lazier	Hemelgarn Racing/Delta Faucet/ Coors Light/Xerox	D/A/G	206	running	28	227	7	45,300	0	45,300
7	16	3	Robbie Buhl	Johns Manville/Menards Special	D/A/F	205	running	26	148	16	44,300	0	44,300
8	27	19	Stan Wattles	Metro Racing Systems/NCLD	R/A/G	205	running	24	71	27	21,200	0	21,200
9	6	6	Davey Hamilton	Reebok/Nienhouse Motorsports	D/A/G	202	running	22	281	2	43,200	0	43,200
10	4	28	Mark Dismore	Kelley Automotive	D/A/G	202	running	20	165	14	42,200	1,000	43,200
11	22	12	Buzz Calkins	Bradley Food Marts/Sav-O-Mat	G/A/G	201	running	19	115	20	19,100	0	19,100
12	23	40	Dr. Jack Miller	Crest Racing	D/I/F	201	running	18	98	22	18,000	750	18,750
13	25	81 R	Brian Tyler	Team Pelfrey	D/A/F	172	engine	17	112	21	39,000	0	39,000
14	1	11	Billy Boat	Conseco AJ Foyt Racing	D/A/G	162	running	19	187	11	37,900	132,500	170,400
15	28	15 R	Andy Michner	Reebok R&S MK V	R/A/G	158	engine	15	92	24	36,900	0	36,900
16	15	16	Marco Greco	International Sports Limited/Mexmil	G/A/F	133	accident	14	194	8	35,800	0	35,800
17	13	30	Raul Boesel	TransWorld Racing/Beloit/ McCormack Motorsports	G/A/G	133	accident	13	120	19	12,700	0	12,700
18	21	18 R	Steve Knapp	Earl's Performance Products/Parker	G/A/G	131	running	12	96	23	34,700	250	34,950
19	26	98 R	Donnie Beechler	Cahill Auto Racing/ Sleep-tite Mattress Factory	D/A/F	122	accident	11	64	28	11,700	0	11,700
20	2	1	Tony Stewart	Glidden/Menards Special	D/A/F	80	engine	14	271	3	32,600	12,000	44,600
21	12	97	Greg Ray	Best Access Systems/TKM/ Dallara/Genoa	D/A/F	75	engine	9	123	18	9,600	0	9,600
22	7	4	Scott Goodyear	Pennzoil Panther G Force	G/A/G	71	clutch	8	236	6	31,000	0	31,000
23	3	8	Scott Sharp	Delphi Automotive Systems	D/A/G	67	accident	8	254	4	30,700	0	30,700
24	11	43 R	David Steele	Pennzoil Panther G Force	G/A/G	39	accident	6	14	36	8,700	0	8,700
25	9	51	Eddie Cheever Jr.	Rachel's Potato Chips/ Team Cheever	D/A/G	30	engine	5	192	9	30,700	0	30,700
26	8	77	Stephan Gregoire	Blue Star Batteries/ Chastain Motorsports	D/A/G	18	accident	4	188	10	30,700	0	30,700
27	24	99	Sam Schmidt	Best Western Gold Crown Racing Special	D/A/F	5	engine	3	146	17	30,700	0	30,700
28	20	5	Arie Luyendyk	Sprint PCS/RadioShack/Qualcomm Brayton Engineering	G/A/F	5	fuel pump	2	175	13	30,700	1,400	30,700 1,400
										TOTAL -	$1,000,000	$247,000	$1,247,000

Texas, Lone Star 500   Time of Race: 2:21:53.557   Average Speed: 131.931 mph   Margin of Victory: 1.577 seconds   Fastest Lap: #35 Jeff Ward (Lap 172, 224.243 mph)
Fastest Leading Lap: #35 Jeff Ward (Lap 189, 223.399 mph)   PPG Pole Winner: Billy Boat   True Value Pole Winning Chief Mechanic: Craig Baranouski/AJ Foyt Enterprises
MBNA America Lap Leader: Tony Stewart   MBNA Charge through the Field: Robby Unser

Lap Leaders						
Lap-Lap	Driver	43-50	#30 Boesel, Raul	110-116	#15 Michner, Andy	164-182 #23 Guerrero, Roberto
		51	#8 Sharp, Scott	117-130	#91 Lazier, Buddy	183-191 #35 Ward, Jeff
		52-75	#1 Stewart, Tony	131-136	#10 Paul Jr., John	192-208 #10 Paul Jr., John
1-27	#1 Stewart, Tony	76-80	#35 Ward, Jeff	137-140	#23 Guerrero, Roberto	
28-41	#28 Dismore, Mark	81-87	#10 Paul Jr., John	141-162	#52 Unser, Robby	74 Total Caution Laps for 1:24:00.000
42	#35 Ward, Jeff	88-109	#30 Boesel, Raul	163	#10 Paul Jr., John	

Legend: R-Indy Racing League Rookie   Chassis Legend: D- Dallara; G- G Force; R- Riley & Scott   Engine Legend: A- Oldsmobile Aurora; I- Nissan Infiniti   Tire Legend: F- Firestone; G- Goodyear

Inset: Arie Luyendyk and Treadway Team weathered the victory drought and came up with a memorable one at Las Vegas. Luyendyk had to keep Sam Schmidt at bay to take the victory.

Triumph and Tears at Las Vegas Showdown

LUYENDYK WINS AND BRACK CLINCHES THE CHAMPIONSHIP

by Bruce Martin

SUNDAY, OCTOBER 11, 1998

Las Vegas is the gambling capital of the world, and the Pep Boys Indy Racing League couldn't find a more fitting venue for the final race of the 1998 season, a race that would decide the drivers' championship. While high-stakes gambling took place at the gaming tables in Vegas, Indy car teams and drivers were playing their own high-speed, high-risk game. Pride, prestige, a race win, a championship, and $1 million was on the line.

After a season-long quest, two teams and drivers hit the jackpot, while many others struggled with engine problems, chassis setup, and a slick track. Kenny Brack, who drives for team owner A. J. Foyt, entered the race with a 31-point lead over

There is still life in the old dog. Arie Luyendyk proved he can mix it up with anyone in the IRL and win. With a Comptech engine behind his shoulders and a good setup, he was able to control the lead and easily win.

Three of these five IRL stars were in contention for the championship at Las Vegas. From left to right, Scott Goodyear, Kenny Brack, Scott Sharp, Davey Hamilton, and Tony Stewart. Stewart and Hamilton had to win the race and hope Brack suffered from problems in order for one of them to steal the title away. All three drivers struggled with problems. Brack finished 10th, Stewart 14th, and Hamilton 19th.

Davey Hamilton and a 41-point lead over defending IRL champion Tony Stewart. Brack had the opportunity to wrap up the title with an eighth place or better finish. Davey Hamilton, who drives for Neinhouse Racing, has been the model of consistency in the last two IRL seasons, finished within the top 10 in the last eight races. Team Menard's Stewart entered third in the title chase, but trailed Brack by 41 points. He has won two IRL races and four poles in 1998, has nine career IRL poles, and a league record with three career wins. For Hamilton and Stewart, their strategy was simple: try to lead the most laps, win the race, and hope for the best.

Sam Schmidt, driving a Dallara/Oldsmobile Aurora/Firestone machine, put in a inspired drived on his hometown track and was challenging for the lead late in the race. He overhauled Buddy Lazier and John Paul Jr. in the waning stages of the race to claim second position.

Arie Luyendyk's win in the Pep Boys Indy Racing League 500K was a highlight in a largely dismal season. The win rejuvenated his stagnating career and had him reconsidering his racing future. It was his fourth career IRL victory. He defeated Las Vegas native Sam Schmidt by 0.926 seconds, and led the race five times for 88 laps, the most of any driver in the race. He took the lead for good on the 169th lap and held on to the checkered flag to collect

$120,200 in front of an estimated 25,000 spectators. Hemelgarn Racing's Buddy Lazier was third followed by John Paul Jr. and 1998 Indianapolis 500 winner Eddie Cheever.

After the race, Luyendyk, who had hinted at retirement while struggling this season, said, "You start to doubt yourself that you actually belong in the car. I've had a lot of crashes this year that certainly weren't my fault, but you get a lot of self doubt when you have a lot of bad luck and things don't go your way. Then, a day like today turns everything around, and one race makes up for the misery I had before."

Although Brack and the AJ Foyt Power Team didn't dominate the season finale or notch another race win, they did what the had to do—clinch the championship. Brack was hampered by engine problems, which kept him from running at the front. His 10th place finish brought him the Pep Boys Indy Racing League Championship and the $1 million that goes along with it. It was an amazing feat for the former Formula 3000 driver in only his second season of racing in the United States.

While Luyendyk and Brack celebrated their victories and the impact the wins would have on their careers, many others competitors experienced heartbreak and disappointment. In order for Davey Hamilton to steal the championship from Brack, he needed to win the Las Vegas race and have Brack finish outside the top 10. Instead, Hamilton fought his setup and never showed race-winning speed. As for Stewart, his final race as a full-time IRL competitor left him distraught to the point where he contemplated "jumping head-first off the back of this transporter."

Billy Boat wasn't in contention to win the 1998 championship but when it comes to qualifying, there is nobody better in the IRL. Boat and his a Dallara/Oldsmobile Aurora/Goodyear Indy car won a fourth-straight pole, his sixth of the season. For the Las Vegas 500, Boat ran a lap at 214.567 miles per hour around the 1.5-mile, 11-degree banked oval to knock Stewart off the pole after the defending IRL champion ran a lap at 212.934 miles per hour just two attempts before Boat.

Boat's partner in the front row was Stewart, who ran a lap at 212.934 miles per hour in a Dallara/Aurora/Firestone, followed by Marco Greco (212.331 mph), Greg Ray (212.272 mph), Robbie Buhl (212.047 mph), and Brack (211.715 mph).

Ironically, Brack's car failed technical inspection before qualifying, which dropped his qualification attempt to one lap instead of two. "Our rear wing was a little high," Brack explained. "Failing tech actually helped us. That reduces the drag. It's not often that you get sent back and it helps you. Maybe the one lap of qualifying hurt us a little, but not too much. We may have been able to improve on the second lap, just squeeze out a touch more. But I'm happy with what we got. Tomorrow, we will do what we normally do and not change strategy much."

So with a season-long buildup for the title, it was finally time to decide the championship. When

Buddy Lazier was in the thick of the racing action once again. An inconsisent set of tires cost him his shot at the lead and he had to back off. But Lazier was still hard on the gas and brushed the wall in the closing stages of the race.

John Paul Jr. showed that his winning performance in the Lone Star 500 at Texas Motor Speedway was no fluke. Sam Schmidt collided with Paul on a late race restart, which ripped off his front wing. Minus a front wing, Paul was able to finish fourth.

Kenny Brack and AJ Foyt wanted to rack up another win in their championship season. Instead they fought an electrical problems from the beginning, but they finished in front of their competition and won the championship.

133

the green flag waved to start the race, Stewart dropped back in the field as his rev limiter and the engine's electronic control unit failed. Boat sped away in front of Greg Ray, Jeff Ward, Marco Greco, and Brack. Stewart's car fell all the way to 20th by the second lap. By the end of the fifth lap, he was last in the 28-car field.

"Man, let's bring this thing in. This is stupid," Stewart radioed to his crew. He attempted to come into the pits on the seventh lap but spun out to bring out the first caution. Team Menard was using a Comptech engine for the first time in an effort to get more reliability after suffering engine problems while using its own in-house motors built by Sonny and Butch Meyer. Stewart qualified with a Team Menard engine but switched to the Comptech for the race.

"I just couldn't believe it," Stewart said. "We got the green, and the car wouldn't go. We couldn't get any rpms. We don't know for sure what it was. It was something electrical. It was the first lap of the damn race, and the whole damn field went by me. I'm leaving the IRL feeling disappointed. Today is a bad day—not the way I wanted to end my IRL career."

With Stewart in the pits, the race was restarted on the 12th lap with Boat in front. Ward went to the inside of Ray in the first turn but couldn't complete the pass. Stewart returned to the race on the 14th lap, and shortly thereafter debris from the bottom of Scott Sharp's car brought out another caution flag. Meanwhile, Brack also suffered an electrical gremlin in his engine that made his car perform as if it was only firing on seven cylinders. As his crew took the engine cover off the car, Brack fell two laps down while in the pits when the race was restarted on Lap 18. Ward passed Boat for the lead on the 28th lap.

Further back in the pack, Luyendyk began to make his charge to the front. After starting 14th, the two-time Indianapolis 500 winner was up to fourth by the 25th lap and was third after 30 laps. Boat's car began to experience handling problems and fell back in the field while Ward was in the lead followed by Cheever, Luyendyk, and Boat. With Brack two laps down, Hamilton appeared to be in position to win the championship, but chassis and engine problems kept him out of the top 10.

Ward pitted on the 40th lap, handing over the lead to Cheever. Luyendyk took his first lead of the race when he passed Cheever on Lap 42. He was in front when a caution flag waved on the 45th lap after rookie David Steele brushed the wall in the fourth turn. Luyendyk pitted during the caution and was back in front when the green flag waved to continue the race on Lap 49. Paul, Scott Goodyear, Cheever, Lazier, and Donnie Beechler were giving chase.

Brack was three laps down when his teammate Billy Boat crashed into the fourth turn wall on the 54th lap. When the race was restarted 10 laps later, Lazier was in the lead followed by Luyendyk, Cheever, Goodyear, and Beechler. Schmidt moved up to third when he passed Cheever in the second turn on the 86th lap. Beechler's bid ended when he crashed in the fourth turn on the 110th lap to bring out another caution flag. When the green flag flew on the 119th lap the field did not make it through the second turn without another crash. As Goodyear went high in the second turn, Ward ran

into the back of his car sending it into the second turn wall to knock both out of the race. During the caution, pace car driver Johnny Rutherford crashed the pace car when it ran into one of the errant wheels from the Goodyear-Ward crash. After switching cars, Rutherford led Luyendyk, Paul, Lazier, and Schmidt to the green flag to resume racing on Lap 129. It was this fateful lap that ended Hamilton's title hopes. Hamilton was running 14th at the time while Brack was 17th. As the field went into the second turn, Roberto Guerrero bumped Hamilton, sending him into the wall.

Hamilton finished 19th in the 28-car field and ended the season second in the IRL, 40 points behind series champion Brack. Hamilton said, "It was brutal out there today. We didn't have a good setup. We were really loose, then we had motor problems where it was cutting out and misfiring. We thought we had the motor fixed and thought

we had a chance. We went down on that restart, and it got pretty congested. Roberto Guerrero came from the outside and it all happened so fast. All of a sudden, I saw a blue car and we were together."

This was the second season in a row that Hamilton has ended up second in the IRL championship race. "It means we've had two good years," Hamilton said. "We're the first loser, but I've done it with two different teams. It makes me feel good. I've done it with A. J. and I've done it with this team. I feel this team is building power right now. We aren't where we need to be, but the team is meshing really well."

Luyendyk stayed in front when the race resumed on Lap 139 followed by Paul, 2.24 seconds behind the leader. Luyendyk had the most consistent car in the field and said later he adjusted the cross-weight bar inside his car, worked the rear bar a bit, and his crew adjusted the front wing in his car on the first pit stop. Luyendyk made his final pit stop on the 163rd lap, but that strategy nearly backfired as the caution flag waved two laps later when Stan Wattles spun out in the fourth turn. When Luyendyk returned to the race, he was behind the pace car, which waved him by. Luyendyk radioed to his crew to ask if he should pass the pace car. His crew never responded, so Luyendyk followed the pace car's orders and drove by to get back on the rear of the lead lap.

The green flag waved on Lap 171 with Luyendyk driving the car to beat as he sped away from Paul, Lazier, Schmidt, rookie Brian Tyler, and Cheever. Robby Unser's engine blew on the 176th lap, and the yellow flag waved on the 180th lap to check for oil on the race track. When green flag racing resumed on the 182nd lap, Luyendyk got a tremendous jump on the field and put some daylight between his car and Paul's. Stan Wattles crashed in the fourth turn to bring out the final caution of the race on Lap 195. The green flag waved on the 204th lap for a five-lap dash to the checkered flag. Luyendyk was turning the same trick on this restart; he roared away into the lead and left the field in his wake. Schmidt went to the outside to pass Paul in the first turn. As he made the pass, part of the wing on Paul's car broke off sending him back to fourth place as Lazier passed him for third.

Schmidt recalled, "I was really apprehensive on that last restart. I was loving the opportunity to have another shot at him, but we guessed a little wrong on the gearing. Buddy would eat my lunch on the restarts, but two or three laps into it, we would have a great car. We were concentrating on not losing him, because I thought we could get John Paul Jr. at some point. I thought we had cleared him and right when my spotter said clear, I saw a big white flash going by his mirror. It must have been his wing. I'm

The city of Las Vegas is a picturesque backdrop to Las Vegas Motor Speedway. In this high-speed, high-stakes game, the Pep Boys Indy Racing League Championship hung in the balance.

Scott Goodyear and the Panther Racing crew demonstrated a textbook pit stop in the gambling capital of the U.S.

were able to go the final eight laps of the race after we hit the wall like that."

Tony Stewart, the 1997 IRL Drivers' Champion, was leaving the series less than fulfilled. For the past three seasons, Stewart embodied the heart and soul of the Pep Boys Indy Racing League. A young, enormously talented American racing star who cut his teeth in USAC Midget, Sprint, and Silver Crown racing, Stewart seemed like a perfect fit for the Indy Racing League, but the driver from Rushville, Indiana, always wanted more. He wanted to compete in NASCAR Winston Cup racing. So last year, he signed a contract with Joe Gibbs Racing where he would split his time between the IRL and the NASCAR Busch Series in 1998 and then move up to Winston Cup full time in 1999. Stewart finished the Las Vegas race 14th, 30 laps off the lead. It was a low-note ending to an impressive IRL career.

On the surface, A. J. Foyt, the fiery Texan, and Kenny Brack, a sedate Swede, seemed like an odd couple. Pundits wondered if the pairing could succeed. At the core of their being, these two men shared a common goal—winning races. It took several races before the team, the driver, and machine meshed, but when it did, the results were spectacular. By mid-season, Brack was obviously the fastest man on the IRL tour. He became the first driver in IRL history to win three races in a row when he won at Charlotte, Pikes Peak, and Atlanta. That put him in position to win the IRL title. The Las Vegas race didn't turn out to be a triumphant end to the season, but they seized the championship. After the race he said, "We had a plan to stay in contention until the end and then see what we could do, but it didn't turn out that way when we had our own problems. We had to do our best from that point. All in all, we had a good season and had our ups and downs and had to make good use of our opportunities."

Brack and Foyt had to overcome some unexpected adversity when the crew discovered a problem with the engine early on race morning. "This morning when we got here, we found a little water in the intake port so we had a cracked cylinder head," Foyt said. "We elected to change the engine and the crew worked hard on that. We didn't have any practice or check for oil leaks when we fired it up in the garage. We went out there cold turkey hoping we didn't have

Kenny Brack and AJ Foyt Power Team Racing were an unknown quantity entering the 1998 season. They started off the series on a less than impressive note with 13th and 14th place finishes in the first two races. Starting with the Indy 500, the results took an upswing and, by mid-season, Brack and Foyt were clearly the combination to beat.

sorry we did that. I thought I had given him enough room and thought we had cleared him."

Over the closing laps, Luyendyk was able stretch his lead with ease and spread the field like a broken accordion. He was able to cruise to the checkered flag to win the race. "The last few laps, I made sure I got through the third turn nice and smooth because I had a little bit of a gap on Sam," Luyendyk said. "When you have a gap like I had with a few laps to go, it's easy to defend that. But I'm real happy for Sam having such a good race. He hasn't had a great year, either, running on a tight budget. For the first time this year, he finally had an engine in the car."

Luyendyk credited the switch to Comptech engines for helping him win the race. "The one thing I can say about the Comptech engine is it ran all day, and that is pretty key to our success," Luyendyk said. "I'm not going to say it was faster, but it was better on response when you get back on the throttle. It ran smooth and had pretty good fuel mileage to go with it."

Sam Schmidt's team had to find another engine after qualifications when one of their motors was lost in transit to the race track. He was able to obtain an engine from Kelley Racing after qualifications. Schmidt said the engine made a tremendous amount of difference in the race.

Lazier may have had the car to beat through the first two-thirds of the race before Luyendyk took charge. "When the sun went away, we got really tight," Lazier said. "We just started trying to get the push out. I touched the wall in Turn 2 pretty hard. That's a testament to how good these cars are. We

any lines or anything leaking. At the start of the race, on the first yellow, Kenny went backwards. The motor wasn't running. We knew we were having some sort of electrical problems going on because all the cylinders were hot. Then, the problem went away but we were already down three laps. You win championships because things have to fall your way. You have to take the good with the bad and hope the good offsets the bad."

While Foyt got most of the attention that came with the championship, Brack could enjoy the greatest accomplishment of his racing career. "This is my biggest success so far in my career," he said.

"I've won championships before, but this is the biggest achievement I've had so far. I don't know what it means yet."

With a championship in a major racing series in just his second year, Brack has been contacted by teams in the CART FedEx Championship Series. But Brack likes where he is at and said he will be back to defend his title in the IRL. "I think I'll be staying here with A. J.," Brack said. "We get along good, and I feel I have a lot to learn in this series, still, and a lot of goals to achieve. I'm in no hurry to move anywhere. I really like this team. It's the best team I've ever been with."

OFFICIAL BOX SCORE
PEP BOYS INDY RACING LEAGUE
Las Vegas 500K at Las Vegas Motor Speedway
Sunday, October 11, 1998

FP	SP	Car	Driver	Car Name	C/E/T	Laps Comp.	Running/ Reason Out	IRL Pts.	Total IRL Pts.	IRL Standings	IRL Awards	Designated Awards	Total Awards
1	14	5	Arie Luyendyk	Sprint PCS/RadioShack/QUALCOMM	G/A/F	208	running	52	227	8	$94,200	$26,000	$120,200
2	23	99	Sam Schmidt	Best Western Gold Crown Racing Special	D/A/F	208	running	40	186	14	78,200	21,100	99,300
3	17	91	Buddy Lazier	Hemelgarn Racing/Delta Faucet Coors Light/Xerox	D/A/G	208	running	35	262	5	66,600	7,150	73,750
4	7	10	John Paul Jr.	Jonathan Byrd's VisionAire Bryant Heating & Cooling	G/A/F	208	running	32	216	11	54,900	850	55,750
5	10	51	Eddie Cheever Jr.	Rachel's Gourmet Potato Chips Team Cheever	D/A/G	207	running	30	222	9	50,700	5,000	55,700
6	22	81 R	Brian Tyler	Team Pelfrey/Baytan/Enginetics	D/A/F	207	running	28	140	18	45,300	0	45,300
7	5	3	Robbie Buhl	Johns Manville/Menards/Special	D/A/F	206	running	26	174	17	44,300	0	44,300
8	3	16	Marco Greco	International Sports Limited/Mexmil	G/A/F	206	running	25	219	10	43,200	2,000	45,200
9	21	18 R	Steve Knapp	Earl's Performance Products	G/A/G	204	running	22	118	22	43,200	1,000	44,200
10	6	14	Kenny Brack	AJ Foyt Power Team Racing	D/A/G	202	running	20	332	1	42,200	0	42,200
11	12	12	Buzz Calkins	Bradley Food Marts/Sav-O-Mat	D/A/G	202	running	19	134	19	19,100	0	19,100
12	11	8	Scott Sharp	Delphi Automotive Systems	D/A/G	198	running	18	272	4	40,000	750	40,750
13	25	19	Stan Wattles	Metro Racing Systems/NCLD	R/A/G	187	accident	17	88	25	17,000	0	17,000
14	2	1	Tony Stewart	Glidden/Menards/Special	D/A/F	178	running	18	289	3	37,900	3,000	40,900
15	9	28	Mark Dismore	Kelley Automotive	D/A/G	176	suspension	15	180	15	36,900	250	37,150
16	27	52 R	Robby Unser	The Children's Beverage Group Team Cheever	G/A/G	174	engine	14	176	16	35,800	0	35,800
17	24	77	Stephan Gregoire	Blue Star Batteries/Chastain Motorsports	G/A/G	160	running	13	201	12	34,700	0	34,700
18	20	30	Raul Boesel	TransWorld Diversified Services BELOIT/McCormack Mtrspts.	G/A/G	144	timing chain	12	132	20	12,700	0	12,700
19	13	6	Davey Hamilton	#6 Reebok/Nienhouse Motorsports	D/A/G	124	accident	11	292	2	33,700	8,000	41,700
20	18	23	Roberto Guerrero	CBR G Force/Infiniti/Firestone	G/I/F	123	accident	10	83	26	10,600	5,000	15,600
21	8	35	Jeff Ward	Thermo Tech/Prolong/Superflo Goodyear/Aurora	G/A/G	120	accident	9	252	6	31,600	3,000	34,600
22	15	4	Scott Goodyear	Pennzoil Panther G Force	G/A/G	117	accident	8	244	7	31,000	3,000	34,000
23	16	98 R	Donnie Beechler	Cahill Auto Racing/Sleep-tite Mattress Factory	D/A/F	107	accident	7	71	28	8,700	2,500	11,200
24	19	15	Jim Guthrie	Reebok R&S MK V	R/A/G	90	suspension	6	41	33	30,700	0	30,700
25	4	97	Greg Ray	TKM/Genoa Racing/Best Access Systems	D/A/F	76	handling	5	128	21	8,700	0	8,700
26	1	11	Billy Boat	Conseco AJ Foyt Racing	D/A/G	51	accident	7	194	13	30,700	32,500	63,200
27	26	43 R	David Steele	Pennzoil Panther G Force	G/A/G	42	suspension	3	17	36	8,700	0	8,700
28	28	40	Dr. Jack Miller	Crest Racing	D/I/F	38	handling	2	100	23	8,700	0	8,700
			Speedway Engines			800		800					
			Comptech Engines			600		600					
										TOTAL -	$1,000,000	$122,500	$1,122,500

Las Vegas 500K   Time of Race: 2:18:19.202   Average Speed: 135.338 mph   Margin of Victory: 0926 seconds   Fastest Lap: #5 Arie Luyendyk (Lap 142, 206.367 mph)
Fastest Leading Lap: #5 Arie Luyendyk (Lap 142, 206.367 mph)   PPG Pole Winner: Billy Boat
True Value Pole Winning Chief Mechanic: Craig Baranouski/AJ Foyt Enterprises   MBNA America Lap Leader: Arie Luyendyk   MBNA Charge through the Field: Sam Schmidt

Lap Leaders				
Lap-Lap	Driver		Caution Flags	
1-27	#11 Billy Boat	50-97 #91 Buddy Lazier		110-138 #98 Beechler, Accident T4,
28-38	#35 Jeff Ward	98-99 #5 Arie Luyendyk		#35 Ward, #4 Goodyear, Accident T2
39-41	#51 Eddie Cheever	100-109 #35 Jeff Ward	Laps Reason/Incident	#6 Hamilton, #23 Guerrero, Accident T2
42-46	#5 Arie Luyendyk	110-112 #10 John Paul Jr.	7-11 #1 Stewart, Spin T4	165-171 #19 Wattles, Spin T4
47	#98 Donnie Beechler	113-124 #91 Buddy Lazier	15-18 Debris on front straight	180-182 Debris on track
48-49	#5 Arie Luyendyk	125-163 #5 Arie Luyendyk	45-48 #43 Steele, brushed wall	198-203 #19 Wattles, Accident T4
		164-168 #10 John Paul Jr.	between T3 & T4	8 Caution Flags, 68 Laps
		169-208 #5 Arie Luyendyk	54-63 #11 Boat, Accident between T3&T4	

Legend: R-Indy Racing League Rookie   Chassis Legend: D- Dallara; G- G Force; R- Riley & Scott   Engine Legend: A- Oldsmobile

Inset: The goal these three championship-contending drivers, Kenny Brack (left), Tony Stewart (middle), and Davey Hamilton (right), were after: the Pep Boys Indy Racing League Cup. As fate would have it, the final race in Las Vegas was a race of survival as mechanical problems plagued all three drivers.

THE 1998 PEP BOYS IRL CHAMPIONS

Kenny Brack and AJ Foyt Power Team Racing Beat the Odds

by Jonathan Ingram

There's rarely been a contrast between a championship team owner and a championship driver in major league motor racing as great as the one between A.J. Foyt and Kenny Brack, the duo that won the Pep Boys Indy Racing League title in 1998.

The team owner is a Texan with an imposing physical stature, famed for alternating between down-home charm and an explosive temper. He's so well recognized in American sports history for his driving exploits that people still stop him on the street and in airports just to shake his hand. His initials alone invoke misty-eyed memories of an outsized hero who towered above the racing world like a real life Paul Bunyan.

The driver is a precise, soft-spoken Swede. During his championship season, at age 32, he still looked like the kid next door. Despite his success in both the United States and Europe, the 5-foot-9, 150-pound Brack could wander through an airport with nary a head turn—although that could change after a three-race winning streak and a title-winning season aboard an Indy car prepared in Houston shops that carried the famed number 14 of A J Foyt Enterprises.

You certainly can't find a greater contrast between the home towns of Foyt and Brack. The

For many of Kenny Brack's competitors his car was a blur just like this photo. He was the driver to chase on the track. The team didn't have a mistake-free season, but they raced within themselves, seldom pushing the equipment past the limit. Thus, they won when they could win and collected the strong finish when they couldn't win.

team owner grew up in Houston, a bustling metropolis located in the hot, semi-tropical climate of the Gulf Coast. Brack grew up in a small village near Karlstad in the wintery wonderland of central Sweden known for its forests and lakes.

When you consider the difference between Foyt's entry into motor racing and the beginnings of Brack's driving career, there's not much in common either. Foyt's father, Tony, and a partner ran a garage in an area of Houston known as the Heights, where they built midget cars in their spare time to compete on the local dirt ovals. When school-aged A.J. tore up his family's yard after "borrowing" his absent father's powerful midget to race it around the house, Tony decided to help his son's hell-bent desire to become a race car driver by making sure he had good equipment to race.

Brack, on the other hand, came from a family with virtually no interest in racing. His father Bert and a partner ran an electrician's shop. The only race cars Brack and his father saw came blasting down forest roads once a year in the Swedish round of the World Rally Championship. But when it comes to racing, the team owner and the driver share the same crucial passion, although developed in different generations and in vastly different environments. From an early age, each was determined not only to succeed, but to be the very best, someone recognized at the top of the racing heap, whether in a single race, a season, or an entire career.

For Foyt, that initially meant convincing his

father Tony, who was tougher than a tire iron, that he could handle the responsibility of driving a race car. It also meant pestering the hell out of anybody who knew anything about racing who came to his father's garage. From there, Foyt worked his way up through the ranks of midget and sprint car racing to become the first four-time winner of the Indy 500.

For Brack, getting to the top meant finding a way out of the forest and frozen lakes of central Sweden. His compass became a Swedish driver named Ronnie Peterson, a nonpareil when it came to car control and fame in Formula 1 racing. While it may have been rally cars that first ignited his burning desire to race, the goal was to emerge from the back roads of Sweden into the realm of single seaters, where the driver is alone in an open cockpit for all the world to see.

"I had to do it on my own," said Brack. "I had to raise my own money. I've done everything on my own. Done my own thing. In the end you benefit from that. You get your own values, good values, hopefully. It's done a lot of good for me in racing and in life."

Where A.J. initially raced a go-kart around the family's house, Brack flogged mopeds on and off the local roads with his buddies. Where A.J. "borrowed" his father's midget racer to test his prowess as a teenager while secretly driving it solo at night on a local track, Brack bought a scruffy used Saab for $250 at age 12 and raced it on homemade circuits atop frozen lakes.

Once he got his driver's license, A.J.'s first car was an Oldsmobile that he modified himself and illegally drag raced on the streets of Houston versus all comers and in the inevitable police chases. For his part, the underaged Brack took his Saab onto

the local roads late at night to practice rally racing. "Driving on the frozen lakes was [legal]," he said. "Driving on the roads was a bit more tricky. You had to pick your moments. But you can do a lot of fun stuff up there, because no one sees you."

In vastly different generations and locations, thus began the makings of a championship combination. It wasn't until the 1997 Pep Boys IRL season, when the Swede competed for Rick Galles' team, that Foyt first saw Brack race. "I noticed him when he was running for Galles," said Foyt. "He worked hard, and he was pretty educated [about racing]. And he looked like he had a lot of car control. The moves he made were smart moves. When he made a move, he made it. He didn't stick his nose in and then get out of it."

Brack came to the IRL after 16 years in road racing. In 1996, he had finished as the runner-up in the Formula 3000 championship, the stepping stone to Formula 1. "I had some offers from F-1 teams," he said, "but all of them were from teams that were not winning races. I always want to win races. I had a good experience when I raced in the United States, when I won the Barber Saab series championship in 1993. So when I got an offer to race in the IRL, I thought that would be the best place for me."

When Foyt decided to make driver changes for the 1998 season, Brack was one of the first he called. "I thought that if he had some help, he would become a winning driver," said Foyt. For his part, Brack liked the idea of working with Foyt as both a business partner and a team owner. "A.J. is the team," said Brack. "If you want to learn how to drive on ovals, there's no better person to learn from than him. He's a genius when it comes to ovals."

While Foyt is indeed a walking repository of expert knowledge on how to race open-wheel cars on superspeedways, studying as one of his pupils is not always the easiest of experiences. The car control that Brack honed on the ice and snow of Sweden, for example, led to a problem early in the season.

"Kenny has a lot of confidence," said Foyt. "We were tire testing at Indy one day, and he kept running right up by the wall in Turns 3 and 4, letting the tires brush up against the wall. I said, 'Kenny, that wall is going to reach out and grab you.' So he did it again. He wouldn't listen. Finally I had to say, 'That's it' and sit him down for the rest of the afternoon. We ended our test early that day."

Another situation concerning tires and a decision by Foyt may well have saved the team's championship. During the season's next to last round at the Texas Motor Speedway, Brack reported a vibration while running second. He had entered the

race with a 23-point lead over Davey Hamilton and a 25-point margin over Tony Stewart.

"We can win this race," Brack reported to Foyt as they discussed, via radio, the Power Team Dallara's vibration during a yellow-flag period. The Swede wanted to ride out the problem until the next pit stop, thinking the vibration resulted from the wrong air pressure or a blister on his Goodyear tires. "One thing about Kenny," said Foyt, "he's aggressive, and he doesn't like to finish even second. But I told him, 'Kenny, the only guys we gotta beat are Davey Hamilton and Tony Stewart. If you've got a problem with the tire, the only thing you're going to hear is a big bang, and then there's going to be a big crash.'"

Brack replied, "Thank you very much A.J. I appreciate that." Just before officials dropped the green flag, Foyt decided to order Brack into the pits from his second-place position. "It was just a gut feeling that I had," said Foyt. "We brought him in, and the right rear tire had a cut right in the middle of it. There were some tires blistering that day, but this was a cut, which probably came from something he picked up on the track during the caution."

Although Brack eventually finished fifth, he increased his lead in the championship by finishing ahead of both Hamilton and Stewart. "I didn't like finishing fifth," said Brack. "But once the race was over, I began to appreciate what we had accomplished."

Despite the fact that Brack's car suffered an electrical problem at the Las Vegas Motor Speedway during the season finale, his huge points lead enabled the team to ride out that problem. Though Brack finished 10th with an engine that ran 1,000 rpms below its usual speed, he beat runner-up Hamilton by 40 points to win the championship.

Sometimes, however, the learning process within the championship team was a two-way street. Once he had Brack on board, Foyt had to

Kenny Brack was diligent in his pursuit of improving the car's performance. He wrote many reports on the car's behavior to Foyt. Throughout the season, the working relationship between driver, crew, team manager, and team owner strengthened, which was pivotal in their championship charge. Here he confers with Foyt while teammate, Billy Boat, listens in.

learn how to work with a driver who gave him detailed written reports and comments after each weekend and sometimes during race weekends. "That's something I've always done since I started racing," said Brack, who looks quite studious when he wears his glasses.

Foyt, who never before had a driver send him written reports, found them useful. "I really like that," he said. "He and I go over them, and a lot of what he has is really good. I can see what goes on during the race. For example, he'll write that we took two turns of front wing at one point in the race, and that maybe we should have put in three."

There were, of course, more noticeable scenarios. When Team Manager Tommy LaMance, Foyt's nephew, made a mistake during the Indy 500 on fuel mileage calculations, it cost two laps on a day when Brack had already led 23 circuits in the "Greatest Spectacle in Motor Racing." During his driving career, when Foyt got angry, he did things like jump out of his car and start banging on it with a hammer on Indy's pit road. This time, Foyt threw the team's lap-top computer in a rage.

Foyt himself can muddle the picture. During what became Brack's first victory at the Charlotte Motor Speedway in a mid-summer race, the team owner decided to take over the direction of Brack's car once his Conseco entry driven by Greg Ray, who was substituting for injured regular Billy Boat, retired from the race. He started to give so many instructions to Brack over the radio that the driver missed the entrance to pit road during the race's final caution.

The Swede had to wait one more lap to pit and then re-started from the back of the field with 34 laps remaining. Sometimes going three wide, Brack passed every car on the track within 21 laps to take the lead and went on to his first IRL victory. "Sometimes," said the Swede, "it's hard to understand what A.J. is saying over the radio." In any event, Foyt didn't get mad at his driver. "It was all up to Kenny, and he made us look like champions," said Foyt, whose words turned out to be prophetic.

In the next race, LaMance redeemed himself when Brack won his second straight race at the Pikes Peak International Raceway by virtue of a fuel mileage gambit. But at the Atlanta Motor Speedway in the last

of Brack's three straight victories, LaMance elected to service Brack's Power Team entry during a yellow, which cost a lap that eventually his driver made up on the track. "I told them to send the car on through the pits," said Foyt. "I chewed some hiney on that one."

"You never know what direction A.J. is going to take," said Brack, who by contrast maintains a perennially even temper. "It can be very entertaining. There's always some surprises. I think he expects the best from himself, and that's the same that he expects from other people. If you do your best and really do your job 100 percent and things don't go right, he won't get angry with you. He knows how it is to drive a car. If you make a mistake, he knows you can do that. If you don't do your best or you're not the right man for the job, then he gets angry. That's why he won 67 Indy car races. There's nothing strange about that. I think it's good."

It appeared to be a bit strange that teammate Billy Boat's Conseco Dallara-Aurora won six poles in his eight races, including an IRL record four straight at the end of the season. Yet Brack won three straight races and nary one pole. "Kenny likes the front end loose," said Foyt. "I think that's what the problem was with Kenny when it came to qualifying. But in the race he's a very smooth driver. Every now and again he'll make me hold my breath like when he went three wide down there in Charlotte."

"The way Billy and I drive the cars is different," acknowledged Brack, who like most road racers tends to go deeper into a corner on an oval than those who grew up on them. "It's mostly in what type of feel you like to have in the car. I like to have a little more push in the car, which is perhaps good in a race

Although Brack wrote many reports on the car's behavior over the course of the season, he verbally explained the car's attitude to Foyt and his crew. Here Brack shows Foyt what the car is doing through use of his words and hands.

situation and not as good in a qualifying situation. You can change the driving style a little bit if you feel like it. But I feel for now that my style is working good. But I have a lot to learn. That's what I'm doing, that's why I'm racing ovals with A.J."

The lowest point in the season came when Boat's car was T-boned during an accident at the New Hampshire International Speedway in June, occurring just one race after Boat had posted a spectacular victory at the Texas Motor Speedway. The talented driver had to sit out two months and two races while a broken pelvis and leg healed. "You don't want to have this kind of thing happen, and we all felt sorry for Billy," said Brack. "You don't wish that for anyone. We're great friends and teammates, and he's a great driver."

It was a tribute to Foyt's philosophy of having two cars on one team that Brack's streak began during Boat's absence. Typically, Foyt had a hand in both the development of the cars and engines. The execution of the team's overall development of the cars was handled by Craig Baranouski, who also worked as the chief mechanic for Boat's entries. John King, meanwhile, was the chief mechanic for Brack's cars. On race day, Team Manager LaMance directed Brack's races from the pits while Foyt called the shots for Boat.

"Everything just fell into place [during Brack's streak]," said Foyt. "Craig Baranouski overlooks both cars. Even though I have two chief mechanics, one for each car, we work together as a crew. I'm just trying to teach 'em all right from wrong. But we were all sick over what happened to Billy." What made Foyt most upset and angry during the 1998 season were accusations from Team Menard owner John Menard that his team's Aurora engines produced more horsepower from means outside the rule book. Menard never verified the charges. "We all go through the same inspection line," said Foyt.

It was clear from Boat's poles and the team's combined four victories that Foyt's Dallaras had strong power from their Aurora engines. The team owner said that came from his exclusive arrangement with engine builder Katech and from his own investments in camshafts, engine air horns, exhaust manifolds, and fuel injectors.

Other team owners "might have megabucks more than me," said Foyt. "But the one thing you can't beat is experience. It doesn't matter whether its professional baseball, football, or anything. Through the mistakes I made over the years, I've got a lot of experience. I try not to make them again."

"Let's face it," continued Foyt. "You've got a rule book, and you work the edge of it. It's not that you're cheating. You work in the gray area. Anybody who's successful, they're working right on the edge. That was also true for me as a driver. I drove right on the edge, and that's what made the difference from me and some other guys."

Foyt freely admits he gained some advantage concerning aerodynamics. He introduced folding mirrors during qualifying, for instance. "The rule book says you have to have two mirrors on the car. But it doesn't say you can't fold 'em back during qualifying to reduce the wind resistance." Foyt also used a technique of having rough paint on his rear wing to buffet air and help reduce drag during qualifying, a choice that IRL officials rejected once it was discovered in pre-race inspection.

"Every pound of drag you lose at 200 miles per hour is one more horsepower," said Foyt. "We picked up 40 pounds less drag in testing in the wind tunnel at Texas A&M. That's 40 more horsepower."

After Brack won the championship at Las Vegas, Foyt walked down pit road for a less than cordial visit with Menard regarding the team owner's accusations of an unfair playing field. But most of the afternoon, the evening, and the wee hours of the morning in the city that never sleeps were reserved for celebrating a championship which paid $1 million to the winning team from Pep Boys. It was the eighth title in the Indy car history of Foyt Enterprises, but the first in 20 years.

"To win the championship for A.J. Foyt in car number 14 is a little something special, I must say," said Brack.

The driver said he was not overly disappointed about not winning the $1 million bonus posted by MCI and offered to any driver able to sweep the races in Charlotte, Atlanta, and Las Vegas. He won the first two legs of the bonus but failed to take the third round when the electrical problem took him out of the running at Las Vegas. "We came away with the biggest prize of everything, which is winning the championship," said Brack. "I was very happy to win the championship. Within a week or two it won't really matter that we didn't win that last race."

Besides, the Swedish driver had already agreed to try his luck once again with Foyt in the 1999 Pep Boys IRL season. "The goals are always to try to win more races," said Brack. "You never think about the one you just won, but about the next one. So my goal is to win more races. Obviously there's the Indy 500 to be thinking about. So there are many more goals to be achieved in this league for me. I've come a good way. I knew I would be able to win races this year with A.J. To be able to win the championship in my second full season in Indy car racing is fantastic."

THE PURSUIT OF SAFETY

IRL DEVELOPS A SAFER CHASSIS

by Bruce Martin

In 1997, the Indy Racing League forged its own destiny by adopting a completely new chassis formula. While the new cars produced exceptionally close racing at a reduced cost, a high number of drivers were injured in raceway crashes. The Indy Racing League responded quickly and dedicated itself to making the new cars safer, while maintaining their cost effectiveness. On both fronts, the IRL has succeeded.

Two chassis manufacturers, G Force of England and Dallara of Italy, were enlisted to build the IRL's new open-wheel racers. These cars are larger and structurally stronger and have more carbon-fiber thickness than older types of Indy cars made by Reynard, Lola, and Penske. In addition, the new IRL machines have aerodynamic packages that produces less downforce. Therefore, the chassis place a higher demand on driving ability and make the cars slower, compared to past machinery.

However, any type of race car design is an evolutionary process. Although the chassis manufacturers performed an outstanding job in building enough cars to fill the grids at 1997 IRL races, the cars weren't finished products. In order to reduce the number of driver injuries that occurred during the 1997 season, chassis testing continued, and the IRL searched for ways to improve driver safety.

When cars crashed rearward into a race track retaining wall, the gearbox would usually hit the wall first. In this scenario, the energy from the impact was transmitted through the chassis to the driver and often caused an injury. With several top drivers out of competition because of serious head injuries, including 1996 co-IRL champion Scott Sharp, IRL officials recognized changes needed to be made to the cars in order to protect their stars.

The IRL met the challenge and made significant changes to the G Force and Dallara. In addition, the new Riley & Scott chassis, an American car introduced in late 1997, was designed with added safety in mind. The main areas of improvement are in the transmission, bellhousing, and driver cockpit. Design changes help components in those areas absorb more energy from an impact and dissipate the force of an accident, providing more protection for the driver. Of the accidents that have occurred in the Pep Boys Indy Racing League during 1998, there have been no serious head injuries. Most have resulted in leg injuries, which are unfortunately common in high-speed, open-wheel racing.

"Our Safety Committee has worked hard all winter, and I am pleased with their progress," IRL Executive Director Leo Mehl said. "We are learning more about our race cars at each race, and I am sure we can improve them more in the future."

Even before the 1997 season was completed, extensive laboratory testing on the design changes was conducted. One area where IRL discovered a problem was the type of foam used in both the seats and headrests. In 1997, the headrest foam would often collapse up to the inner edge of the carbon fiber tub under a hard impact. It became apparent that the foam was too soft.

Before the 1997 Las Vegas race last year, IRL removed the headrests from 12 cars, and, according to Casey, impact tests were conducted by the IRL with the help of General Motors. This confirmed that the foam was too soft. The IRL took recorded information from the cars involved in a crash and analyzed the impact to find solutions to the problems. Then the IRL went about developing a firmer, safer headrest foam with the collaboration of such companies as Technofab, E.G. Composites, and Mark One. "We

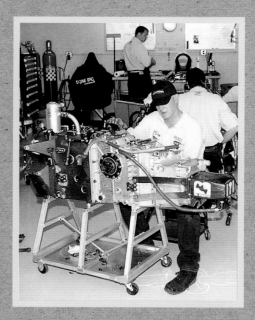

The IRL technical staff acquired and tested more supportive helmet safety foam. The stiffer headrest foam resisted collapsing and provided improved support in crash situations. The result was safer cars and fewer injuries.

made up new headrests," Casey said. "We had several different models and worked with blocks of different foam with different types of covering to see which had the least amount of rebound."

The team of IRL technical officials also went to work on the transmission and related components. It was another area where serious gains in safety could be made through testing. Casey explained that some of the items, like the transmissions and bellhousings, were tested on an impact sled at Wayne State University in Detroit by John Melvin, research manager at GM's Motorsports Technology Research program, and John Pierce, an IRL safety consultant.

The data gathered from the tests was used to improve both the strength and the impact characteristics of the parts. They measured how much energy the existing bellhousing design absorbed on impact. The force necessary for crushing or deforming the transmission and its components was found to be too high. Essentially, the transmission needed to be reliable, yet start deforming with less force when a crash occurred.

"We lightened them, did the tests on them," Casey said. "We decided to extend the attenuator, and that helped quite a bit. They started crushing more easily. Emco worked on the gearbox and made the collapsible shafts inside. They also made some sleeves and everything together made it crush easier." The combination of changes worked together and significantly improved the absorption of energy.

Before teams were allowed to compete in the 1998 Pep Boys Indy Racing League, they were required to purchase update kits for their 1997 chassis, which are legal through the 1999 season. New chassis included the updates and are sold at a set price of $280,000 per car. "G Force built a new bellhousing," Casey said. "The update kit included engine covers, an underwing, and sidepods, and Dallara actually did an update on the nose of their car."

Despite the changes, IRL officials said they will never be satisfied that any race car is completely safe. And in reality, a race car will never be completely safe. Casey said, "There is still room for improvement. We are doing more testing trying to make things better, but the cars are a lot better than they were last year."

In addition, more safety improvements will be implemented and announced throughout the 1998 Pep Boys IRL season. "This is a continuing process," said IRL Technical Director Phil Casey. "We're constantly in a state of development. As soon as one race is over, we go back and work harder on improvements. Even though we've made things better, you're always looking for new ways to do things."

By providing a safer car, which can provide close, wheel-to-wheel racing at high speeds, IRL officials are confident they have a formula for success.

A summary of the changes instituted for the 1998 season follows:

• The transmission case was made more crushable during a tail-end impact. Redesign also has lightened the case by nearly 40 pounds, allowing it to break easier and absorb more impact.

• The transfer shaft that holds the gears was lightened and now has a telescopic mechanism that allows it to collapse 1 inch upon impact.

• The diameter of various transmission bolts was reduced, allowing the bolts to snap more easily during impact and absorb force. A fixed main transmission nut was replaced by a snap-ring that pops off during impact, allowing the shaft to dissipate force.

• An aluminum spacer was added between the third, fourth, fifth, and sixth gears, providing 1 inch of crushable area between those gears during a rear-end impact.

• The bellhousing was redesigned and lightened by nearly 10 pounds, allowing it to break easier and absorb more impact.

• The driver cockpit now includes special headrests for all three types of chassis— G Force, Dallara, and Riley & Scott. The headrests, made of special energy-absorbing foam, wrap around the cockpit near the driver's head. The inserts are 3 inches thick behind the driver's head and 2 inches thick on each side. The top of the headrest can be no lower than 4 inches from the top of the driver's helmet, providing more protection during impact.

An Indy Racing League mechanic works on an improved gearbox. Changes to the gearbox were instrumental in improving safety and reducing injuries. The housing, shaft, spacers, rings, and gears crushed under less impact and absorbed more energy. Thus, less energy was transferred to the tub, which greatly reduced the chance of injury.

THE 1998 PEP BOYS INDY RACING LEAGUE CHAMPIONSHIP SERIES

IN FACTS, FIGURES, AND STATISTICS

Point Standings

Position	Driver	Points
1.	Kenny Brack	332
2.	Davey Hamilton	292
3.	Tony Stewart	289
4.	Scott Sharp	272
5.	Buddy Lazier	262
6.	Jeff Ward	252
7.	Scott Goodyear	244
8.	Arie Luyendyk	227
9.	Eddie Cheever Jr.	222
10.	Marco Greco	219
11.	John Paul Jr.	216
12.	Stephan Gregoire	201
13.	Billy Boat	194
14.	Sam Schmidt	186
15.	Mark Dismore	180
16.	Robby Unser (R)	176
17.	Robbie Buhl	174
18.	Brian Tyler (R)	140
19.	Buzz Calkins	134
20.	Raul Boesel	132
21.	Greg Ray	128
22.	Steve Knapp (R)	118
23.	Dr. Jack Miller	100
24.	Andy Michner (R)	92
25.	Stan Wattles	88
26.	Roberto Guerrero	83
27.	Tyce Carlson	73
28.	Donnie Beechler (R)	71
29.	Eliseo Salazar	60
30.	Mike Groff	56
31.	Jimmy Kite	52
32.	J.J. Yeley (R)	50
33.	Jim Guthrie	41
34.	Jack Hewitt (R)	23
35.	Stevie Reeves (R)	20
36.	Dave Steele (R)	17
37.	Billy Roe	11
38.	Paul Durant	9
39.	Scott Harrington	8
40.	Johnny Unser	5
41.	Robbie Groff	2

(R) - Rookie

Sprint PCS Rookie of the Year Point Standings

Position	Driver	Points
1.	Robby Unser	176
2.	Brian Tyler	140
3.	Steve Knapp	118
4.	Andy Michner	92
5.	Donnie Beechler	71
6.	J.J. Yeley	50
7.	Jack Hewitt	23
8.	Stevie Reeves	20
9.	Dave Steele	17

1998 Pep Boys IRL Series Money Leaders

1.	Eddie Cheever Jr.	$1,811,200
2.	Kenny Brack	$1,096,700
3.	Billy Boat	$1,004,150
4.	Tony Stewart	$1,002,850
5.	Buddy Lazier	$984,850
6.	Davey Hamilton	$856,850
7.	Jeff Ward	$811,650
8.	Scott Sharp	$808,900
9.	Scott Goodyear	$761,750
10.	Arie Luyendyk	$746,100

1998 Pep Boys IRL Series Wins

1.	Kenny Brack	3
2.	Scott Sharp	2
	Tony Stewart	2
3.	Billy Boat	1
	Eddie Cheever Jr.	1
	Arie Luyendyk	1
	John Paul Jr.	1

Chassis Manufacturer Wins

1.	Dallara	8
2.	G Force	3

Engine Manufacturer Wins

1.	Aurora	11

Tire Manufacturer Wins

1.	Goodyear	7
2.	Firestone	4

IRL Series Total Laps Completed

1.	Kenny Brack	2,085
2.	Davey Hamilton	2,032
3.	Scott Sharp	1,935
	Buddy Lazier	1,935
5.	Marco Greco	1,869
6.	Scott Goodyear	1,859
7.	Tony Stewart	1,738
8.	Jeff Ward	1,696
9.	Arie Luyendyk	1,685
10.	John Paul Jr.	1,604

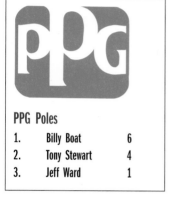

PPG Poles

1.	Billy Boat	6
2.	Tony Stewart	4
3.	Jeff Ward	1

True Value Pole Winning Chief Mechanic

Craig Baranouski, AJ Foyt Enterprises	6
Scott Marks, Team Menard	4
Mitch Davis, ISM Racing	1

MBNA Lap Leaders

1.	Tony Stewart	598
2.	Jeff Ward	326
3.	Scott Sharp	210
4.	Billy Boat	159
5.	Scott Goodyear	153
6.	Kenny Brack	145
7.	Buddy Lazier	143
8.	Arie Luyendyk	121
9.	Eddie Cheever Jr.	85
10.	John Paul Jr.	76

Car		Driver	Car Name	Chassis/Engine/Tire	Entrant
1		Tony Stewart	Gliddens/Menards Special	D / A / F	Team Menard Inc.
1T		Tony Stewart	Gliddens/Menards Special	G / A / F	Team Menard Inc.
3		Robbie Buhl	Johns Manville/Menards Special	D / A / F	Team Menard Inc.
3T		Robbie Buhl	Johns Manville/Menards Special	G / A / F	Team Menard Inc.
4		Scott Goodyear	Pennzoil Panther G Force	G / A / G	Panther Racing LLC
4T		Scott Goodyear	Pennzoil Panther G Force	G / A / G	Panther Racing LLC
5	W	Arie Luyendyk	Sprint PCS/Radio Shack/Qualcomm	G / A / F	Treadway Racing LLC
5T	W	Arie Luyendyk	Sprint PCS/Radio Shack/Qualcomm	G / A / F	Treadway Racing LLC
6		Davey Hamilton	Nienhouse Motorsports G Force Aurora	G / A / G	Nienhouse Motorsports
6T		Davey Hamilton	Nienhouse Motorsports G Force Aurora	G / A / G	Nienhouse Motorsports
7	R	Jimmy Kite	Royal Purple Synthetic/"Synerlec"/Scandia	D / A / G	Team Scandia
7T	R	Jimmy Kite	Royal Purple Synthetic/"Synerlec"/Scandia	D / A / G	Team Scandia
8		Scott Sharp	Delphi Automotive Systems	D / A / G	Kelley Racing
8T		Scott Sharp	Delphi Automotive Systems	D / A / G	Kelley Racing
9		Johnny Unser	Hemelgarn Racing	D / A / G	Hemelgarn Racing, Inc.
10		Mike Groff	Jonathan Byrd's VisionAire Bryant Heating & Cooling	G / A / F	Jonathan Byrd Cunningham Racing LLC
10T		Mike Groff	Jonathan Byrd's VisionAire Bryant Heating & Cooling	G / A / F	Jonathan Byrd Cunningham Racing LLC
11		Billy Boat	Conseco AJ Foyt Racing	D / A / G	AJ Foyt Enterprises
11T		Billy Boat	Conseco AJ Foyt Racing	D / A / G	AJ Foyt Enterprises
12		Buzz Calkins	Bradley Food Marts/Sav-O-Mat	G / A / G	Bradley Motorsports
12T		Buzz Calkins	Bradley Food Marts/Sav-O-Mat	G / A / G	Bradley Motorsports
14		Kenny Brack	AJ Foyt PowerTeam Racing	D / A / G	AJ Foyt Enterprises
14T		Kenny Brack	AJ Foyt PowerTeam Racing	D / A / G	AJ Foyt Enterprises
15		Eliseo Salazar	Reebok R&S MK V	R / A / G	R & S Cars, Inc.
15T		Eliseo Salazar	Reebok R&S MK V	R / A / G	R & S Cars, Inc.
16		Marco Greco	Int. Sports Ltd. Phoenix Racing	G / A / F	Phoenix Racing
17		Andy Michener	Chitwood Motorsports, Inc.	D / A / G	Chitwood Motorsports, Inc.
18		John Paul Jr.	PDM Racing, Inc.	G / A / G	PDM Racing, Inc.
19	R	Stan Wattles	Metro Racing Systems/NCLD	R / A / G	Metro Racing Systems
19T	R	Stan Wattles	Metro Racing Systems/NCLD	R / A / G	Metro Racing Systems
20		Tyce Carlson	Immke Auto Group	D / A / G	Immke Racing, Inc.
21		Roberto Guerrero	Pagan Racing Dallara-Oldsmobile	D / A / G	Pagan Racing
21T		Roberto Guerrero	Pagan Racing Dallara-Oldsmobile	D / A / G	Pagan Racing
22		TBA	rsm Markoe	D / A / F	rsm Marko
23		Paul Durant	CBR G Force Aurora	G / A / G	Cobb Racing-Price Cob.
23T		Paul Durant	CBR G Force Aurora	G / A / G	Cobb Racing-Price Cobb
24	R	Danny Drinan	D.B. Mann Development	D / A / G	Mann Motorsports
27		Claude Boubonnais	Blueprint Racing, Inc.	D / A / F	Blueprint Racing, Inc.
28		Mark Dismore	Kelley Automotive	D / A / G	Kelley Racing
28T		Mark Dismore	Kelley Automotive	D / A / G	Kelley Racing
30		Raul Boesel	Beloit/Fast Rod/Team Losi McCormack Motorsports	G / I / G	McCormack Motorsports

Indianapolis 500 Entry List

Car		Driver	Car Name	Chassis/Engine/Tire	Entrant
30T		Raul Boesel	Beloit/Fast Rod/Team Losi McCormack Motorsports	G / I / G	McCormack Motorsports
31		TBA	Menards/Glidden Special	D / A / F	Team Menard Inc.
31T		TBA	Menards/Glidden Special	G / A / F	Team Menard Inc.
32		TBA	Menards/Johns Manville Special	D / A / F	Team Menard Inc.
32T		TBA	Menards/Johns Manville Special	G / A / F	Team Menard Inc.
33		Billy Roe	Royal Purple/ProLink/Scandia	D / A / G	Team Scandia
33T		Billy Roe	Royal Purple/ProLink/Scandia	D / A / G	Team Scandia
34		TBA	Team Leisy McCormack Racing Scituate Pipe Bengalog	G / A / G	Team Leisy/McCormack Racing
35		Jeff Ward	ISM Racing	G / A / G	ISM Racing
40		Dr. Jack Miller	Crest Racing	D / I / F	Crest Racing/SRS
40T		Dr. Jack Miller	Crest Racing	D / I / F	Crest Racing/SRS
41		TBA	Team Coulson Racing	G / A / F	Team Coulson Racing
43		TBA	Harbaugh Hill/Pennzoil Panther Racing	G / A / G	Panther Racing LLC
44	R	J.J. Yeley	One Call Communications Quaker State Menards SRS	D / A / F	SRS
50		TBA	Eurointernational-Dececco Liberty Racing	D / A / F	Eurointernational/Liberty Racing
51		Eddie Cheever Jr.	Team Cheever	D / A / G	Team Cheever
52	R	Robby Unser	Team Cheever	D / A / G	Team Cheever
53		Jim Guthrie	ISM Racing	G / A / G	ISM Racing
54		Hideshi Matsuda	Beck Motorsports	D / I / F	Beck Motorsports
55	R	Steve Knapp	ISM Racing	G / A / G	ISM Racing
66		Scott Harrington	LP Racing, Inc./HWI	D / A / F	LP Racing, Inc./HWI
68	R	Jaques Lazier	CBR G Force Aurora	G / A / G	Cobb Racing-Price Cobb
77		Stephan Gregoire	Chastain Motorsports/Miller-Eads	G / A / G	Chastain Motorsports
81		TBA	Team Pelfrey	D / A / F	Team Pelfrey
84		TBA	AJ Foyt Enterprises	D / A / G	AJ Foyt Enterprises
84T		TBA	AJ Foyt Enterprises	D / A / G	AJ Foyt Enterprises
88		TBA	Jonathan Byrd's Cafeteria	G / A / F	Jonathan Byrd Cunningham Racing LLC
90		Lyn St. James	Lifetime TV for Women Special	G / I / G	Lyn St. James Racing, LLC
91	W	Buddy Lazier	Delta Faucet/Coors Light Hemelgarn Racing	D / A / G	Hemelgarn Racing Inc.
91T	W	Buddy Lazier	Delta Faucet/Coors Light Hemelgarn Racing	D / A / G	Hemelgarn Racing Inc.
97		Greg Ray	Aptex Dallara Mercury outboards cruisers yachts	D / A / F	Thomas Knapp Mtrspts/Genoa Racing
98	R	Donnie Beechler	Cahill Auto Racing	G / A / F	Cahill Auto Racing, Inc.
99		Sam Schmidt	Best Western Gold Crown Racing Special	D / A / F	LP Racing, Inc./PCI
99T		Sam Schmidt	Best Western Gold Crown Racing Special	D / A / F	LP Racing, Inc./PCI

LEGEND: A = Aurora V8, D = Dallara, G = G Force, I = Nissan Infiniti, R = Indy 500 Rookie, W = Indy 500 Winner

PPG Pole Award
$100,000
PPG INDUSTRIES
Billy Boat

Chevrolet
Chevrolet Camaro Convertible
($27,000 value)
Billy Boat

Harley-Davidson of Indianapolis
1998 Harley Davidson XL 1200
($12,000 value)
Billy Boat

GTE "Front Runner" Award - $30,000
$10,000 *awarded to each front row driver*
GTE
Billy Boat, Greg Ray, Kenny Brack

True Value "Pole Winning Chief Mechanic" Award - $10,000
COTTER AND COMPANY
Craig Baranouski (Billy Boat)

Ameritech "Youngest Starting Driver" Award - $7,500
AMERITECH
J.J. Yeley

Buckeye Machine/Race Spec "Final Measure" Award - $5,000
awarded to last team to pass inspection and qualify for the race
BUCKEYE MACHINE/RACE SPEC
Billy Roe

COLD FIRE "Hottest Pit Crew" Award - $5,000
(awarded to the pit crew of the highest qualifying rookie)
FIREFREEZE WORLDWIDE SRS (J.J. Yeley)

Ferguson Steel "Most Consistent Qualifier" Award - $5,000
awarded to the veteran who records the most consistent qualifying laps
FERGUSON STEEL COMPANY, INC.
Mike Groff

Ferguson Steel "Most Consistent Rookie Qualifier" Award - $5,000
awarded to the rookie who records the most consistent qualifying laps
FERGUSON STEEL COMPANY, INC.
Stan Wattles

Mi-Jack "Top Performer" Award - $5,000
awarded to the driver recording the fastest single qualifying lap
MI-JACK PRODUCTS
Billy Boat

S R E Industries "My Bubble Burst" Award - $5,000
awarded to the last driver to be bumped on last day of qualifying
SRE INDUSTRIES
Eliseo Salazar

Snap-On Tools/CAM "Top Wrench" Award - $5,000
awarded to the chief mechanic (voted by peers) demonstrating skill in preparation for qualifying
SNAP-ON TOOLS/CAM
Jon Ennik (Greg Ray)

T.P. Donovan "Top Starting Rookie" Award - $5,000
OLINGER DISTRIBUTING COMPANY, INC.
J.J. Yeley

$495,000

$150,000

$45,000

BOSCH

$45,000

AURORA
by Oldsmobile
$30,000

**RAYBESTOS
BRAKE PARTS**
$30,000

**FIRST
BRANDS
STP RACING**
$24,000

**EARL'S
PERFORMANCE
PRODUCTS**
$11,000

**PREMIER
FARNELL
CORP.**
$10,000

**SIMPSON
HELMETS**
$10,000

LOCTITE
$9,500

BELL HELMETS
$6,000

BART WHEELS
$5,000

CANON
$5,000

EMCO GEARS, INC.
$5,000

FIRESTONE
$5,000

FIRST GEAR
$5,000

HYPERCO INC.
$5,000

**IDEAL DIVISION STANT
CORP.**
$5,000

KECO COATINGS
$5,000

**KLOTZ SPECIAL
FORMULA PRODUCTS**
$5,000

**MECHANIX
WEAR**
$5,000

NISSAN
$5,000

**SNAP-ON
TOOLS**
$5,000

STANT MFG.
$5,000

WISECO PISTON
$5,000

BORG-WARNER TROPHY AWARD

$130,000 plus trophy replica
$80,000 bonus if the 1997 winner repeats his victory
($20,000 added to the bonus each year until a back-to-back win is recorded)
Borg-Warner Automotive, Inc.
Eddie Cheever Jr.

CHEVROLET OFFICIAL PACE CAR AWARD

1998 Chevrolet Corvette
Eddie Cheever Jr.

$90,000 - Coors Brewing Company
(contest held May 21, 1998)
Panther Racing (Scott Goodyear)

SCOTT BRAYTON DRIVERS TROPHY

$25,000 - Royal Purple Motor Oil
(awarded to the driver who most exemplifies the attitude, spirit and competitive drive of Scott Brayton) Roberto Guerrero

AMERICAN DAIRY AWARDS

$10,750 - American Dairy Association
(winner, fastest rookie, winning chief mechanic) Eddie Cheeve, Jr., Jimmy Kite, Owen Snyder III

LOCTITE AWARDS

$10,500 - Loctite Corporation and Permatex Fast Orange *(winner, winning chief mechanic, pole position) Eddie Cheever Jr., Owen Snyder III, Billy Boat)*

BANK ONE "ROOKIE OF THE YEAR" AWARD

$10,000 - Bank One, Indianapolis
Steve Knapp

FASTLANE FOOTWEAR "FASTEST RACE LAP" AWARD

$10,000 - Fastlane Footwear, Inc.
Tony Stewart

KODAK "PHOTO FINISH" AWARD

$10,000 - Eastman Kodak Company
Eddie Cheever Jr.
(race winner)

MBNA MOTORSPORTS "LAP LEADER" AWARD

$10,000 - MBNA Motorsports
(awarded to the driver who leads the most laps during the 1998 Indianapolis 500)
Eddie Cheever, Jr.

MARSH "MOST IMPROVED POSITION" AWARD

$10,000 - Marsh Supermarkets
Steve Knapp

NBD "LEADERS' CIRCLE" AWARD

$10,000 - NBD Bank
Eddie Cheever, Jr.

NATIONAL CITY BANK "CHECKERED FLAG" AWARD

$10,000 - National City Bank, Indiana *(race winner)*
Eddie Cheever, Jr.

C & R RACING "TRUE GRIT" AWARD

$5,000 - C & R Racing, Inc.
(awarded to the mechanic that exemplifies outstanding achievement and excellence in preparation and management)
John King (Kenny Brack)

CLINT BRAWNER "MECHANICAL EXCELLENCE" AWARD

$5,000 - Clint Brawner Mechanical Excellence Foundation
Brad McCanless (Jimmy Kite)

"CRAFTSMAN TRACTOR" AWARD

$5,000 - Frigidaire Home Products
(awarded to the team using the Craftsman Tractor during the entire month of May at the Speedway)
Team Hemelgarn (Buddy Lazier)

GOODYEAR "WINNING CAR OWNER" AWARD

$5,000 plus ring - The Goodyear Tire and Rubber Co.
Eddie Cheever Jr.

INDIANA OXYGEN "PERSEVERANCE" AWARD

$5,000 - Indiana Oxygen
(presented to the team on race day that exemplifies the most exceptional sportsmanship in a non-winning effort) ISM Racing (Jeff Ward)

LINCOLN ELECTRIC "HARD CHARGER" AWARD

$5,000 - Lincoln Electric Racing's #1 Choice in Welding
(awarded to the lowest qualifier to lead the race)
Arie Luyendyk

MOTORSPORTS SPARES INT'L "PERSISTENCE PAYS" AWARD

$5,000 - Motorsports Spares Int'l., Inc.
(awarded to the highest finishing last day qualifier)
Jimmy Kite

PREMIER/D-A "MECHANICAL ACHIEVEMENT" AWARD

$5,000 - Premier Farnell Corp.
Jimmy Kite

"STIHL THE LEADER" AWARD

$5,000 - Stihl Inc.
(Stihl is the technological leader in the power tools industry and would like to recognize the team/car on the leading edge of technology in the Indianapolis 500)
R & S Cars, Inc. (Eliseo Salazar)

TENNECO AUTOMOTIVE "EFFICIENCY" AWARD

$5,000 - Tenneco Automotive
(awarded to the team that runs the most miles between pit stops)
Kenny Brack

Indianapolis 500 Scoring Positions at 10-Lap

POS	Driver	Car No.	SP	1	10	20	30	40	50	60	70	80	90	100	110	120	130	140	150	160	170	180	190	200	Driver	Car No.
1	Eddie Cheever Jr.	#51	17	20	25	21	9	5	5	3	1	1	2	6	5	1	4	3	1	1	2	1	1	1	Eddie Cheever Jr.	#51
2	Buddy Lazier	#91	11	10	9	32	25	22	2	1	9	9	1	5	6	2	6	5	5	2	2	2	2	2	Buddy Lazier	#91
3	Steve Knapp	#55	23	21	17	13	7	7	13	11	10	8	8	7	7	3	5	6	4	3	3	3	3	3	Steve Knapp	#55
4	Davey Hamilton	#6	8	7	5	7	3	2	4	8	6	6	5	2	2	5	3	4	3	5	5	5	4	4	Davey Hamilton	#6
5	Robby Unser	#52	21	18	20	20	15	11	7	9	7	5	7	3	3	7	7	7	8	7	7	6	5	5	Robby Unser	#52
6	Kenny Brack	#14	3	3	7	3	2	1	3	2	2	3	13	13	11	10	9	9	9	8	8	7	6	6	Kenny Brack	#14
7	John Paul Jr.	#81	16	16	15	16	13	10	9	6	3	2	3	1	1	4	1	1	6	4	4	10	7	7	John Paul Jr.	#81
8	Andy Michner	#17	19	19	21	22	19	16	11	13	11	11	12	11	14	12	15	12	12	9	9	8	8	8	Andy Michner	#17
9	J.J. Yeley	#44	13	32	32	31	29	24	18	15	14	14	15	14	12	14	12	11	11	10	10	9	9	9	J.J. Yeley	#44
10	Buzz Calkins	#12	18	13	12	11	14	14	1	7	12	13	4	10	9	15	11	14	14	13	14	13	10	10	Buzz Calkins	#12
11	Jimmy Kite	#7	26	26	26	28	28	25	15	14	15	16	14	17	16	16	16	15	15	14	13	12	11	11	Jimmy Kite	#7
12	Jack Hewitt	#18	22	24	30	29	27	23	17	16	16	15	16	15	13	11	13	16	13	12	12	11	12	12	Jack Hewitt	#18
13	Jeff Ward	#35	27	23	18	14	31	28	26	17	17	17	17	16	15	13	14	16	16	15	15	14	13	13	Jeff Ward	#35
14	Marco Greco	#16	14	15	14	15	12	12	24	19	19	18	18	18	17	17	17	17	17	16	16	15	14	14	Marco Greco	#16
15	Mike Groff	#10	32	30	31	30	26	26	16	18	18	19	19	19	19	18	18	18	18	18	17	17	16	15	Mike Groff	#10
16	Scott Sharp	#8	7	11	11	10	5	3	6	4	5	7	9	8	8	9	8	8	7	6	6	4	15	16	Scott Sharp	#8
17	Stephan Gregoire	#77	31	29	23	25	23	19	10	10	8	10	10	9	10	8	10	10	10	11	11	16	17	17	Stephan Gregoire	#77
18	Greg Ray	#97	2	2	2	1	1	30	30	29	21	20	20	20	20	19	19	19	19	19	18	18	18	18	Greg Ray	#97
19	Raul Boesel	#30	30	33	33	33	33	33	33	32	30	29	23	23	23	23	22	21	20	20	20	20	19	19	Raul Boesel	#30
20	Arie Luyendyk	#5	28	27	24	24	24	18	8	5	4	4	6	4	4	6	2	2	17	19	19	19	20	20	Arie Luyendyk	#5
21	Dr. Jack Miller	#40	15	14	16	17	21	27	27	20	20	22	22	22	22	22	24	24	24	22	22	22	21	21	Dr. Jack Miller	#40
22	Roberto Guerrero	#21	9	8	10	9	10	8	21	22	23	23	25	25	25	25	25	25	25	25	24	23	22	22	Roberto Guerrero	#21
23	Billy Boat	#11	1	1	1	4	8	21	14	21	22	21	21	21	21	20	20	20	21	21	21	21	23	23	Billy Boat	#11
24	Scott Goodyear	#4	10	9	6	6	30	31	31	31	32	31	24	24	24	24	23	22	22	23	23	24	24	24	Scott Goodyear	#4
25	Johnny Unser	#9	25	25	28	27	22	20	12	12	13	12	11	12	18	21	21	23	23	24	25	25	25	25	Johnny Unser	#9
26	Sam Schmidt	#99	6	6	8	8	6	6	19	23	24	24	26	26	26	26	26	26	26	26	26	26	26	26	Sam Schmidt	#99
27	Mark Dismore	#28	12	12	13	12	11	9	20	24	25	25	27	27	27	27	27	27	27	27	27	27	27	27	Mark Dismore	#28
28	Stan Wattles	#19	29	28	27	23	17	15	22	25	26	26	28	28	28	28	28	28	28	28	28	28	28	28	Stan Wattles	#19
29	Jim Guthrie	#53	20	17	19	18	16	13	23	26	27	28	29	29	29	29	29	29	29	29	29	29	29	29	Jim Guthrie	#53
30	Billy Roe	#33	33	31	29	26	20	17	25	27	28	30	30	30	30	30	30	30	30	30	30	30	30	30	Billy Roe	#33
31	Robbie Buhl	#3	5	5	4	5	4	4	28	28	29	27	31	31	31	31	31	31	31	31	31	31	31	31	Robbie Buhl	#3
32	Donnie Beechler	#98	24	22	22	19	18	29	29	30	31	32	32	32	32	32	32	32	32	32	32	32	32	32	Donnie Beechler	#98
33	Tony Stewart	#1	4	4	3	2	32	32	32	33	33	33	33	33	33	33	33	33	33	33	33	33	33	33	Tony Stewart	#1

	WDW SP	WDW FP	PIR SP	PIR FP	IMS SP	IMS FP	TMS SP	TMS FP	NHIS SP	NHIS FP	DDIS SP	DDIS FP	CMS SP	CMS FP	PPIR SP	PPIR FP	AMS SP	AMS FP	TMS SP	TMS FP	LVMS SP	LVMS FP	Number of Races	Best Start	Running at Finish	Best Finish	Laps Completed	Races Led	Laps Led
Donnie Beechler	-	-	-	-	24	32	17	27	15	20	-	-	24	19	21	10	24	22	25	19	16	23	8	15	1	10	868	1	1
Billy Boat	3	21	2	3	1	23	2	1	1	21	-	-	-	-	1	9	1	12	1	14	1	26	9	1	4	1	1262	4	159
Raul Boesel	9	18	13	8	30	19	19	28	9	19	9	14	9	24	12	25	15	10	13	17	20	18	11	9	4	8	1225	2	37
Kenny Brack	2	13	5	14	3	6	11	3	8	18	12	10	3	1	5	1	6	1	10	5	6	10	11	2	9	1	2085	5	143
Robbie Buhl	14	20	12	12	5	31	3	6	12	10	-	-	-	-	6	2	21	11	16	7	5	7	9	2	6	2	1532	2	13
Buzz Calkins	10	14	17	9	18	10	10	15	23	15	-	-	-	-	15	24	12	28	21	11	12	11	9	10	7	9	1343	1	4
Tyce Carlson	27	11	27	13	-	-	28	12	-	-	-	-	19	11	-	-	-	-	-	-	-	-	4	19	4	11	753	0	0
Eddie Cheever Jr.	23	24	20	10	17	1	20	26	11	9	17	16	12	20	16	8	11	3	9	25	10	5	11	9	6	1	1465	3	85
Mark Dismore	22	5	15	16	12	27	6	21	13	8	3	18	4	15	4	19	5	7	4	10	9	15	11	3	6	5	1597	3	62
Paul Durant	-	-	26	21	-	-	-	-	-	-	-	-	-	-	-	-	-	-	-	-	-	-	1	26	0	21	99	0	0
Scott Goodyear	21	17	14	6	10	24	7	4	5	2	6	6	7	3	11	18	4	4	7	22	15	22	11	5	7	2	1859	4	153
Marco Greco	25	27	16	20	14	14	5	8	14	13	21	3	5	5	9	6	7	13	15	16	3	8	11	3	7	3	1869	1	3
Stephan Gregoire	15	4	22	4	31	17	16	25	16	24	11	5	18	8	18	4	8	20	8	26	24	17	11	8	7	4	1550	0	0
Mike Groff	4	7	24	15	32	15	-	-	-	-	-	-	-	-	-	-	-	-	-	-	-	-	3	4	2	7	558	0	0
Robbie Groff	12	28	-	-	-	-	-	-	-	-	-	-	-	-	-	-	-	-	-	-	-	-	1	12	0	28	0	0	0
Roberto Guerrero	6	26	11	27	9	22	8	24	-	-	-	-	-	-	10	21	28	19	18	4	18	20	8	6	2	4	754	2	29
Jim Guthrie	-	-	-	-	20	29	-	-	-	-	20	7	21	22	-	-	-	-	-	-	19	24	4	19	1	7	416	0	0
Davey Hamilton	19	3	7	26	8	4	15	7	22	4	2	4	8	7	7	5	10	2	6	9	13	19	11	2	9	2	2032	5	67
Scott Harrington	-	-	-	-	-	-	-	-	-	-	22	22	-	-	-	-	-	-	-	-	-	-	1	22	0	22	0	0	0
Jack Hewitt	-	-	-	-	22	12	-	-	20	25	-	-	-	-	-	-	-	-	-	-	-	-	2	20	1	12	206	0	0
Jimmy Kite	28	16	4	18	26	11	-	-	-	-	-	-	23	23	-	-	-	-	-	-	-	-	4	4	2	11	502	0	0
Steve Knapp	-	-	-	-	23	3	-	-	-	-	5	13	-	-	14	14	19	14	20	18	21	9	6	5	4	3	1043	0	0
Buddy Lazier	8	15	9	28	11	2	23	11	3	7	14	2	14	13	17	7	18	17	19	6	17	3	11	3	7	2	1935	6	143
Arie Luyendyk	5	8	19	24	28	20	4	13	7	5	10	9	15	4	22	22	9	8	28	28	14	1	11	4	6	1	1685	3	121
Andy Michner	-	-	-	-	19	8	-	-	-	-	-	-	16	12	20	17	14	9	27	15	-	-	5	14	4	8	913	2	9
Dr. Jack Miller	11	23	-	-	15	21	21	22	19	16	15	20	17	9	25	23	27	27	22	12	28	28	10	11	4	9	896	0	0
John Paul Jr.	7	10	21	19	16	7	12	16	10	26	13	21	13	6	13	15	17	23	14	1	7	4	11	7	7	1	1614	3	78
Greg Ray	16	25	18	11	2	18	14	2	-	-	7	15	2	17	-	-	16	24	12	21	4	25	9	2	2	2	1067	3	23
Stevie Reeves	-	-	-	-	-	-	-	-	-	-	-	-	20	10	-	-	-	-	-	-	-	-	1	20	0	10	184	0	0
Billy Roe	-	-	-	-	33	30	25	20	-	-	-	-	-	-	-	-	-	-	-	-	-	-	2	25	1	20	156	0	0
Eliseo Salazar	26	12	6	23	-	-	18	23	17	6	-	-	-	-	-	-	-	-	-	-	-	-	4	6	2	6	476	0	0
Sam Schmidt	17	9	25	7	6	26	24	18	24	12	18	17	22	14	19	13	22	15	23	27	23	2	11	6	6	2	1568	0	0
Scott Sharp	20	6	8	1	7	16	9	5	4	3	4	1	6	18	8	11	3	18	3	23	11	12	11	4	7	1	1935	4	210
David Steele	-	-	23	22	-	-	-	-	-	-	-	-	-	-	-	-	-	-	11	24	26	27	3	11	0	22	140	0	0
Tony Stewart	1	1	3	2	4	33	1	14	6	1	1	8	1	21	3	3	25	5	2	20	2	14	11	1	7	1	1738	10	598
Brian Tyler	13	19	28	17	-	-	-	-	25	14	19	12	11	16	24	16	23	21	24	13	22	6	8	11	5	6	1475	0	0
Johnny Unser	-	-	-	-	25	25	-	-	-	-	-	-	-	-	-	-	-	-	-	-	-	-	1	25	0	25	98	0	0
Robby Unser	-	-	-	-	21	5	27	9	18	11	16	11	-	-	23	12	13	16	17	2	27	16	8	13	5	2	1504	1	22
Jeff Ward	24	2	1	5	27	13	13	17	2	22	8	19	10	2	2	20	2	6	5	3	8	21	11	1	6	2	1696	8	326
Stan Wattles	18	22	-	-	29	28	26	10	26	17	-	-	-	-	-	-	20	26	26	8	25	13	7	18	2	8	794	0	0
J.J. Yeley	-	-	10	25	13	9	22	19	21	23	-	-	-	-	-	-	26	25	-	-	-	-	5	10	2	9	600	0	0

Series Ranking	Series Total	Car No.	Entrant
1	332	14	AJ Foyt Enterprises
2	292	6	Nienhouse Motorsports
3	289	1	Team Menard
4	272	8	Kelley Racing
5	262	91	Hemelgarn Racing
6	252	35	ISM Racing
7	244	4	Panther Racing
8	227	5	Treadway Racing
9	224	11	AJ Foyt Enterprises
10	222	51	Team Cheever
11	219	16	Phoenix Racing
12	215	10	Byrd-Cunningham Racing
13	201	77	Chastain Motorsports
14	186	99	LP Racing/PCI
15	180	28	Kelley Racing
16	176	52	Team Cheever
17	174	3	Team Menard
18	160	81	Team Pelfrey
19	156	18	PDM
20	142	15	R&S Cars Inc.
21	134	12	Bradley Motorsports
22	132	30	McCormack Motorsports
23	105	23	CBR Cobb Racing
24	100	40	Crest Racing/SRS
25	98	97	Thomas Knapp Motorsports
26	88	19	Metro Racing
27	71	98	Cahill Racing
28	57	44	SRS
29	48	17	Chitwood Motorsports
30	45	7	Team Scandia
31	41	21	Pagan Racing
32	36	20	Immke Racing
33	35	55	ISM Racing
34	12	27	Blueprint Racing Inc.
35	9	43	Panther Racing
36	8	22	rsm Marko Inc.
37	5	9	Hemelgarn Racing
38	1	33	Team Scandia
39	1	53	ISM Racing

	Date	Winner (start)	Time of Race	Average Speed	Margin of Victory	Second	Third	Fourth	Fifth
WDW	1/24/98	Tony Stewart (1)	2:06:07	95.140	8.579 sec.	Ward	Hamilton	Gregoire	Dismore
Phoenix	3/22/98	Scott Sharp (8)	2:02:18.735	98.110	2.366 sec.	Stewart	Boat	Gregoire	Ward
Indianapolis	5/24/98	Eddie Cheever Jr (17)	3:26:40.524	145.155	3.191 sec.	Lazier	Knapp	Hamilton	R. Unser
Texas	6/6/98	Billy Boat (2)	2:08:45.543	145.388	0.928 sec.	Ray	Brack	Goodyear	Sharp
New Hampshire	6/28/98	Tony Stewart (6)	1:51:30.262	113.861	1.788 sec.	Goodyear	Sharp	Hamilton	Luyendyk
Dover	7/19/98	Scott Sharp (4)	2:29:49.262	99.318	0.689 sec.	Lazier	Greco	Hamilton	Gregoire
Charlotte	7/25/98	Kenny Brack (3)	1:58:10.555	158.408	5.602 sec.	Ward	Goodyear	Luyendyk	Greco
Pikes Peak	8/16/98	Kenny Brack (5)	1:29:52.649	133.515	7.542 sec.	Buhl	Stewart	Gregoire	Hamilton
Atlanta	8/29/98	Kenny Brack (6)	2:17:15.289	140.026	0.944 sec.	Hamilton	Cheever Jr.	Goodyear	Stewart
Texas	9/20/98	John Paul Jr. (14)	2:31:53.557	131.931	1.577 sec.	R. Unser	Ward	Guerrero	Brack
Las Vegas	10/11/98	Arie Luyendyk (14)	2:18:19.202	135.338	0.926 sec.	Schmidt	Lazier	Paul Jr.	Cheever Jr.

	Date	Pole (finish)	Pole Time	Pole Speed	Starters	Number of Cars Running at Finish	Number of Cars on Lead Lap at Finish	Number of Leaders	Number of Lead Changes	Number of Yellows	Number of Laps under Yellow
WDW	1/24/98	Tony Stewart (1)	Rain/Points	Rain/Points	28	15	4	5	8	10	77
Phoenix	3/22/98	Jeff Ward (5)	20.839	172.753	28	17	3	5	6	10	80
Indianapolis	5/24/98	Billy Boat (23)	2:41.072	223.503	33	18	3	10	23	2	61
Texas	6/6/98	Tony Stewart (14)	24.059	224.448	28	17	5	6	21	6	45
New Hampshire	6/28/98	Billy Boat (21)	23.490	162.146	26	16	4	6	9	6	50
Dover	7/19/98	Tony Stewart (8)	19.438	185.205	22	10	2	5	8	7	99
Charlotte	7/25/98	Tony Stewart (21)	24.490	220.498	24	12	3	8	19	7	43
Pikes Peak	8/16/98	Billy Boat (9)	20.16	178.571	25	19	3	6	11	3	28
Atlanta	8/29/98	Billy Boat (12)	24.734	224.145	28	10	7	6	13	6	56
Texas	9/20/98	Billy Boat (11)	23.896	225.979	28	14	4	10	18	8	74
Las Vegas	10/11/98	Billy Boat (26)	25.167	214.567	28	14	4	7	13	8	68

Indianapolis 500 Winners

AAA SANCTIONING

Year	St. Pos.	Car #	Driver	Car Name & Sponsor / Chassis / Engine	Qualify Speed	Race Time	Race Speed
1911	28	32	Ray Harroun	Nordyke & Marmon / Marmon / Marmon		6:42:08.000	74.602
1912	7	8	Joe Dawson	National Motor Vehicle / National / National	86.130	6:21:06.000	78.719
1913	7	16	Jules Goux	Peugeot / Peugeot / Peugeot	86.030	6:35:05.000	75.933
1914	15	16	Rene Thomas	L. Delage / Delage / Delage	94.540	6:03:45.000	82.474
1915	2	2	Ralph DePalma	Mercedes/E.C. Patterson / Mercedes / Mercedes	98.580	5:33:55.510	89.840
1916	4	17	Dario Resta	Peugeot Auto Racing / Peugeot / Peugeot	94.400	3:34:17.000	84.001 a
1919	2	3	Howdy Wilcox	Peugeot/Indpls Spdway Team / Peugeot / Peugeot	100.010	5:40:42.870	88.050
1920	6	4	Gaston Chevrolet	Monroe/William Small / Frontenac / Frontenac	91.550	5:38:32.000	88.618
1921	20	2	Tommy Milton	Frontenac/Louis Chevrolet / Frontenac / Frontenac	93.050	5:34:44.650	89.621
1922	1	35	Jimmy Murphy	Jimmy Murphy / Duesenberg / Miller	100.500	5:17:30.790	94.484
1923	1	1	Tommy Milton	H.C.S. Motor / Miller / Miller	108.170	5:29:50.170	90.954
1924	21	15	L.L. Corum-J. Boyer	Duesenberg / Duesenberg / Duesenberg	93.330	5:05:23.510	98.234
1925	2	12	Peter DePaolo	Duesenberg / Duesenberg / Duesenberg	113.080	4:56:39.460	101.127
1926	20	15	Frank Lockhart	Miller/Peter Kreis / Miller / Miller	95.780	4:10:14.950	95.904 b
1927	22	32	George Souders	Duesenberg/William White / Duesenberg / Duesenberg	111.550	5:07:33.080	97.545
1928	13	14	Louie Meyer	Miller/Alden Sampson, II / Miller / Miller	111.350	5:01:33.750	99.482
1929	6	2	Ray Keech	Simplex Piston Ring/Yagle / Miller / Miller	114.900	5:07:25.420	97.585
1930	1	4	Billy Arnold	Miller-Hartz / Summers / Miller	113.260	4:58:39.720	100.448
1931	13	23	Louis Schneider	Bowes Seal Fast/Schneider / Stevens / Miller	107.210	5:10:27.930	96.629
1932	27	34	Fred Frame	Miller-Harry Hartz / Wetteroth / Miller	113.850	4:48:03.790	104.144
1933	6	36	Louie Meyer	Tydol/Louie Meyer / Miller / Miller	116.970	4:48:00.750	104.162
1934	10	7	Bill Cummings	Boyle Products/Henning / Miller / Miller	116.110	4:46:05.200	104.863
1935	22	5	Kelly Petillo	Gilmore Speedway/Petillo / Wetteroth / Offy	115.090	4:42:22.710	106.240
1936	28	8	Louie Meyer	Ring Free/Lou Meyer / Stevens / Miller	114.170	4:35:03.390	109.069
1937	2	6	Wilbur Shaw	Shaw-Gilmore / Shaw / Offy	122.790	4:24:07.800	113.580
1938	1	23	Floyd Roberts	Burd Piston Ring/Lou Moore / Wetteroth / Miller	125.680	4:15:58.400	117.200
1939	3	2	Wilbur Shaw	Boyle Racing Headquarters / Maserati / Maserati	128.970	4:20:47.390	115.035
1940	2	1	Wilbur Shaw	Boyle Racing Headquarters / Maserati / Maserati	127.060	4:22:31.170	114.277
1941	17	16	F. Davis-M. Rose	Noc-Out Hose Clamp/Moore / Wetteroth / Offy	121.100	4:20:36.240	115.117
1946	15	16	George Robson	Thorne Engineering / Adams / Sparks	125.540	4:21:16.700	114.820
1947	3	27	Mauri Rose	Blue Crown Spark Plug/Moore / Deidt / Offy	120.040	4:17:52.170	116.338
1948	3	3	Mauri Rose	Blue Crown Spark Plug/Moore / Deidt / Offy	129.120	4:10:23.330	119.814
1949	4	7	Bill Holland	Blue Crown Spark Plug/Moore / Deidt / Offy	128.670	4:07:15.970	121.327
1950	5	1	Johnnie Parsons	Wynn's Friction/Kurtis-Kraft / Kurtis / Offy	132.040	2:46:55.970	124.002 c
1951	2	99	Lee Wallard	Murrell Belanger / Kurtis / Offy	135.030	3:57:38.050	126.244
1952	7	98	Troy Ruttman	J.C. Agajanian / Kuzma / Offy	135.360	3:52:41.880	128.922
1953	1	14	Bill Vukovich	Fuel Injection/Howard Keck / KK500A / Offy	138.390	3:53:01.690	128.740
1954	19	14	Bill Vukovich	Fuel Injection/Howard Keck / KK500A / Offy	138.470	3:49:17.270	130.840
1955	14	6	Bob Sweikert	John Zink / KK500C / Offy	139.990	3:53:59.130	128.213